History and Totality

The question of modernity is a key issue in contemporary cultural debate. Through an examination of the modern historicist concept of totality, Totality and History brings together in a single volume the views of a number of influential theorists on this issue. Accessibly written, it introduces students to sophisticated philosophical debates often confined to specialists.

In this work John Grumley establishes a tradition of radical historicism from Hegel to the Budapest School. He charts both its continuous evolution from the early nineteenth century to the present and its transformation in the context of European social, economic and cultural change. Through his careful reappraisal of historical interpretation from Hegel to Foucault, Grumley demonstrates the contemporary relevance of radical historicism and vindicates its emancipatory spirit in the face of the post-structuralist critique of 'totality thinking'. He also includes detailed analyses of Marx, Dilthey, Simmel, Weber, Lukács, Horkheimer, Adorno and Habermas. This book will find a wide readership among students and scholars of social and cultural theory, history, philosophy and Marxism.

John Grumley is Tutor in Philosophy at the University of Sydney.

'*History and Totality* analyses the high points in the development of a problematic that has dominated much of European social thinking for over a century and a half from the confident holism of Hegel to the radical anti-holism of the later Foucault. It is both a major contribution to the understanding of this development and an accessible introduction to it for those who are grappling with it for the first time.' – John Burnheim, University of Sydney

History and Totality
Radical historicism from Hegel to Foucault

John E. Grumley

Routledge
London and New York

First published 1989
by Routledge
11 New Fetter Lane, London EC4P 4EE
29 West 35th Street, New York, NY 10001

Printed in Great Britain by TJ Press (Padstow) Ltd, Padstow, Cornwall

British Library Cataloguing in Publication Data
    Grumley, John E.
    Totality and History: radical historicism
    from Hegel to Foucault
    1. European philosophy
    I. Title
    190

    ISBN 0-415-01292-9

Library of Congress Cataloging in Publication Data
also available

Certainly all historical experience confirms the truth – that man would not have attained the possible unless time and again he had reached out for the impossible.

Max Weber

For my daughter Harriet

Contents

Preface and acknowledgements

An earlier version of the present study was submitted for a Doctorate at the University of Sydney in 1985 under the title 'Lukács and Totality: The Historical Transformation of a Concept'. Having the opportunity to revise and rewrite the text for publication, I decided to shift the focus of the study although most of individual expositions remain largely as they were. The reason for the change should be familiar to anybody who has undertaken a large study over a number of years. The submitted title was a compromise between the dissertation as initially conceived and the way it eventually emerged. My original aim was a study devoted to Lukács. However, as my research proceeded it exploded temporally both forward and backwards in the effort to fully understand his work. As time went on I became much more interested in the tradition of radical historicism as a whole stretching back to Hegel and forward to Lukács' fraternal critics in the Budapest School. The title and subtitle of the dissertation amounted to an uneasy resolution of this tension. The present study more accurately reflects the later conception. To take account of the strident critique of totality coming from post-structuralist quarters a completely new chapter on the work of Michel Foucault has also been added. Despite his emphatic anti-totalising and anti-humanist credentials, the strong historicising element in his thought and his interest in philosophy as critique makes him something more than just a counter-point to the radical historicist tradition.

During the writing I have received a great deal of assistance and accummulated a number of heavy debts. In the early days of my research, Michael Eldred helped me take the first steps in reading Lukács in the original German. I owe more than I can say to my friend and colleague George Márkus. His work and personality has been a source of continual inspiration. As my supervisor, he scrupulously read various versions of the chapters and sent me back to the drawing board on a number of occasions. He also kindly read the new Foucault chapter offering a number of penetrating criticisms and suggestions. I would also like to thank Agnes Heller, John Burnheim and Martin Jay who examined the dissertation and supplied me with helpful comments. In particular, I would single out Martin Jay who generously sent me a very detailed commentary on the earlier text.

Last but certainly not least comes Pauline Johnson. She has lived with this text for a number of years and has always been very supportive. In discussions with her I first rehearsed and clarified many of the basic ideas and in the final stages she edited each chapter suggesting many useful changes.

Finally a big thanks to my parents Isabel and Jack Grumley who have never ceased to support and encourage my work.

Introduction

Philosophy, Georg Lukács once observed, originally arose as a cultural response to loss. The unified totality of immediate, meaningful social experience characterising integrated, closed societies had begun to dissolve. The utopian aim of philosophy was to *theoretically reimpose* the lost unity, to overcome the emergent rifts between essence and appearance, subject and object, engendered by changing historical conditions. This understanding of the cultural meaning of philosophy is also relevant to any contemporary interpretation of the modern historicised concept of totality. The idea of a totalising historical process can be viewed as a modern reaction to a later, seemingly permanent, historical crisis; the epochal transition to dynamic, bourgeois socio-economic relations and forms.

In dynamic conditions of accelerated socio-economic change, philosophy's traditional, static view of the world as a cosmos or fixed totality, which in various forms had endured since antiquity, collapsed. With the crisis of traditional institutions, the old forms of experience supported by inherited worldviews and totalised meanings were found wanting. The philosophical response to this great historical challenge began to take shape at the end of the eighteenth century. If social experience was to be rendered meaningful, the phenomenon of rapid historical change had to be assimilated into the traditional picture. Hegel's response to this challenge was the introduction of an immanent dynamism into the old concept of totality.

The following study proposes to chart the story of this very influential modern historicist version of 'totality thinking' which took its bearing from Hegel. This tradition has been, and continues to be, a very rich and fertile source for contemporary cultural reflection. Its influence on modern Marxism, philosophy, historiography, social theory and many other cultural disciplines cannot be overestimated. Martin Jay's recent work <u>Marxism and Totality</u> has painstakingly analysed the significance and vicissitudes of the concept of totality within the tradition of Western Marxism.The present study aims to reconstruct the *historicist stream* of 'totality thinking' from Hegel to the present. This task demands a careful analysis of the quite startling evolution of the *cultural meaning* of the totality concept; tracing its surprising interpretative metamorphoses under the impact of changing historical conditions; following the course of the tradition's own ongoing philosophical self-critique and examining the most recent challenge to the traditions' *emancipatory credentials*. Finally, a tentative appraisal of its contemporary significance shall be offered.

Given this survey will be occupied only with the key evolutionary stages of the 'historicist' tradition, it cannot claim to be a modern history of the concept of totality. As Jay points out, this concept has appeared in many other modern guises even within the Marxist tradition. It has also found employment with such notable modern philosophers as Heidegger and Sartre. Within the historicist tradition, the name of Georg Lukács holds a special place. He was responsible for the positive reinstatement of the concept into Marxist discourse, for rediscovering the link between Marx and the great philosophical tradition of classical German Idealism and effecting a paradigmatic reading of 'totality' that ensured its modern transmission and critical development. Lukács' importance at least partly explains the otherwise strange inclusion of the leading thinkers of the *fin de siècle Geisteswissenschaften*. His achievement is inexplicable without some understanding of the radical *re-evaluation* of the concept of totality ventured by Dilthey, Simmel and Weber. Lukács' revival of the concept of totality allows us to *philosophically reconstruct* a radical historicist tradition from Hegel to the present. Yet even Lukács appears in this story only as a contributor to the historicist tradition. The later course of his very long philosophical development in which he repudiated his early emphasis on 'totality' falls outside this history.[1]

To appreciate the truly revolutionary character of the historicist concept of totality we must briefly recall the traditional understanding of totality which it supplanted. There is every reason to believe that the notion of totality was central to religious mythology and therefore antedates the philosophical tradition altogether. Max Weber argued that totalising religious images were the result of a long process of rationalisation which replaced the fragmented, polyphonic, magical beliefs of earliest antiquity with unifying interpretations of the cosmos as a whole. In any case, we can safely say that the concept of totality is at least as old as philosophy itself. Both religious myth and philosophy purported to supply comprehensive, 'total' explanations/interpretations of the cosmos. We need not dwell on the specificities of myth and philosophy.[2] What is significant is that both these cultural forms seem to indicate the invariant cultural need for orientation in the world.

It would, however, be a considerable error to interpret this cultural need in ahistorical terms. Interpretation of the cosmos was not always associated with the search for human meaning. Classical metaphysics presupposed the unity and meaningfulness of being; the task of *theoria* was the apprehension of the regularity and timeless order of the natural cosmos. The Greeks were disinterested in the later Christian question of the ultimate divine purpose of the cosmos. The natural order and lawful beauty of the cosmos provided a perfect model of the essence they sought. Beyond the presumed immutability of the rational, harmonious, cosmic processes of seasonal change, growth and decay, of eternal recurrence, they felt no need to inquire.

This naïve naturalism generates the idea of a *cosmic totality*. The constant change of empirical circumstances does not touch the immutability of the cosmic order. Although history first came into its own with the Greeks, it had no place in *theoria* proper. Originally it was concerned only with the extraordinary mortal deed or work which momentarily suspended the circular movement of the natural order. It celebrated 'immortal' acts in a domain that was itself empirical, transient and inexorably mortal. The meaning of these deeds and words were self-contained and a Herodotus needed only to preserve their memory by stabilising in writing that which was ordinarily perishable and futile.[3] For the later Greek historians, the interpretation of history was reconciled with metaphysics by patterning its understanding on the eternal model of the natural cosmos. But the intent of studying history was always essentially practical: to publicly relate the great event so as to establish a yardstick of greatness or to understand the causal factors which determined the fate of the *polis*.

Thucydides, Aristotle and Polybius viewed human institutions and affairs in terms of recurrent cycles and sequences. Classical interpretation of history and nature converged in the idea of cyclical eternity. However, truth was never disclosed in such an impermanent realm as human affairs. Knowledge of its cycles was deemed practically useful as it enabled men to recognise the present in the past and adapt their conduct accordingly. Yet the transitory did not rate as a real object of theoretical contemplation. Plato speaks with contempt of human affairs because they fail to reveal eternal Being.[4] Karl Löwith explained this very unfamiliar aspect of Greek thought as follows:

> In this intellectual climate, dominated by the rationality of the cosmos,
> there was no room for the universal significance of a unique,
> incomparable historic event. As for the destiny of man in history, the
> Greeks believed that man had resourcefulness to meet every situation with
> magnanimity – they did not go further than that. They were primarily
> concerned with the logos of the cosmos not with the Lord and the
> meaning of history.[5]

As Löwith suggests, the Greek view contrasts sharply with the Judeo-Christian one that finally superseded it. In the latter, which gradually absorbed elements of neo-Platonism, the static eternal idea of totality retained its central cosmo-theological place. Particularly in medieval society, the idea of the organic whole, understood as the totality of the spiritual and physical order, was both a societal ideal and explanatory principle.

The distinguishing feature of the Judeo-Christian view was the unique position occupied by the transcendent God. God was the apex of a clearly hierarchicised moral-religious order providing its *telos* and ultimate meaning. The entire cosmos was infused with a transcendent theological meaning and it no longer seemed sufficient to contemplate eternity in the manifest recurrence of natural cycles. How this divine promise was to be fulfilled remained a matter of dispute and vacillation between *escatological hope* and *patient faith* in eternal salvation. Doctrinal schism clearly reflected temporal divisions. The established church counselled subordination to a 'natural' thiswordly hierarchy where each individual was allocated a place and purpose. The reward was everlasting afterlife. Periodically, however, radical social unrest exploded the patient endurance of earthly suffering. This generated chiliastic expectations of the 'second coming'; present misery and religious fervour were potent forces for doctrinal heresies.[6]

The Judaic and Christian religions were essentially historical.Their essential religious message focused on a future-directed historical sequence of events (the Covenant – its betrayal – God's punishment – the coming of the Messiah; Original Sin – Redemption – Last Judgement). In both cases the future was integrated as a constitutive moment in the interpretation of the present and of history. Yet, as sacred history, this divine temporal story was essentially prefigured and teleologically closed. It sustained only a tenuous connection with the secular history of real events. As Habermas observes, this conception preserves the distinction 'between the subject of history and the subject who acts historically, between the lord of history and those who are merely subjected to it'.[7]

For medieval Catholicism, a single unique event became the axis of a meaningful interpretation of the world as a whole. This promise of redemption, however, did not impinge on the cosmic stability of existing social structures and the official hierarchical, teleologically ordered view of the world. Aside from the marginalised heretical doctrines engendered by chiliastic hopes, – Joachim of Flora, for example, providing a revolutionary new periodisation of history while simultaneously projecting the immanent historical realisation of the Christian promise in the immediate future[8] – the orthodox Catholic cosmology retained its static character despite the essentially historical structure of its founding tradition. The scholastic tradition endorsed this legitimising static cosmology. Augustine deprived secular events of any religious value. His *Civitas Dei* was situated beyond the temporal sphere; only one book relates to secular events. The *Civitas Dei* was essentially a *supra-historical ideal;* the secular was relegated to virtual insignificance and the meaning of history fixed in a dogmatic, sacred interpretation.

With only slight modification, the essentials of this static concept of totality survived until the seventeenth century. This was the case despite the gradual emergence of theoretical tensions as the impact of slow socio economic change began to take its toll. Of course, some tensions can be detected as early as the Renaissance. However, they never really threatened the pervasive dominance of the static, religious cosmology. Nevertheless, at the margin a new awareness of history is perceptible in some of the outstanding thinkers of the age. Cusanus and Ficino both demonstrated a clear appreciation of the historical plurality of religion. They viewed the idea of religion as the totality of its historical forms.[9] Clearly these marginal cracks in the edifice of a timeless, static, divinely ordered cosmos hardly ruffled the surface of orthodoxy. They *merely* opened the *theoretical possibility* of the philosophy of history and the sense of a diverse, dynamic history. Only the multiple forces of profound historical change finally challenged the basic conceptual/ideological structure of the christian medieval worldview.

The rise of the natural sciences and the transition from the traditional idea of a closed cosmos to an infinite, mechanical universe represented a fundamental challenge to the traditional philosophical understanding of totality. Yet far from signifying the collapse of the traditional concept, it occasioned only the gradual restriction of the ontological concept of totality to the organismic realm. The great early modern metaphysicians still relied on a static concept of totality. Leibniz (1646-1716) still conceived the universe as a cohesive system in pre-established harmony and correspondence. All the elements or parts of the cosmos function in harmony and as a totality achieve a unified action and possess a single overall significance.[10] This Leibnizian conception retained the fundamental features of the traditional static, closed theological understanding of totality. Yet theoretical tensions of increasing significance abound. On the one hand, his seminal and ominous insistence on the self-subsistence of each monad, on the positive uniqueness of every individual, anticipates the modern age and a new sense of historical individuality, while, on the other, the optimistic pronouncement that we live in the 'best of all possible worlds' denies man any active participation in the production of a better one.[11] This tension is exemplified in the Leibnizian concept of progress which further exacerbates the strains on his essentially static system.[12] Hans Blumenberg has even argued that in demonstrating the rationality of absolute ends on the model of divine action, Leibniz 'rationalised' evil and paved the way for the modern concept of history.[13]

Soon after, subterranean historical movements became visible fissures and added impetus to the contest for ideological hegemony. As the socio-economic forms of nascent bourgeois society developed an irreversible momentum and the *ancien régime* approached political crisis, traditional ideas became increasingly untenable. Numerous commentators have remarked that philosophical interest in history grew dramatically throughout the eighteenth century. It reached a milestone when Vico problematised the totality of history and Voltaire coined the term 'philosophy of history'. And yet, even Vico's achievement falls short of the great epoch of philosophy of history soon to follow. His philosophy of history remained retrospective. Comprehension of the whole of history presupposed its cyclicality.[14] This idea of the recurrence of the past was soon brushed aside by truly revolutionary events.

The expansion of the market economy and other bourgeois forms, together with increasing social mobility, already heralded the increasing dynamism of modern social life. Even before the French Revolution translated these underlying socio-economic trends into an explicit political challenge to the old order, the educated public had already become more aware of history as dynamic change. The widespread popular optimism of the eighteenth century signified this new public consciousness. Nevertheless, amongst the diverse streams of thought contributing to the French Enlightenment, one also recognises a sobering consciousness of complexity of historical change and even of the contradictions of 'historical progress'. Turgot viewed the steady accumulation of knowledge as a clear index of real human progress. But both Voltaire and Rousseau were much more cautious and pessimistic. Contemporary decadence and over-refinement were perceived by Rousseau as the basis for a critique of the modern idea of 'progress'. Voltaire's Philosophy of History (1766) catalogued the vast spectrum of cultures and epochs exposed by commercial expansion, travel and historical enquiry. From the perspective of increasing socio-political crisis, his consciousness of the unity of mankind and its development made possible the thought of an empirical subject of history and problematised the question of the total historical process but without yielding a conclusive philosophy of history.[15]

The French Revolution clearly marks the great historical watershed of modernity. Its repercussions overturned all conventional perceptions of history. No longer at the mercy of the ossified traditions and institutions satirised by Voltaire, the future offered new social possibilities requiring urgent philosophical consideration and integration.

The impact of the dramatic social, economic and intellectual turmoil of the late eighteenth century was felt in Germany, if not as severely. This is evident in the programmatic works of Kant and Herder. While history did not find a prominent place in Kant's pre-revolutionary critical philosophy, his later speculations on this topic paved the way for the trajectory of classical German Idealism and the radical historicisation of rational metaphysics. Kant experimented with a new reflective mode of understanding organic and historical development. In conformity with his critical approach, Kant proposed a philosophically informed concept of history liberated from the grip of both Bossuetian historical theology and Bayleian scepticism. Human history follows neither a divine plan of salvation nor is it a repetition of past evils.[16] Against these dogmatisms, Kant demanded a methodological separation of cosmology, morality and history that allowed the situation of men in the world to be judged in its own right in accordance with the practical, regulative idea of philosophical teleology. On an opposite tack, Herder laid down the foundations for nineteenth- century German historicism by celebrating the immense diversity of historical cultures and their essential incommensurability.[17]

These developments show that by the end of the eighteenth century the theoretical metamorphosis of the static, metaphysical concept of totality into a dynamic notion of historical processuality was definitely under way. The accelerated transformation of existing 'lifeworlds' engendered a cultural-existential need to interpret the new experience of rapid change and explain its meaning. In the work of Hegel and his contemporaries who lived through the initial phase of this crisis, this need found urgent expression. José Ripalda has provided us with a thoughtful evocation of this historical impact on the experience of Hegel's generation:

> When one has lived so consciously through the most turbulent moment of the development of bourgeois society, the French Revolution, a goverment of law, the development of nationalism, the victories of reaction, the unstable advances of an epoch as rich in hopes as in deceptions, it is impossible to overlook the epoch and absorb oneself in the metaphysical background. Its place is in the historical moment.[18]

The young Hegel was to perceive the contemporary problems of his age in terms of history and as a question of historical crisis. The relatively closed socio-political cosmos of the *ancien régime* had dissolved under the pressure of dynamic, immanent forces produced by the new bourgeois forms. This new dynamism was clearly not the old temporal category of change so contemptously dismissed by the old metaphysics. Contemporary change was not that of 'natural cycles' manifesting the immutable, cosmic order. The proliferation of bourgeois forms destroyed all natural hierarchies and liberated the voracious, new productive system. In this new world, change was no longer repetition but perpetual transformation. A revolution which permeated every crevice of social existence transforming the very essence of all institutions and relations.

This brief overview has brought us to the historical threshhold of the period with which the following chapters are concerned. This epoch gave rise to a new understanding of history associated with a progressively nuanced historicisation of the concept of totality. One in which the meaning of the total historical process will vacillate wildly between imminent emancipation and ever narrowing entrapment and dehumanisation.

Birth of the emancipatory, historicist concept of totality

Chapter One

Hegel: between metaphysics and history

Georg Wilhelm Fredrich Hegel (1770-1831) lived through one of the most turbulent periods of European history. Ripalda's evocation of the existential impact of these historical changes underlines the fact that Hegel's philosophy was forged in a continuous interplay with the dramatic and rapidly changing events which shaped the modern bourgeois world. The period of Hegel's philosophical productivity was circumscribed by the two great historical watermarks of the emergent bourgeois industrial age. As a young theological student attending the Tübinger Stift, he was an avid follower of the revolutionary events in Paris. His last article was a commentary on the British Reform Bill. These two events symbolise a momentous process of historical transformation which delivered the dynamic, antagonistic bourgeois society from the crisis of the *ancien régime*. As Ripalda suggests, Hegel's philosophy was wrought from a conscious reflection upon the significance of this profound process of transformation. In his mind historicity became an essential moment of metaphysical speculation and this involved a radical rethinking of the traditional, static concept of totality.

This chapter analyses the character of Hegel's philosophical revolution, how he came to effect it and the philosophical tensions that were passed on to his successors with this new understanding of totality. The gestation of his mature system involved a gradual synthesis of insights into a whole range of theoretico-practical dilemmas – historical, political, cultural, philosophical. To appreciate this complex synthesis, we must venture into the original problem complexes that fuelled his intellectual development.

The problem of diremption

In his earliest published work, Hegel offered a succinct reading on the crisis of the age:

> Division *(Entzweiung)* is the source of the need for philosophy, and as the culture *(Bildung)* of the age, the unfree given side of the structure. In our culture, that which is an appearance of the Absolute has isolated itself from the Absolute, and determined itself as independent. At the same time, however, the appearance can not deny its origin, and must therefore proceed to form the multiplicity of determinations into a whole.[1]

This passage from the Difference Between the Fichtean and the Schellingian Systems of Philosophy (1801), written at Jena, presents a cultural diagnosis, a view of philosophy and a programme. Hegel nominates the central problem of his early work and an interpretation of the philosophical task as the reconstitution of the 'whole'. Much of Hegel's early endeavour revolved around this problem of 'division'. To understand the significance of this problem and its dimensions, sometimes also termed 'diremption' *(Trennung)*, it is essential to reconstruct to the problematics of Hegel's early work.

Much social commentary in the late eighteenth century was directed at the increasingly visible impact of accelerated socio-economic change. Major literary figures remarked on the increasing complexity of modern society, growing inequalities of wealth and the expanding division of labour. In spite of a general optimism and the assurances of nascent political economy that these were all signs of increasing national prosperity, these thinkers expressed a real disquiet over the destructive consequences of modernity. Each to varying degrees, articulated regrets over the loss of community and the resulting social and individual fragmentation. Schiller's dramatic evocation of the fate of all those 'victims' of the new bourgeois forms of specialisation in his Letters on the Aesthetic Education of Man was typical:

> Eternally chained to only one single fragment of the whole, man himself grew to be only a fragment; with the monotonous noise of the wheel he drives everlastingly in his ears, he never develops the harmony of his being, and instead of imprinting humanity upon his nature he becomes merely the imprint of his occupation, his science.[2]

The inroads of economic specialisation and societal complexity induced not merely a concern for the 'totality 'of the individual but also a keen awareness of the increasing social divisions wrought by a dynamic economy. Especially in comparsion to the idealised homogeneity attributed to the classical Greek *polis,* late eighteenth century society seemed to be characterised by rigid divisions between between social ranks and professions. We possess a fragment from Hegel's school essays which draws some of the cultural consequences of this increasing social division:

> The ideas and culture of the classes are too distinct for a poet in our times to be read and universally understood.[3]

German society at this time represented a unique configuration of these problems. In it the pervasive socio-economic trends of bourgeoisification were aggravated by political 'backwardness'. Unlike the leading European nations England and France, Germany was politically fragmented and beset with parochialisms. The loose confederacy of large and small states could not challenge inveterate local interests. As a result, local trade barriers and currencies hindered economic development and stifled the provision of auxiliary services.[4] Dissipated political authority was compounded by the deep religious divisions which remained as the legacy of the Reformation. Religious differences intensified social and cultural rifts between classes and professions and rendered even more fragile the tenuous sense of cultural unity provided by a common language.

For the educated, these manifestations of German underdevelopment were the cause of deep frustrations. Political disunity only heightened the sense of social division and personal atomisation arising from the new social forms and the disintegration of the traditional community. Hegel was especially concerned with the disintegration of cultural unity. Social inequalities and cultural divisions accentuated the other manifestations of German backwardness.

The rediscovery of classical literature was crucial in shaping the critical perspective of this educated milieu. Like most of his contemporaries, Hegel was capitivated by the cultural vision of classical Greece as represented in the writings of Winckelmann, Lessing, Herder and Schiller. The existing fractures of cultural and social life were only magnified when compared to this ideal of a homogeneous, harmonious culture. Hegel's early writings often compare the deplorable privatisation of modern individual existence to this ancient communality that integrated the individual into a higher social unity affirmed in a common religion and morality. This vital unity was *polis* life.

Hegel's earliest diagnosis of his society's contemporary crisis was framed from this historical perspective. The Berne essay 'The Positivity of the Christian Religion' (1795-6) employed the contrast between contemporary social division and cultural diremption and the homogeneous culture and unity of *polis* society. Hegel maintained that the *polis* citizen obeyed laws and officials they had helped to determine; their morality was a free product organically nurtured from everyday life and sustained by a willing self-sacrifice to the needs of the *polis*, not a set of rules imposed by transcendent authority.[5] Hegel underlined that even the poor Athenian citizen who was unable to vote and forced into salvery still shared with illustrious citizens the myths of a homogeneous culture. He could attend and appreciate the public dramas of Sophocles and Euriphides as well as the other religious festivals.[6]

The important issue in this analysis is not Hegel's idealisation of actual conditions. In the late eighteenth century climate of cultural worship surrounding Greek civilisation such idealisation was inevitable. More significant is the way this ideal functioned. Hegel consistently employed it as a critical standard against which he criticised the deficiencies of his own society:

Thus we are without any religious imagery which is homegrown or linked with our history, and we are without any political imagery whatever; all that we have is the remains of an imagery of their own lurking amid the common people under the name of superstition... These are sad and indigent remains of an attempted independence and an attempted possession, and the general attitude to them is that it is the duty of all enlightened people to extirpate them altogether. As a result of this temper in the upper classes, quite apart from the coarseness and intractability of the available material, it has become totally impossible to ennoble these remnants of mythology and thereby refine the imagination and sensibility of the common people.[7]

In this typical passage Hegel bemoans the cultural rupture between the educated classes and the common people.The educated were captivated by Greek mythology which had no organic relation to German history or the struggles of its common people. The old Teutonic myths of the people did bear some relation to the dim historical past but they were far removed from present conditions and simply incompatible with modern ideas.[8] Neither option offered any alternative to the ossified Christian orthodoxy as a seedbed for cultural renewal. Christianity had become a fixed institutional doctrine dependent upon authority but no longer spontaneously and freely affirmed by the people. It had become a 'positive' religion; one severed from its original public function of propagating morality and therefore symptomatic of the pervasive privatisation of modern life.[9] It had played a major role in the enervation of public life and communal solidarity by explicitly denouncing secular commitment in favour of the life hereafter.

Hegel's analysis clearly linked together the phenomena of personal fragmentation and cultural diremption. Although Schiller had an idea of the 'aesthetic state'which transcended the isolated individual, he had focused on the question of the individual's harmonious development. By contrast, Hegel emphasised the absence of cultural unity as the direct cause of the contemporary fragmented condition of the individual. The Christian dichotomy between the public and private person, the split between the spiritual and the secular in the individual was for him a symptom of a fundamental socio-political problem: the dissolution of cultural harmony and communal unity. For Hegel, the individual was always more than a mere 'part', the individual was a reflection of the 'whole', expressing the ideals and culture of the society to which he belonged. Therefore, fragmentation of the individual was symptomatic of social and cultural fractures.

This emphasis is significant because it hints that Hegel's critique of 'positive' religion was something more than a typical Enlightenment defence of reason and moral autonomy against faith and the power of tradition. While at this early stage Hegel's ethical standpoint was Kantian – equating the idea of rational self-legislation with the Rousseauian model of participatory democracy – , his critique clearly implied much more than a narrow defence of subjective moral autonomy.[10] 'Positivity' was for Hegel primarily a critical concept implying the historical decay of a set of religious beliefs into a lifeless, fixed, objective doctrine. Historical change rendered the beliefs rigid and detached from the living needs and spiritual powers which had originally been their soil. Consequently, these beliefs no longer commanded the commitment of the whole person but received only ritualised, formal acknowledgement. If religious belief was to again recapture a truly subjective dimension, Hegel maintained it had to consume the whole person as had the 'folk' religions of Greece. They had permeated the whole lifeworld and expressed all the ancient citizens' hopes and fears.[11] Hegel's identification of authentic subjective religion with the organic 'folk' religions shows clearly that his critique of positivity was primarily activated by a condemnation of contemporary cultural diremption. The critique depended upon and took its bearing from the ideal of cultural integration exemplified by classical Greece. It implied that religion could engender spontaneous commitment and be a force for individual affirmation only when it was tightly interwoven into the very fabric of the individual's everyday life, only when it harmonised with the other cultural and political aspects of life.

This was Hegel's initial insight into the contradictions of his own society. He focused on the problem of cultural diremption from the critical perspective supplied by the historical ideal of classical Greek cultural harmony and vitality. This ideal furnished a normative concept of totality with which he criticised his own society. We now need to examine the way in which this practical and theoretical problem instigated Hegel's philosophical development and contributed to the shaping of his mature concept of totality.

By Hegel's time there was nothing particularly original in a historical approach to contemporary social critique. Rousseau had viewed modernity as a tragic degeneration from an earlier barbaric 'golden age'. He also idealised the classical *polis*. Yet, despite the profound awareness of historical contradiction in his thought, in Rousseau's hands this historical perspective could only issue in a deep historical pessimism. Faced with modern civilised decadence he renounced all hope of social regeneration in the developed European nations. As mentioned in the Introduction, the French Revolution completely swept away this pessimism and opened up the future as a source of messianic cultural hopes. For the young Hegel, the same historical perspective now produced an entirely different historical interpretation and outlook.

In the context of contemporary revolutionary events, Hegel's first tentative moves towards a philosophy of history escaped the practical dilemma of pessimistic retreat into a lost, idealised past. Anticipating radical historical possibilities, he projected his vision of a revitalised, unified, harmonious culture into an immediate future within the grasp of the revolutionary present.[12] He may have been a political moderate but there can be little doubt he held genuine hopes that the French events would bring radical reforms to southern Germany. He expected the collapse of the moribund Holy Roman Empire and with it the end of the most archaic and backward states and institutions. He perceived them as an obstacle to the effective rejuvenation of political and cultural unity in the German states. Among Hegel's manuscripts are draft proposals for the constitution of a reunited Germany. The centrepiece of this scenario was the utopian idea of revitalised, authentic, 'folk' religions as the basis of renewed social cohesion and cultural homogeneity. This was an optimistic programme of emancipatory socio-political renewal which sustained Hegel until his move to Frankfurt.

This problem of socio-cultural diremption remained with Hegel in Frankfurt where he absorbed the most recent philosophical developments under the tutelage of his schoolfriend Hölderlin. But in the major essay of this period 'The Spirit of Christianity and Its Fate' (1798-1800), he definitely revised his previous very critical stance toward the Christian religion. In the Berne essay Socrates had been praised above Jesus as an ethical teacher.[13] This now changed. Hegel came to appreciate Jesus' espousal of love as the expression of the higher moral principle. He still maintained that orthodox Christianity had degenerated into a 'positive' religion but this judgment was qualified by the recognition that it was a sublime ethical teaching which had been corrupted and transformed into a rigid set of doctrines and merely outward religious observances. Hegel attributed much of the blame for this degeneration to traditional Judaism.

Jesus was fated to deliver his reconcilatory message in an unfree culture scarred by diremption. The contemporary cultural diremption which Hegel was later to characterise in the <u>Difference</u> essay as the disjunction between the isolated Absolute and the world was simply a residual legacy of the original Judaic belief in a separate, unforgiving, omnipotent Deity. This dualistic religious idea was symptomatic of a culture born from alienation and social diremption. Abraham, the founder of the Jewish faith, had divorced himself from all communal and family ties, avoided close relations with all other foreign peoples and been unwilling to settle in any single territory. This all-consuming estrangement denied even the intimate nexus with a 'home' arising from the occupation and cultivation of land. Hegel argued that this sense of complete alienation was deeply ingrained in Judaic culture. It received its most profound cultural expression in the absolute bifurcation between the all-powerful, vengeful Deity and the abject, powerless and obedient subjects.[14]

Hegel concluded that Jesus' message was inevitably distorted by these unique cultural conditions. This society was praying for divine deliverance from alien conquest; the institutionalisation of the doctrine occurred in a milieu that had lost the taste for freedom and retreated into the solace of private life and the promise of individual immortality.[15] The original teachings of Jesus were intended to challenge the tyranny of the Judaic law which stultified the growth of living, natural relationships. He aimed to promote a communal spirit founded on love and mutual faith. Yet, in the context of Judaism and the later Roman persecution, the community remained only a small enclave of believers. Because the original faith had not permeated the existing institutions of public life, the kingdom of heaven had to be reinterpreted as a beyond, as another promise dislocated from secular life. This spirit of diremption infiltrated all historical versions of the Christian tradition and was discernible as the specifically religious dimension of the contemporary historical crisis.[16]

It is not easy to explain the abrupt transformation of Hegel's attitude to Christianity. Outside of a profound religious conversion,[17] it is likely that his reassessment of the Christian religion was the result of a number of independent converging factors. Of these, both theoretical and practical perspectives played equally important roles.

The Terror in France marked a crucial point in the evolution of Hegel's view of contemporary political prospects. From the Phenomenology of Spirit we know that the experience of the Terror dampened Hegel's enthusiasm for direct democracy. He came to believe that this was an inappropriate political form for the populations of the absolutist states who possessed no living democratic traditions.[18] Disillusionment with the course of radical politics encouraged a reconsideration of the existing institutional arrangements with more sympathy for their possible rationality. At the same time, the general direction of these political mediations was confirmed by Hegel's own further studies. Around this time Hegel became acquainted with Sir James Steuart's theory of political economy. From Steuart's work, An Inquiry into the Principles of Political Economy (1767), he gained a new perspective on the apparent fragmentation and disunity of the emergent bourgeois order. There he found an evolutionist understanding of historical development based on the idea of the progressive unfolding of society's economic structure.[19] This optimistic theory of historical progress allowed Hegel to review his previous pessimistic philosophy of history and perceive an essential rationality underlying the apparent chaos of the new order.

The crux of this reassessment again centred on the problem of diremption. The new typology of history acquired from Steuart overturned Hegel's earlier view of history as a process of decline from the previous circumstances of cultural unity and political freedom towards increasing alienation. Now an underlying progress of reason in history could be discerned even within the contradictions of historical development. Raymond Plant argues convincingly that this new historical typology is already present in the essay 'The Spirit of Christianity'.[20] However, at the same time that Hegel was being influenced by the developments in the 'new science' of political economy he was also beginning to experiment with an organicist interpretation of life as totality. This theoretico-philosophical development complemented the influence of political economy. Regarding life as a totality allowed him to view diremption not as a 'distortion' of some ideal unity but as a moment or a phase in a totalising process which overcame and encompassed it.

The inspiration for this important new perspective was implicitly present in Hegel's admiration for the unity and organic harmony of Greek culture. Until this time Hegel had reconciled his Kantianism with this ideal by interpreting the citizen of the polis state as an embodiment of the autonomous Kantian ethical subject. Obviously this interpretation ignored tensions. For example, it is difficult to reconcile the Kantian dualistic opposition of duty and inclination, moral law and natural impulse, reason and passion with the Greek ideal of the harmonious personality. Hegel's surprising shift from Kant to Jesus in 'The Spirit of Christianity' represents a final rejection of Kantian moral asceticism. That he had become conscious of the previously unnoticed theoretical tensions between his Kantianism and classicism is reflected in his relentless attack on the life-destroying rigorism of the Judaic law. Dieter Henrich has argued that Hölderlin was probably responsible for alerting Hegel to this theoretical discrepancy.[21] The unbridgeable gulf posited by Kant between the eternal moral law and its empirical-historical realisation was simply another expression of the fragmented individual personality that Hegel's historical ideal of cultural harmony and individual wholeness was meant to combat.

Against this ethical dualism, Hegel now recognised Jesus as the bearer of a higher, harmonious principle. He promoted community and reconciliation; he disposed of the dirempted view of humanity as internally torn between law and impulse in favour of a vision of overcoming and the inward unification of the divided personality through the assimilation of an immanent divine love. The essential meaning of Jesus' teaching had nothing to do with external imperatives or commandments. Jesus was the bearer of divine love; this love was an inherent life force, the expression of life as an integral whole. The original Christian ethics was an ethics of life.[22]

This new evaluation of Jesus' message was clearly related to the new organicist conception of life now promoted by Hegel. This view of life as an indivisable, interconnected, self-maintaining unity that preserves itself through internal diremption and the process of perpetual, self-reproductive overcoming came to figure prominently in Hegel's thought. The motif of organic diremption played a very significant part in Hegel's reassessment of the Christian spirit in 'The Spirit of Christianity'. He employed this idea in his intricate analysis of punishment and fate to distinguish between the former as an effect of transgressed law and the latter as a punishment engendered from the essential unity of life itself.[23] Attacking all dualist conceptions, he maintained that law always remained a external and alien universality to the individual it punished, while fate, on the other hand, arose immediately out of the living action of the individual; fate disposes of the cleavage between the universal and particular:

> Only through a departure from that united life which is neither regulated
> by law nor at variance with law, only through the killing of life, is
> something alien produced. Destruction of life is not the nullification of
> life but its diremption, and the destruction consists in its transformation
> into an enemy. It is immortal, and, if slain, it appears as its terrifying ghost
> which vindicates every branch of life and lets loose its Eumenides.[24]

These reflections have an obvious import for the concept of love and the organicist interpretation of life Hegel was then absorbing. The sphere of lawful punishment always remained a domain of rigid oppositions without prospect of genuine reconciliation. In life, however, reconciliation was part of an organic process where the forces of life *itself* actually annulled its own diremption.[25] For Hegel, love was an exemplification of this living, organic reconciliatory force. In love, opposition and diremption were merely external judgements not really touching the essential unity of the lovers. Lovers constitute a living whole and the appearance of distinctness and separation referred only to their eventual mortality.[26]

Not surprisingly, these intricate ethical reflections had profound metaphysico-religious ramifications. In his analysis of fate and love Hegel elaborated a new paradigm for the interpretation of historico-social diremptions and divisions. In this framework, fixed oppositions and polarities were relativised and subsumed as moments in greater unities of organic wholeness and living totalisation. Diremption and opposition are not illusory but necessary moments of a living process irreducible to fixed categories and oppositions. In the famous Fragment of a System (1800), attributed to Hegel, the author states: 'Life is a union of union and non-union'.[27] In his Frankfurt period, in conjunction with Hölderlin and Sinclair, Hegel embarked on a radical new programme to formulate a religious philosophy of unity. On the basis of the model of organic life, he translated the principle of diremption into a spiritual account of the immanent unity of the natural and historical worlds. Just as living organisms preserved themselves through internal processes of diremption, assimilation and regeneration, so too, he believed, the diremptions of these macro-realms were comprehensible in the same terms. Every phenomenon was encompassed in this immanent developmental unity: the spiritual unity of the life process.

To make this new programme fully intelligible we must say a few words about the vibrant philosophical debates occurring around the turn of the eighteenth century. In the 1790s, Fichte had revised the Kantian transcendental notion of pure consciousness with an activist interpretation. He was, however, unable to escape the radically subjectivist conclusion that both the natural and social worlds were thereby conceived as constructs of the ego. Hegel's new metaphysics of unity was intended as a critical retort to Fichte's needless rejection of metaphysics and the consequent extreme subjectivisation of reality. With his more famous young friend Fredrich Schelling, Hegel was determined to extend the limits of the Fichtean system and revive metaphysics by ignoring the Kantian strictures against thinking the Absolute. Only by infringing this proscription would the natural and historical worlds be granted a real objectivity. Hegel wanted to construe both these domains as animated by an immanent spiritual principle without reducing them to mere constructs of the ego.[28] Hegel achieved this goal of overcoming radical subjectivism with his revolutionary new concept of totality. He simply proposed to conceptualise the Absolute in terms of an immanent processual unity of both the natural and historical worlds.

Hegel's systematic achievement is commonly interpreted as the culmination of theoretical developments within the philosophical tradition of classical German Idealism. While this is undoubtedly a valid perspective, it tends to minimise the contributions of the other problematics outlined above. As far as Hegel's own development is concerned we know that he turned to metaphysics and theoretical philosophy only to resolve problems which first occurred to him as historical, political, religious – essentially practical – questions. The nub of these questions revolved around the diagnosis of the historical crisis of the age.

At the centre of Hegel's practical concerns stood the problem we have been analysing: socio-cultural diremption. The dramatic turn of historical events and the destruction of his political hopes obviously precipitated the process of rethinking this problem. Understandably, this revision was couched in the terms of contemporary philosophical debates. They allowed Hegel to engage with the underlying interpretative framework of this problem and accelerated his discovery of a radically changed perspective. With this new framework whereby cultural diremptions and social conflicts could be perceived as not fixed nor as manifestations of decline but as moments within a more encompassing historical process of spiritual development, Hegel modified his earlier negative attitude towards emergent bourgeois society and completely overturned his earlier historical pessimism.

Contrary to conventional interpretations, this famous reconciliation with bourgeois society did not signify the complete abandonment of his initial normative concept of totality, i.e. the ideal of perfect cultural unity. The collapse of Hegel's political hopes for the rebirth of the ancient republics in modern form necessitated decisive theoretical and diagnostic adjustments. He eventually *historicised* and *ontologised* the concept of totality as a comprehensive total process of a self-unfolding and self-recognising reality. Hegel's ethico-religious reflections on diremption, his awakened economic insights into the historical evolution of productive organisation and his struggles with the dilemmas of contemporary systematic philosophy all coalesced to suggest a radically alternative interpretation of present socio-cultural diremption.

Clearly this historicised/ontologised concept of totality was also imbued with a familiar Christian significance.[29] The experience of diremption was assimilated to the traditional Christian motif of Original Sin and Redemption. Hegel annulled the opposition between the infinite God and finite humanity with the idea of a necessary processual development through progressive phases of alienation to, finally, complete unity in difference. This ultimate schema is already prefigured in 'The Spirit of Christianity':

> The culmination of faith, the return of the Godhead whence man is born,
> closes the circle of man's development. Everything lives in the Godhead,
> every living thing is its child, but the child carries the unity, the
> connection, the concord with the entire harmony, undisturbed through
> development, in itself. It begins with faith in gods outside itself, with fear,

until through its actions it has isolated and separated itself more and more; but then it returns through associations to the original unity which now is developed, self produced and sensed as a unity. The child now knows God, i.e., the spirit of God is present in the child, issues from its restrictions, annuls the modification, and restores the whole. God, the Son, the Holy Spirit.[30]

Clearly, however, this passage only offers an interpretative schema and is far from Hegel's mature conception. Historical development is here couched in religious images.[31] Religion was not bound by the reflective oppositions of philosophical thought. This hierarchy will be inverted in Hegel's final conception. His mature idea of totality involved the processual self-actualisation of an infinite, *rational* subject in the natural and historical worlds thereby realising its own adequate self-knowledge.

Hegel's *ontologico-historicisation* of the concept of totality had a double significance. It attacked the problem of diremption on two, albeit related, theoretical levels. Firstly, Hegel challenged the traditional Christian diremption between humanity and God in an effort to humanise contemporary religion. Secondly, he offered a meaningful interpretation of the historico-social crisis of his time with the idea of an immanent rationality behind the appearance of chaos and conflict. In short, his concept of totality expressed a cautious, humanistic optimism. In an epoch of revolutions, of exceedingly rapid social change, this faith could be ascribed to immanent historical forces. Emancipation from the historical remnants of enslavement and alienation could be judged as, in principle, realised. Hegel's successors have judged that he was overly optimistic and that he failed to solve the problem of diremption. To assess these judgments Hegel's mature concept of totality must be explored, his 'reconciliation with reality' and its tensions examined, while also considering its cost to his youthful ideal of totality.

Totality as the unfolding of spirit

The truth is the whole. But the whole is nothing other than the essence consummating itself through its development.[32]

This formulation from the Preface to the Phenomenology of Spirit (1807) encapsulates the idea of Hegel's philosophy of unity. It articulates a revolutionary programme to revise the entire philosophical tradition and resolve the practical questions summarised above as the problem of diremption.

In the Introduction it was noted that classical *theoria* involved the idea of contemplative immersion in the cosmic 'whole'. Hegel too wants to comprehend the truth as a 'whole' but his understanding of it is radically different. The classical totality was natural, timeless and static, his is a living, dynamic, developmental, processual totality. Hegel identifies the dynamism of

21

his concept of totality with the processual unfolding of a spiritual essence. Clearly alluding to the Christian Trinity and its figurative victory over diremption, he viewed the divine *as a process* encompassing all reality. Spirit is not an isolated element but the 'whole' itself.[33] Only as Spirit, according to Hegel, this 'whole' is expressed in its subjective aspect.

Hegel's concept of spirit is the conceptual realisation of his early desire to overcome the religious and social phenomenon of diremption. Spirit refers to a 'general consciousness' that also activates practical reason and action. This intersubjective medium is both human and divine. In order to avoid the debilitating socio-cultural consequences of the dirempted orthodox Christian interpretation of the relation between humanity and divinity, Hegel opted for a radically humanist undertanding of the divine. The full realisation and emancipation of the human spirit is perceived by him as both the culminatior of, and identical to, the broader theologico-ontological process in which reality as a whole was actualised. The divine and the human fuse into a spiritual unity and history becomes its immanent processual self-determination and self-unfolding.

Hegel elaborates this idea of spirit most fully in the Encyclopaedia of the Philosophical Sciences (first edition, 1817),[34] in arguing that the idea of God in opposition to its finite manifestations was a mere abstraction. He continues: 'the true God' is nothing else than 'the living process of positing the Other, the world'.[35] This 'Other' Hegel understood to be the two great realms of finite existence: nature and human history. These realms are spheres of 'Otherness' because they are characterised by estrangement and the discrepency between perfect spiritual self-sufficiency and their own specific mode of determination. As matter, nature is external and dependent upon something else for its determination. It is an eternal site wherein spirit plays out its return to its own essential unity and such dependency means it is always other than it is.[36] Unconscious of the species imperialism latent in this view of nature as a 'being for humans', Hegel depicts nature as *lack;* it merely abides in space, without freedom or any immanent development; it is a realm of 'eternal change and chaos' characterised only by contingency and necessity.[37]

While Hegel also views the realm of human history as a sphere of Otherness, it carries the potentiality to transcend estrangement. The sphere of history is the domain of finite spirit. Spirit is essentially self-dependent, self-contained and free. In fact, it is everything that nature is not. Independent of all external determination, it is divine infinitude. Yet, this is a one-sided portrait in as much as it concerns finite spirit. The essential attribute of this finite spirit is its need for disclosure, 'to posit this other outside itself and to take it back into itself, in order to be subjectivity and Spirit'.[38] In conditions of estrangement and diremption, spirit is finite and human. As a finite, sensuous being, man is dependent upon the world of objects as an alien power.[39] His activity in nature reveals an immanent spiritual *telos*. His practical and theoretical activity (in willing and thought) transforms the alien givenness making it his own and activating his potential rationality. This practico-theoretical activity of internal diremption allows spirit to constitute itself, to both form its latent spiritual potential and acquire emancipatory self-knowledge. Formulated in such abstract terms, Hegel's characterisation of spirit remains rather obscure and will require a more detailed elaboration shortly.

At first sight this concept of finite spirit appears as a profoundly antiquated view of humanity. This divided, but godly, being rises through diremption and contemplation to the recognition of its inherent spirituality. The only thing distinguishing this view from earlier Christian teleologies is Hegel's incorporation of modern ideas like freedom and subjectivity as truly essential aspects. Yet this appearance is deceptive. His seminal understanding that the actualisation of these values involved their temporalisation and a process of historical realisation was revolutionary. The realisation of spirit's full self-knowledge is conceived as a single, unified historical enterprise. Spirit is the substance of history and its self-cultivation signifies the actualisation of humanity's inherent spiritual perfection. Before saying anything more about Hegel's interpretation of history and his insights into its significance, we must return to his account of finite spirit. In particular, Hegel's anthropology reveals some crucial elements of his understanding of humanity's historical dynamism. The spiritual capacities of the human species are 'pre-historical' in the sense that they underlie historical development.They exist as latent potentialities only fully realised in history. They are, therefore, only accessible to *post factum* analysis.

In the Encyclopaedia Hegel designated 'ideality' and 'manifestation' as the distinctive and interwoven determinations of 'natural' finite spirit. Ideality is defined by Hegel as spirit's capacity to reduce the external to its own inwardness.[40] It is the intellectual capacity to classify particular objects of the external world as members of a class existing only 'ideally' yet, at the same time, constituting their essence. These objects are appropriated as universals and lose their apparent independence and concrete particularity. Universality is an essential property of spirit.[41] The capacity for abstraction manifest in idealisation strips the representation of subjective immediacy and raises it to the universal, intersubjective domain of thought.

The complementary capacity to 'ideality' is humanity's ability to objectify itself in determinate being. This ability to posit itself in the 'Other', to impress it with one's own nature Hegel terms 'manifestation'. By means of this transformative process of positing its other, spirit actualises itself in the external world. Both of these capacities 'ideality' and 'manifestation' involve the diremption of spirit. Simultaneously, spirit appropriates/negates the existing and posits itself through self-objectification. In the shape of a continuous dynamic process these spiritual capacities together constitute the spiritual core of humanity. For Hegel, they signify spiritual subjectivity.[42]

These latent faculties of subjectivity are possessed as a spiritual *telos* of humanity requiring realisation. Humanity cannot remain an inert being in the condition of nature but immediately commences its gradual self-transcendence and becoming to spirit. In contrast to the animal immersed in mere sensuous feeling and suitably adapted to a pre-existing natural environment, the human species is furnished with its own means of self-transcendence and it capable of making a home virtually anywhere.

Hegel's anthropology provides an account of man as a thinking being that challenges the classical conception of human thought. In keeping with his dynamic understanding of spirit, his emphasis falls on the *willed essence of thought* as an active interaction between humanity and its world. While Hegel preserved disinterested contemplation as an indispensible moment of theoretical activity, he understands thought as a grasping *(greifen)* constitution of its object. Not confined to feeling, man interposes thought between impulses and their satisfaction. But this realm of thought is an active appropriation. The human capacity to enter the domain of ideal ends depends upon this essential unity of thinking and willing.[43] Animals are chained to their inorganic nature because they lack the dual capacity to think it as other and willfully transform it into their own. This universality and potential unlimitedness of man that gives him 'a much more extensive environment and makes all objects' his 'inorganic nature and objects of knowing' resides in the spiritual capacity to perceive the immediate natural environment as lacking, inessential, as object and be driven to transform it.

The corollary of Hegel's dynamic, appropriating view of human spirituality is his radically anthropocentric conception of nature. He no longer sees nature in Kantian terms as a realm of appearances operating according to its own necessary laws and alien to human freedom. On the contrary, it is truly a 'being for humans'. Nature is the pre-condition of human spiritual unfolding and its instrument. As the terrain and means of humanity's development towards self-recognition, nature is an always changing determination of spirit. Always changing because in his own self-transformation, man constantly reposits nature in new forms and appearances. As we shall see, far from celebrating this emancipatory conception of humanity's increasing power over nature, a vastly changed historical perspective will force the Frankfurt School to radically question this instrumentalisation of nature as an expression of a deformed rationality forged in the domination of both internal and external nature.

Determinants of historical dynamism

Hegel's theory of historical development is multi-faceted and exceedingly rich. The dynamic of spiritual self-diremption plays itself out in numerous dimensions on a number of levels. At the most basic level, organic nature provides a model that specifies 'need' as the pre-condition of all living processes. Need plays a significant role in Hegel's understanding of both natural and social processes. This testifies to the continuing importance of his initial model of organic diremption.

Like the animal, man experiences need engendered by periodic sensations of lack and suffering. Yet, unlike the animal, he possesses a ideational faculty which intercedes between desire and the impulse for immediate satisfaction. It signifies the suspension of appetite. The mediation of thought temporarily postpones satisfaction and animates latent theoretical, constructive and creative powers. Postponement allows for the gradual transformation of needs as thought reshapes and augments their recurrent pattern. So in this most elementary dimension of human life immanent spiritual capacities are already activated.

Once Hegel moves on to a specific consideration of historical development, his discussion of need is always resituated and complicated by an acute recognition of the impact of social and historical mediation. This is perhaps his most profound insight. The dynamic process of man's interchange with nature cannot be abstracted from the constantly changing historico-cultural context in which it takes place.

Hegel gives particular attention to the domain of social interaction. The early sections of the Phenomenology of Spirit outline the principal part played by social interaction in conditioning subjectivity and self-consciousness. The famous depiction of the struggle for recognition and its consolidation in definite social relations of domination and subordination represents a pathbreaking glimpse into the social construction of subjectivity. This point is amplified in the Lectures on the Philosophy of World History:

> The spirit's own consciousness must realise itself in the world; the
> material or soil in which it is realised is none other than the general
> consciousness, the consciousness of the nation. This consciousness
> encompasses and guides all the aims and interests of the nation, and it is
> on it that the nation's rights, customs and religion depend. It is the
> substance which underlies the spirit of a nation, even if individual human
> beings are unaware of it and simply take it for granted. It is a form of
> necessity, for the individual is brought up within its atmosphere and does
> not know anything else. . . . No individual can transcend it, and although
> the individual may be able to distinguish himself and others of his kind,
> he can make no such distinction between himself and the spirit of the
> nation.[44]

All liberal theories of social contract failed to appreciate the significance of the supra-individual social medium conditioning subjectivity. As a spiritual being the human individual was potentially free but this did not mean that he/she was a self-sufficient totality. Subjectivity is always bound to, and conditioned by, certain external circumstances. Freedom and dependency here are not opposed. Hegel stressed that the individual could only attain real freedom within a broader material and socio-cultural context which provided a medium that circumscribed the form of freedom in any given age.[45]

Hegel's keen awareness of this inter-dependency between the individual and society led him to explore the ramifications of social interaction. The historically generated ensemble of social institutions and relations embodied and preserved the essential achievements of human development. Each dimension of collective life presupposed specific inter-subjective rules, forms and relations. Even the most elemental, 'natural' sphere of basic needs was socially organised in the case of human beings. Such obligatory arrangements organised and institutionalised labour as a lawful, regularised activity of need satisfaction.

Hegel broke new philosophical ground in emphasising the importance of labour as a motor of historical development. Yet, it is noteworthy that he conceptualises this activity specifically in terms of generalised social relations. Labour is not a naturalistic response to need. On the contrary, it is a *disciplined, institutionalised* activity always embedded in specific social arrangements and *socialised* needs and abilities. Hegel symbolised this social contextualisation of labour with his account of the dialectic of master and slave. His strategy here was to underline that spirit is not some sort of fundament at the core of individual subjectivity but a *generalised consciousness* born of a shared form of life, a medium in which individuals mutually form one another and are raised to assume the form of subjectivity appropriate to their station and the age.[46]

With this historico-social medium in mind, we should pay some closer attention to Hegel's account of labour. He maintains in the Phenomenology of Spirit that work teaches restraint to the natural individual. Labour requires him to transcend egoism and the impulse of mere appetite. Discipline is an indispensible means of activating theoretical powers. The suspension of consumption and the recognition of the independence of natural objects are landmarks in humanity's quest to dispel the alienness of nature. Work has an educative function in so far as it stimulates the augmentation and extension of spiritual capacities. It consists in both the theoretical and practical appropriation by man of a foreign and limited reality. It permits him to objectify his potential universality in a world of objects. The world increasingly bears the stamp of human productivity and creativity. Work exemplifies a growing human control over nature.[47]

According to Hegel, the slave is the primary bearer of the spiritual developments occasioned by the institutionalisation of labour under conditions of domination. Only the slave is compelled to self-discipline; he is forced to transform an alien objectivity and, in so doing, exercises all of his spiritual potentialities. The slave posits himself as the 'negative power' in reality. In labour he internalises the will of the master and the activity elevates him above his own particularity.[48] The master, on the other hand, is constrained by his social privilege never to escape an 'unalloyed feeling of self'. His own imperious self-will is a freedom enmeshed in servitude to immediate appetites. He is incapable of recognising form as the 'universal formative activity' of self-consciousness.[49]

As mentioned, Hegel's phenomemological analysis of labour indicates the complex inter-meshing of labour (man's relation to nature) and social interaction (man's relation to other men) but it does not really thematise this interpenetration. Both are simply contributory dimensions to the historical unfolding of finite spirit. Yet, this historical unfolding itself presupposes some account of the objective configurations of spirit that unify these two dimensions. The concept of objective spirit was crucial to Hegel's understanding of history. Hegel viewed the formation of human communities into higher social forms like the *polis* states as the beginning of history proper. The objective sphere of social existence not only serves as the foundation of spirit's actual realisation in language and institutions but it also makes possible a high cultural sphere of symbolic representation. The latter sphere is the purest dimension of human self-consciousness and self-recognition. Hegel understood this sphere of Absolute spirit as the highest expression of humanity's faculty for ideality. Yet, while it possesses eternal value, this cultural sphere arises from, and is embedded in, the changing objective configurations of socio-historical life.

History and the spirit of the nation

Hegel's understanding of objective spirit depends upon the idea of spirit as a vital, subjective, self-dirempting, processual universal. The unfolding of spirit in history is manifest in the concrete formation and dissolution of particular societies. Each society contributing to this universal process itself forms a 'totality' which portrays the same organic evolution as spirit. All the unique and diverse characteristics of the society constitute a living whole:

> The spirit's acts are of an essential nature; it makes itself in reality what it already is in itself, and is therefore its own deed or creation. In this way, it becomes its own object, and has its existence before it. And it is the same with the world which also has an existence in space. Its religion, ritual, ethics, customs, art, constitution and political laws – indeed the whole range of its institutions, events and deeds – all this is its own creation, and it is this which makes a nation what it is.[50]

An admirer of Montesquieu, Hegel did not ignore the natural and physical determinants of historical societies which formed the material basis of their specific historical contributions. Nevertheless, his principal emphasis invariably falls on the general consciousness of the society in question. It is this consciousness as expressed in the forms of communal organisation (primarily the political state) which enhances the natural bounty in specific ways and enlivens the whole historical formation with its own unique configuration of spiritual freedom.[51]

This *identity* between the general consciousness or spirit of a nation and the universal spirit of world history was a key to Hegel's interpretation of history. It can also be viewed as an answer to his earlier problem of religious diremption. The divine is actualised in each collective spiritual individuality.[52] Each spiritual whole represents a link in the chain of divine spirit.[53] Hegel's metaphor of the 'chain of spirit' requires careful interpretation to distinguish it from the Rankean idea that each historical epoch was 'equally close to God'. Although Hegel agreed with his younger historicist contemporary in ascribing a theological meaning to the historical process as a whole, he insisted that the teleology of history was rational and implied a *unified developmental process* or *progress*. The spirit of each society was a manifestation of the universal in a more developed form than the one it succeeded. Each new historical form was a unique contribution to the ultimate spiritual meaning of history. More than the mere addition of incommensurable shapes and diversity, history, for Hegel, possessed an immanent cumulative significance. As we shall see, Ranke's more positivist leaning revolted before this rationalist understanding of history. Against this, Hegel's historical optimism permeates his concept of totality:

> World history is the expression of the divine process which is a graduated progression in which the spirit comes to know and realise itself and its own truth. . . .The principles of the national spirits in their necessary progression are themselves only moments of one universal spirit, which ascends through them in the course of history to its consummation in an all-embracing totality.[54]

In Hegel's understanding, historical progress is tied to the idea of diremption. Each historically significant society is fated to reproduce the basic pattern of spiritual self-realisation – actualisation of essential dispositions, unity and immanent self-dissolution. This dynamics of diremption informs Hegel's analysis of all the great historical societies. Each, in the period of its maturation, manifests a unified will. Citizens perceive their own self-identity, interests and destiny as so closely interwoven with whose of the city-state as to be virtually identical.[55] In this early phase, the discrepency between national potential and its actualisation is bridged by a flowering of national creativity that realises the national spirit as a set of institutions, a vital shared consciousness and an appropriate configuration of freedom.

This achievement of communal solidarity and unity is, however, always relatively short-lived. As a universal, spirit cannot bear the constraints of the particularity of the nation's self-satisfied existence. The immanent universality of spirit assumes a destructive, negative form of opposition with the society itself. The result is manifest diremption marked by internal social divisions and the loss of public enthusiasm. The citizen's commitment to communal goals and values slackens as he withdraws into his own private interests and particularity. For Hegel, this was a sure sign of the demise of a national spirit. Yet, his attitude to these symptoms of diremption undergoes an unmistakeable transformation from his initial historical pessimism. Recollection of the ossification and decline of a great national spirit remains an occasion for sad reflection on the transience of even great historical achievements. But this does not prevent him from deriving a positive meaning out of such historical tragedies. Specifically resorting to the biological metaphor of perennial revitalisation,[56] Hegel insists that this process of increasing social divisions must be viewed as the manifestation of a recurrent cycle. But historical recurrence is to be distinguished from the tedious, unchanging cycles of nature:

> There is nothing new under the sun (in the natural cycle). But this is not so with the sun of spirit. Its movement and progression do not repeat themselves, for the changing aspect of the spirit as it passes through endlessly varying forms is essentially progress.[57]

Here Hegel demonstrates his mature reconciliation with the course of contemporary history. It is based on a theory of historical progress which still needs to be spelt out in terms of Hegel's understanding of modern bourgeois society. However, before doing this we should briefly recapitulate the significance of his new conceptualisation of totality.

Hegel's *historicisation* of the totality concept implied a view of history as a process of cumulative human self-definition. In this process, man's spiritual potentialities were developed to their fullest extent. Spiritual self-sufficiency, however, truly applies only to the realm of the spiritual Absolute – art, religion and philosophy. In regard to finite human historical development, it is appropriate to speak only of relative totalities (specific socio-cultural wholes) as moments of the Absolute. This belief in the immanent self-movement of history in the form of human self-development imparted to this conception a striking dynamism and an emphatic humanist meaning. History signified the realisation of human freedom. At the same time, however, Hegel provided history with a metaphysico-theological meaning and a teleologico-finalistic interpretation. The interpretative storms which were later to factionalise the Hegelian School clearly find their theoretical origins in the tensions of this powerful synthesis of emancipatory and conservative elements.[58] Typically, this latter strain in Hegel's synthesis is thought to be exemplified in his reconciliation with his contemporary historical conditions. If history had attained its culmination in modernity, it was *imperative* to perceive the rationality of the present. Yet, as we shall see, Hegel's attitude to modernity is far more complex than is usually credited. The problem of Hegel's historical optimism and his 'reconciliation with reality' requires a closer look at his interpretation of modernity and, especially, of modern civil society.

The system of needs as immanent reason

Our discussion of Hegel's early work has indicated that the transformation of his attitude towards modernity and particularly to the signs of socio-cultural diremption was initiated and facilated by a complex combination of factors: the reinterpretation of Christianity on the organist model of life, the discovery of political economy and its assertion of the immanent economic rationality of the bourgeois forms and the extended division of labour, the recent post-Kantian developments within theoretical philosophy, all against the background of a changed historical outlook and the disappointment of Hegel's optimistic political hopes. The influence of the new political economy was strikingly evident in his appreciation of 'economic rationality' and in the role he attributed to new human needs in his account of historical development.

Within Hegel's new interpretative framework, all manifestations of decline and decadence – individualism, privatisation, cultural heterogeneity, intensified political struggles and increasing social divisions – became susceptible to a more positive alternative reading. The new perspective relied heavily on the dialectic of generality and individuality unearthed and celebrated by the new political economy. As early as the System of Ethical Life (1802) written at Jena, Hegel adopted a developmental account of history based on the new ideas. It stressed the expansion of human labour, the growth of mutual dependence and the evolution of an elaborate network of needs which constantly generated both new needs and new forms of productive organisation.[59]

These economic insights received a much more elaborate and sophisticated treatment in the account of civil society presented by Hegel in the Philosophy of Right (1821). But the key idea remained the same. Beneath the contemporary appearance of private vices, increasing social divisions, class conflict and inequality flowing from bourgeois economic relations was a more fundamental unity. An expanded division of labour had created a complex system of needs which increasingly encompassed all modern individuals. Specialisation and social heterogeneity were not simply negative phenomena to be bemoaned. More essentially, they were signs of a rich, comprehensive system of societal satisfaction of needs possessing its own internal dynamic. The activity of the isolated labourer contributed to a network of mutual social inter-dependence which maintained the unity of society as a constantly self-reproducing totality. From this perspective all individual strivings assumed a new significance: they were the manifestation/instruments of an immanent social reason furthering the welfare of all individuals within the social whole.

Hegel did not accept all the destructive consequences of this dialectic of civil society without reservation but he did clearly affirm the fundamental idea of an *immanent rationality* at the very heart of the new bourgeois social order. The fundamental reason for this affirmation lies not in Hegel's appreciation of civil society as an *separate new* social sphere nor in his positive assessment of its potentiality as a sphere for the free development of individuality. Both these factors were significant in his final assessment but not alone decisive. The great advance of the bourgeois system was that it made progressive change *the principle of its own inherent functioning*.[60] This bourgeois social mechanism, tempered by some state intervention, realised qualitative progress, expansion in both the organisation of production and institutional reform as essential moments of its own dynamism. Bourgeois society could accommodate significant change without precipitating crisis and revolution. Its mechanisms enabled social contradictions and diremption to be ameliorated and transcended (in the Hegelian sense of *aufgehoben)* in the immanent dynamic movement of society itself.

This instance of immanent social reason served as a model for Hegel's broader understanding of the general relation between individuality and universality in history. This schema of underlying rationality behind the apparent chaos of the new commercial system provides a framework for interpreting the entire historical process. Hegel's famous idea of the 'ruse of reason' encapsulates the conviction that history works towards supra-individual spiritual ends through individual passions and private interests without the latter necessarily being conscious of the higher rational principles they advance. This formula is nothing more than a historical generalisation of the dialectic of individuality and generality taken over from the political economists.

It was a simple matter for Hegel to reconcile this idea of an immanent social reason with the unorthodox theological impulses that still permeated his thinking. It was easy to identify in this immanent social reason the modern configuration of the universal reason of spirit. Civil society provides an adequate social arena for the actualisation of a new, higher form of human subjectivity and its aspirations for complete autonomy. Modern civil society greatly expanded the scope of subjective possibilities and of free action. The subterranean workings of bourgeois relations had already almost completely destroyed traditional social relations and the liberalisation of Prussia as an immediate response to defeat at the hands of Napoleon seemed part of the process of dismantling remaining obstacles to the further extension of subjective freedom. In this climate, despite occasional setbacks, Hegel's optimism seemed warranted.

In his Philosophy of Right, he analyses the contribution of this new system of mutual inter-dependence to the modern realisation of freedom. His emphasis falls on the altered form of historicity ushered in by the development of modern civil society. Its immanent dynamism signifies an enormous expansion and multiplication of human needs that constitute a 'second human nature' increasingly corresponding to the spiritual aspiration towards universality.[61] As Hegel says, the modern expanded division of labour and its network of social inter-dependence stimulated a concern for freedom. Subjectivity was no longer submerged in the necessities of natural existence and community but now found a more perfect expression in the complex mutual exchanges of commercial life.[62] The decisive basis of this progressive dynamism was the massive accumulation of wealth and objective skills generated by the new socio-economic mechanism.

Hegel does not, however, attribute all these contemporary achievements to the dynamism of civil society alone. The historical evolution of spirit is the labour of millenniums and Hegel's analysis refuses to simplify the multiple dimensions involved. In this longer perspective, he also viewed the Protestant Reformation as the decisive modern landmark in the awakening of free subjectivity. Nevertheless, he undoubtedly considered bourgeois society the most perfect objective instantiation of rational freedom; an appropriate soil for the full actualisation of all subjective potentialities and a dynamic, flexible institutional framework making possible a non-revolutionary absorption of the social tensions generated by its own progressive internal dynamics.

Reconciliation with reality and the modern state

Hegel's generally positive estimation of bourgeois modernity was not an uncritical endorsement of all aspects of contemporary reality. The surrender of his early normative ideal of a homogeneous, unified culture in favour of a historically immanent standard tied to the evolution of spirit did, however, imply a more positive and deeper analysis of contemporary contradictions. This *historicisation / ontologisation* of the concept of totality as an all-encompassing spiritual unfolding designated the present historical arrangement of socio-political institutions (primarily the state) as the contemporary form of an immanent, universal standard. While this interpretative framework implicitly legitimated modern bourgeois society, it was not intended as an *apologia*. A more detailed account of Hegel's analysis of bourgeois society should clarify his attitude on this point.

The ideas of diremption and contradictory progress which were the corner-stones of Hegel's understanding of history were preserved in his theory of bourgeois society. He viewed the self-regulating dynamism of bourgeois society as the closure of an earlier phase of unconscious historical development that engendered radical breaks and historical discontinuity. The 'automatic' mechanism of bourgeois society incorporated diremption as an internal facet of its normal, rational functioning. Hegel's appreciation of these internal dynamics allowed him to perceive this self-regulation as the culmination of social development. This system could tolerate a certain amount of social friction and institutional dissonance as a normal aspect of its own dynamics. But obviously Hegel imposed definite limits on the manifestations of conflict, division and irrationality he was prepared to accept as the ineradicable accidentality and contingency of finite conditions. His early concern with the social and cultural costs of historical 'progress' is still very much apparent.

The Philosophy of Right presents a frank and balanced account of the gains and costs of the bourgeois commercial system. Hegel recognised the capacity of market relations to reconcile some social contradictions but he also acknowledged that it generated others. The same system of needs and mutual inter-dependence which he extolled as the foundation of contemporary individual freedom was also responsible for an exponential explosion of neediness and want. The other side of rapidly expanding social wealth and objective development was a frightening growth in social distress and pauperisation. Hegel explains the modern division of labour as the main cause of the virtual dehumanisation of a whole class of unemployed (*der Pöbel*). These individuals were thrown into poverty without the opportunity or the means to participate in the material and intellectual benefits or share in the enhanced individual autonomy accruing from the expansionary tendencies of civil society.[63]

Like the early political economists, Hegel viewed these horrific sacrifices as a necessary human cost of economic development, progress and the provision of a social arrangement adequate to the contemporary demands of autonomous subjectivity. It is clear, however, that his idea of modern society incorporated important features that were aimed at ameliorating the conditions of victims, providing institutional support for them and eventually eliminating the worst excesses of the system. While contradictions were inherent in the internal mechanisms of bourgeois society, he maintained that astute social innovations and state intervention would moderate them and cushion their destructive social impact. It is not going too far to say that Hegel anticipated the modern welfare state. His optimistic assessment of modern bourgeois society at least partially rested on the belief that its social contradictions could be checked and alleviated by reform, the modification of civil institutions and the careful supervisory activity and authority of the modern rational state.

Hegel's mature conception of the modern state was the condensation of a long period of reflection on the problem of an appropriate socio-political form for modernity beginning with his early work The German Constitution (1800-2). There he had charted a middle way between a non-interventionist model of social life and one of oppressive state regulation and control.[64] His solution crystallised in the Philosophy of Right where he argued for a complex triparite vision of modern society. Bourgeois civil society formed the basis of this model but the extreme social convulsions it sometimes engendered had to be mediated and offset by interventionary social mechanisms serving a more complete integration of private and universal interests.

This essential integration and amelioration of the contradictory dynamics of civil society was to be aided by guild-like corporations. While trade guilds were historically on the decline in Hegel's Germany, he viewed an reinvigorated version of them as an essential mediating link between individual and general interests. Functioning similarly to a trade guild, the role of the corporations was to represent collective sectional interests – all those in the same profession or trade – and thereby uphold relatively universal concerns in the predominately private, civil sphere.[65] Corporations were not to impose external controls but organically express common concerns and protect the welfare of individual members.[66]

The corporations were not Hegel's only concession to reformatory impulses and the social need to shore up society against the ravages of a competitive economy. He also mentions the existence of a public authority assigned with the task of controlling crime, facilitating the efficient supply of essential commodities and generally regulating the free sphere of commercial activity. [67] Hegel firmly acknowledges the necessity of regulation as a counter to extremes of private interest:

> This (particular) interest invokes freedom of trade and commerce against
> control from above; but the more blindly it sinks into self-seeking aims,

the more it requires such control to bring it back to the universal. Control is also necessary to diminish the danger of upheavals arising from clashing interests and to abbreviate the period in which their tension should be eased through the working of a necessity of which they themselves know nothing.[68]

These theoretical additions and modifications of empirical reality in Hegel's idea of the modern state indicate the existence of a *residual normative element* in his philosophy long after he had determined to reconcile himself with modernity and opt for a philosophy of unity founded on radical historical immanence. While this normativism was strictly precluded by his *historicisation* of the concept of totality, the fact that he was only occupied with the *rational idea of the state* – only in principle realised in existing bourgeois reality – in the <u>Philosophy of Right</u>, enabled him to preserve a crucial *critical distance* from contemporary conditions and institutions.

This critical distance is also embedded in Hegel's concept of the modern state. The sort of social cohesion and public spiritedness he desired was inimical to the domain of civil society primarily orientated to private interests. The measures of reform anticipated by Hegel were never conceived as fundamentally reversing this basic orientation but merely introducing the element of universality into the civil sphere as an organic link to higher, collective interests.

For Hegel, it was the modern state that represented the full instantiation of universality and rationality in the sphere of objective spirit. He categorically rejected the liberal view of the state which reduced its functions to defence, protection of private property and facilitation of free commerce. Hegel's state had a far more significant role to play. He was probably encouraged to take this course by his experience of a relatively enlightened Prussian bureaucracy at Berlin.[69] At the same time, there were important systematic motives for his idealisation of the modern state. According to his understanding of historical development as the divine unfolding of spirit, he was compelled to view the institutional and legal structure of the leading historical nations as the objective manifestation of spiritual essence. In particular, Hegel interpreted the state as the bearer of this higher necessity; it ensured the provision of the essential stable medium of general consciousness; it provided citizens with a concrete universal and end thereby raising them above their own selfish particular interests to a real participation in a communal ethical life. The requirements and needs of the civil sphere, accordingly, were subordinated by Hegel to this higher collective and spiritual end. Individuals would only experience their full individuality by active participation in this universal ethical life.[70]

Although Hegel's conception of the universality of the modern state drew on a number of traditional and contemporary sources, his idealisation of the Greek *polis* was probably still the most significant. While his mature philosophy of history allowed him to look on many features of modernity as historical advances, he held firm to the classical ideal of the citizen's total identification with the political community as the noblest empirical expression of freedom:

> But the subjective will has also a substantial life – a reality – in which it moves in the region of essential being, and has the essential itself as the object of its existence. This essential being is the union of the subjective with the rational Will: it is the moral whole, the state, which is that form of reality in which the individual has and enjoys his freedom; but on the condition of his recognising, believing in and willing that which is common to the whole.[71]

It is clear from this passage that the individual autonomy which Hegel claimed as the great historical advance of modernity is embedded within a definite inter-subjective social world. The institutions of the state form a structural network within which individuals possess reciprocal rights and duties. They are an infrastructure which not only provides a framework for free activities but also constitutes the individuals themselves as legal and moral persons. The task of social integration is one involving all spheres of modern society. Hegel sees the family, civil society and the state all having a specific role to play in the process that raises natural individuality to a full participation in the citizen-body, in moderating social dissensions and promoting a modern sense of community.

The privileged position Hegel allocates to the institutions of the state *vis-à-vis* civil society is another indication of the concealed normative dimension in his mature thought. The idea of the rational state reveals a critical distance to contemporary institutions. But this normative stance was not a complete relapse into the philosophical dualism he formerly criticised. Hegel's rational idea was a synthesis of empirical elements drawn from all Europe.[72] Sometimes they had no empirical basis in Prussia at all. Yet, despite Hegel's efforts to concretise his critical standpoint, his rational state nowhere actually existed in the modern bourgeois world. Implicitly, it remained a *normative, theoretical construct.*

This *suppressed* normativism in Hegel's theory of the state is indicative of a deep tension in his concept of totality between the rational universal and contemporary empirical conditions. He endorsed existing institutions as, in principle, an adequate finite likeness to the Absolute. Bourgeois socio-political forms were potentially capable of retaining their 'self-identity' in the process of rapid change. They eliminated the necessity for radical historical disjunctions by incorporating the mechanisms for immanent, rational transformation within the machinery of their own self-reproduction. In this *idealised* description of bourgeois society as rational, progressive and self-regulating, Hegel revealed both his moderate political reformism and the definite limits of his political imagination. At the same time, there is a strong *realist* element which correctly located the source of the contemporary aspiration towards individual autonomy and social emancipation in the internal dynamism and diremptions of bourgeois society. Most of Hegel's philosophical contemporaries, whether radical or conservative, were convinced that at the heart of his philosophy was the humanist, Enlightenment message of humanity's *historical self-creation and self-legislation*. This widely felt contemporary judgment finds confirmation in the radical 'historicist tradition' of totality thinking from Marx to the Frankfurt School which has drawn so much emancipatory inspiration from Hegel's thought. Yet, Hegel was clearly a transitional figure bridging two epochs. His central concept of spirit unites the *dynamism* of the modern world with historical *tradition* by portraying history as a process of human self-elevation towards freedom and supra-individual rationality in which the cleavage between humanity and divinity is finally overcome.

Hegel's optimistic, humanist message is embedded within a *theological* conception of man's essential spirituality. This metaphysical broadening of the notion of subjectivity enabled him to view history not merely as a process of human self-determination and self-realisation but also as the self- unfolding and self-mediation of a supra-individual universal totality of rational relations. Hegel's modernising synthesis remained, paradoxically, a metaphysics of the eternal Absolute.

The precarious balance of this synthesis rested on the historical compromises of post-revolutionary Prussian politics. Hegel's optimism relied on the tenuous basis of enlightened liberal reform within a authoritarian, bureaucratic state. As this liberalism gave way before the Restoration and the Prussian state met the challenge of new dynamic socio-economic forces with political repression, this fragile historical basis began to disintegrate. From the 1840s, German philosophy repudiated metaphysics and the radical wing of the Hegelian school annexed the critical, historicist dimension of his philosophy reshaping it as basis of a critical theory of bourgeois society. With Marx, its central idea of a historical process bearing the immanent essential meaning of reality was finally submitted to a revolutionary interpretation and put in the service of contemporary radical social praxis.

Chapter Two

Marx: from history to praxis

Hegel's dynamic, processual concept of totality testified to his confident belief in historical progress. The dynamism of the concept reflected the real historical movement of the epoch; the overturning of both the social and political forms of the *ancien régime* and their replacement by emergent bourgeois relations and institutions more in tune with the modern spirit of individual self-determination. Bourgeois society, however much Hegel only anticipated its actualisation in Germany, signified, at least in principle, the instantiation of a rational, self-regulating social organisation. Hegel's thought both expressed and largely endorsed this revolutionary historical transformation. History was conceived as the progressive human attainment of self-knowledge and freedom.

Hegel elevated contemporary revolutionary processes and events to a cosmic-metaphysical significance. His understanding of spirit acknowledged a *decisive historical rupture* while simultaneously confirming *historical continuity and its unified essential meaning*. Contemporary crisis and social diremption were mere moments in the continuous, all-encompassing immanent process that achieved man's complete self-recognition as the realisation of spirit. Chapter One has argued that this interpretation lacked neither a sense of historical contradiction nor a critical social perspective. It was, nevertheless, a peculiar sort of theodicy: human history as a divine historico-ontological process.

This complex synthesis of revolution and tradition could not survive the accelerating processes of bourgeois modernisation. Its tensions surfaced in the squabbles that engulfed Hegel's disciples after his death in 1831. The real struggles between the liberal modernising forces and conservative Restorationists found a philosophical echo in the disputes between young and old, left and right Hegelians.

Marx and the Young Hegelians

Karl Marx (1818-1883) studied philosophy at the time of these conflicts which signalled the ultimate demise of Hegelianism's cultural dominance. He attended the lectures of Eduard Gans, one of Hegel's immediate pupils, and actively participated in the great controversies which marked the dissolution of Hegelianism.[1] Marx's earliest writings represent a critical dialogue with the Hegelian system in which he edged towards a new definition of the problems of the age and his own independent response to them.

Marx's initial attitude to Hegel combines youthful deference with an increasingly critical note. In the dissertation of 1841 Hegel was 'our master' and his thought was the only modern 'total philosophy'.[2] Soon, however, Marx was directing his critique against the totality claim of the Hegelian philosophy.[3] But even this initial critical move is couched in terms of his endorsement of Hegel's method and his philosophical aim. The method involved the idea of the self-mediating concept and the leading principle was the Hegelian goal to realise the unification of the rational and the real. This remained Marx's standpoint only a short while longer until his independent critique broadened to encompass the whole philosophical enterprise. However, until late 1843 he agreed with the other Young Hegelians that Hegel's programme for the reconciliation of the opposition of concept and reality by means of the processual mediation of the concept was both a great philosophical advance and the basis for a radically new practical standpoint. The principles of Hegel's totality claim were not in question; the Young Hegelians, including Marx, were only hostile to its 'purely speculative' realisation.

In the contemporary climate of overt political reaction and censorship of all liberal opposition, Hegel's equation of the rational notion with these antiquated and authoritarian state institutions seemed a farce. The gaping divorce between *the Idea* and existing irrationality completely compromised Hegel's theoretical reconciliation. Formulated in the years when Prussia had led the way in progressive enlightened reform, Hegel's optimistic historical scenario collapsed under the weight of an increasingly repressive Restoration faced with strengthening liberal opposition and economic crisis. Marx echoed the widely shared view that Hegel's one-sided speculative solution to the question of existing irrationality was a purely theoretical answer unable to eliminate actual contradictions.

The opportunity to fully substantiate this fledgling practical critique came when Marx's academic hopes were obstructed and he turned to journalism. Working for the *Rheinische Zeitung* he was obliged to follow everyday politics at close hand. In studying the Prussian legislature and its debates he saw the direct influence of powerful material interests on the resolution of concrete issues. This caused him to radically question the very foundations of Hegel's political philosophy. The idea of the universal state embodying the higher interests of society and overriding the particular interests of the civil order was unmasked as a complete fiction. Marx now made a decisive theoretical advance. At issue now was not just the deficiencies of Hegel's 'philosophical overcoming' of real societal contradictions but, far more importantly, the ideological character of his whole theoretical stance.[4]

The real problem was Hegel's inability to disentangle his philosophy from the existing world. This betrayed not just a premature reconciliation with the present social order but an indirect apologetics. The exhaustive commentary on Hegel's philosophy of state repeatedly ridicules the quite imaginary character of his supposed speculative autonomy from the existing world.[5] The Hegelian *Begriff* had no other manifestation than the realised historical world. Its independent, critical distantiation was a sham; it collapsed into an uncritical affirmation of the existing social arrangements. It legitimised antiquated authoritarian political structures by *theoretically transfiguring them into expressions of historical rationality* therefore *disguising the concrete material interests they served.* Just as damaging was Marx's critique of the other side of Hegel's contemplative standpoint. Pure thought lacked a *practical force* able to initiate real change. This merely confirmed the charge that the Hegelian philosophy was really unable to differentiate itself from the existing world.

Theory and praxis

Marx's initial critique of Hegel had merely expressed the shared belief amongst the Young Hegelians that theory should become practical. The major step in the gestation of his own Marxian perspective was this exposure of the ideological function of Hegel's philosophy. This crucial insight into the real practical determination of theory in contemporary society compelled Marx to rethink the general question of the relation between theory and praxis in the most radical way.

Hegel had already made a significant advance in drawing attention to the practical basis of theory. He recognised the historical conditioning of thought and its embeddedness in man's *active intentional* relation to the socio-natural environment. Yet, his practical, materially conditioned understanding of human thought was ultimately neutralised by the dominance of the contemplative moment within his philosophical system. Speculative thought, the culmination of spiritual self-development, transcended the merely subjective difference between theoretical and practical attitudes. Speculative thinking allowed the conditioned, finite subjectivity to absorb the whole content of world history, while, at the same time, realising a detachment shaped by a knowledge of the self's essential spiritual self-sufficiency. The role Hegel assigned to the state – the bearer of the rational idea above the particular interests and conflicts of civil society – only drew out the concrete political implications of the same idea.

In philosophical terms, Marx's critique of Hegel only extended and radicalised the latter's own understanding of the historical conditionedness of theory. In particular, Marx emphasised that the *practico-materialist determination of all theory and culture by the social interests expressed in it* put paid to the illusory independence of philosophy. In the same way that Marx saw the idea of the rational state as an indirect legitimisation of the dominant *Junker* interests, he viewed philosophy's alleged detachment as serving the same apologetic function.

This seminal discovery of the practico-materialist determination of theory had profound repercussions for Marx's own standpoint. One clear consequence was his recognition that rational theory required its own immanent practico-material force or historical agent. Such a sociological agent was lacking in Hegel's speculative philosophy. Therefore, the great contradictions of emerging bourgeois society remained untouched. Hegel merely assumed that the rational state would alleviate the worst symptoms of these ruptures while the contradictions themselves remained ineradicable costs of modern subjective autonomy. Hegel had seen no real historical agent with sufficient incentive to challenge these residual social irrationalities. This practical impotence was glaringly manifest in the absence of a future perspective in Hegel's philosophy. This only reinforced the ascendency of contemplation. His theory was conveniently limited to the passive, backward-looking role of the 'owl of Minerva'.

The logical outcome of this fundamental critique of Hegel's resolution of the theory/praxis relation was Marx's desire to anchor his own theory in *a concrete socio-practical perspective* and designate *a real historical agent of social transformation* for whom his materialist critique would both express and clarify its own long-term interests. The outlines of this strategy are clearly formulated in his Hegel's Philosophy of Right: Introduction (1843) where he envisages a crucial double connection between a practically constituted, interested theory and a social praxis illuminated and directed by it:

> The point is that revolution needs a passive element, a material basis.
> Theory is realised in a people only in so far as it is the realisation of
> peoples' needs. But will the enormous gap that exists between the
> demands of German thought and the responses of German reality now
> correspond to the same gap both between civil society and the state and
> the civil society and itself ? Will the theoretical needs be directly practical
> needs ? It is not enough that thought should strive to realise itself; reality
> must itself strive towards thought.[6]

In spite of the insight that 'reality must iself strive towards thought', Marx's formulation clearly preserves a residual Young Hegelianism that has not been completely shaken off. The Feuerbachian motif that the proletariat was to be the 'heart' of revolutionary emancipation and philosophy its 'head' still betrayed an exaggerated subjective activism counterposing 'dynamic' theory to the 'passive' material element activated by it. Marx, however, had moved to the point of situating his critical theory within the emerging class struggle of bourgeois society and viewing it as an expression of an incipient revolutionary self-consciousness. Critical theory is now interpreted as the theoretical clarification of the self-understanding and real needs of an immanent objective historical forces: the proletariat.[7]

As mentioned, Marx was not the first Young Hegelian to advocate the redirection of philosophical interest towards praxis and the future. Cieszkowski had championed the 'passage of philosophy beyond itself' and Moses Hess had already connected a philosophy of action with the cause of socialism.[8] Marx was not even the first theorist to view the proletariat as a potential revolutionary agent. To some extent this had already been anticipated by the St Simonians. In the contemporary historical context of intensified socio-political crisis and class struggle which culminated in the European-wide conflagration of 1848, with the propagation of socialist doctrines amongst the workers in nearby France, it is hardly surprising that even conservative thinkers had also recognised a potential social threat in the proletariat. In his Socialism and Communism in France (1842), Lorenz Von Stein had emphasised the potential social dangers of the rapid increase of the class of dispossessed and completely degraded individuals in bourgeois society. Marx's achievement was to synthesize these disparate elements within a very powerful philosophico-theoretical revolution.[9]

Marx's synthesis revolutionized traditional understandings of the theory/ praxis relation and appeared to also overcome the inherent difficulties he had exposed in Hegel's totality claim. It involved viewing the proletariat not just as a 'practical force' but as a dynamic ensemble of expanding human needs. Such a dynamic historical subject generates a new radical perspective on bourgeois society and seeks self-clarification through the theory which expresses it. Marx linked the socio-economic situation of the proletariat and the needs engendered by it with the development of a radical critique of this society and with the *practically neceassary* universal historical task to overthrow bourgeois forms and realise a rational society. The proletariat possessed both the incentive and the potential power to perform the practical act of socio-political reconciliation precluded from Hegel's perspective. It replaces Hegel's spirit as a real, concrete, historical subject. The implications of this immanent, dialectical understanding of the theory/praxis nexus only fully emerge in the German Ideology (1846) when Marx opts for the complete dissolution of philosophy as an independent force separate from the real historical process.[10]

In summary, Marx's initial critique of Hegel's philosophy rejects its totality claim. Hegel's belief that his philosophy presented a concrete totality of all the determinations of spirit involved an illegitame confusion of the descriptive and normative components of his theory. His historico-ontologisation of the concept of totality required the repudiation of a normative dimension. For Marx, this denial resulted in an ideological mystification. Hegel's philosophy provided an indirect *apologia* for the existing socio-political framework and masked the real contradictions between this social reality and rational theory. Hegel's concrete totality was really *a false totality*. The speculative unification of concept and reality surreptitiously elevated *rational prescription* to *description*. As a result, existing social contradictions were theoretically minimised and eternalised. This sanctioned eternalisation signified the premature closure of the historical process. Faced with the manifest irrationalities of the authoritarian Prussian regime, Marx denounced the ideological character of this historical closure and posited the practical necessity of a future emancipatory social struggle. Contemporary history is a site of open struggle between the emerging proletariat and the reactionary forces opposed to it.

This relentless critique does not, however, mean that Marx had completely rejected his erstwhile 'master'. Put simply, he still maintained allegiance to the principle of the Hegelian philosophy and acknowledged that any attempt to surpass it had to assimilate its truth. His very detailed critique of Hegel in the Economic and Philosophical Manuscripts of 1844 provides us with a clear indication of what Marx saw to be the main elements of this 'truth'.

The inheritance of idealism

In his 1844 critique, Marx maintained that the elements of a critical philosophy were already encrusted in Hegel's understanding of the process of mediation. They went 'far beyond Hegel's own point of view'[11] but had not yet attained self-clarity. This embryonic critique was still in a 'concealed' and 'mystified' form.

Hegel's most enduring achievement was his understanding of 'the self-creation of man' as a historical process in which man was the 'product of his own labour'. Moreover, this understanding of history viewed development as a process in alienation where human species-powers became estranged even in the very act of their creation and were henceforth treated as objects.[12] Hegel had interpreted human labour as a process of self-mediation in alienation which, only at the end of the entire historical process, was to be transcended in his own philosophy.

These core insights into a real 'dialectic of negativity' became the positive basis of Marx's own historical interpretation tied the critico-practical project of socialist revolution. He extracted the humanist significance from the Hegelian idea of spiritual self-mediation by reinforcing the *immanentist idea of the historical process*. This critical extraction entailed a materialist translation of Hegel's abstract, theological presuppositions. Marx viewed human labour as the obscured practical motor of the historical process.The incessant expansion of human needs and abilities due to the practical requirements to produce and reproduce the material conditions of life is seen as an ongoing process of practical mediation from which Hegel had abstracted. As we have seen in Chapter One, Hegel's account of historical development is multidimensional and included a keen awareness of the historical role of human labour. Yet, Marx oversimplifies in order to emphasise that Hegel's insights into the vital role of practical mediation are obscured by the inherent philosophical abstraction of his idealist method.

With this method Hegel had hypostasised consciousness in such a way as to reduce the concrete historico-practical development of the human species to a rarified process of unfolding consciousness. By reducing this rich multi-faceted practical process to a singular one of increasing self-consciousness, Hegel had fixed spirit *as an independent propelling force* to which he imputed the real direction and essence of the historical process.[13] Quite independently of the real practical processes of human self-production crystallised in social labour, Hegel had resorted to a *spiritual telos* to ensure the ultimate transcendence of alienation. Productive activity was excluded from such transcendence because Hegel persistently viewed it as a site of human limitation where spiritual aspirations and rationality never escaped accidentiality. In productive activity human freedom was constrained and therefore necessarily estranged. Objectively, it issued in unintended consequences while, subjectively, it was motivated by private, particular needs and petty self-interests. By ascribing a divine essence to human subjectivity, Hegel was able to interpret history as moved by a *telos* and objective meaning at once both *the product of human actors themselves* and, at the same time, in accordance with eternal, divine logic *quite independent of them.* For Hegel, the real bearer of the historical essence was ultimately not concrete individuals but world spirit (*Weltgeist*). In the spirit of Feuerbach, Marx castigated this theological conception as an abstraction of human thought from its natural-material process and therefore as an idealist inversion of the real situation, i.e., Feuerbach's view of the divine as the intellectual projection of human-species powers. Clearly, however, Marx's places far more stress on the practico-historical character of the process from which this abstraction takes place than in Feuerbach's sensualist-naturalist reading.

This critique of idealist abstraction went to the very heart of Hegel's concept of totality. Marx's ridicule of the idea of absolute spirit as a theological spectre undermined its theoretical presuppositions. It destroyed the idealist notion of infinite subjectivity which had shaped classical German Idealism from the time of Kant's revolutionary interpretation of objectivity as a product of transcendental synthesis. Marx's critique fused Feuerbach's materialist anthropology with the humanist historicism contained in Hegel's idealist version of man's historical self-constitution. Against some interpretations of the early Marx it should be emphasised that the latter moment clearly dominates his synthesis.[14] The result of this fusion was a radically new standpoint which became the permanent basis of Marx's own account of history.

Marx's concept of finite subjectivity

Marx's new concept of finite subjectivity is centred on the idea of *objective activity.* His concept of subjectivity, like Hegel's, presupposes consciousness. But, for him, consciousness is not the manifestation of latent spiritual powers; it is tied to the specific character of human activies as their expression. As Marx will later emphasise, consciousness is always consciousness of some specific life activity. This is not spiritual activity but the activities of production; production of material and ideal objects which, in turn, generate objective, essential powers.

This Marxian emphasis on production underscores two crucial features of his concept of finite subjectivity. Firstly, it implies the necessary metabolic exchange with nature as the essence of man's objective being:

> An objective being acts objectively, and it would not act objectively if objectivity were not an inherent part of its essential nature. It creates and establishes only objects because it is established by objects, because it is fundamentally nature. In the act of establishing it does not therefore descend from its 'pure' activity to the creation of objects; on the contrary, its objective product confirms its objective activity, its activity as the activity of an objective, natural being.[15]

Marx views man as a natural being, both active and limited. He posssesses both active and passive powers manifest in the form of vital drives and capacities, suffering and need. His sensuous nature is linked to his essential corporeality shared with animals. The objects of human desire exist outside and independently of it – they are the objects of human needs. Elementary biological needs like hunger exemplify the objective essence of these needs. Yet, while Marx goes to some lengths to stress the natural-objective foundation of human activity neglected by idealism, he is equally, if not more concerned, to register its dynamic, socio-historcial dimension. This fusion of two lines of critique (Feuerbachian and Hegelian) provides him with a comprehensive view of all aspects of determination conditioning the development of concrete finite, individuals.

This second dynamic dimension of human activity is vital to Marx's view. He recognises the human appropriation of objects and the objectification of increasing human powers as a dynamic process of historico-social constitution. Practical activity is conceived as always transforming both the manipulated object and the active subject in accordance with socially mediated rules and norms. Human essential powers are never stationary but are always augmented and expanded in their very use. Human labour is not merely repetitive but *creative* in a double sense. Not only is the world of objects humanised by the imposition of culturally and historically conditioned forms but these 'worked up' objects require new capacities and abilities and generate needs. Through this constant process objective human powers are expanded and the structure of existing human needs enriched.

Marx's dynamic view of the practical activation and accumulation of essential human powers draws heavily on Hegel's emancipatory idea of historical 'becoming'. Even the forming of the human senses is 'a labour of the entire history of the world down to the present'.[16] Human activity is characterised by the constant multiplication and expansion of abilities and needs. Yet, Marx clearly transforms Hegel's idealist bias. This dynamic process occurs within the context of, and is always determined by, a specific historico-social organisation of production. But, in accord with Hegel, Marxian humanism also categorically rejects the reduction of humanity to some purely 'natural' basis; he constantly reinterated the view that human essence and human activity are essentially historical and necessarily shaped by the reigning socio-historical forms.

The humanism of the 1844 manuscripts allows a neat encapsulation. On the one hand, Marx maintained that 'a being which does not have nature outside itself is not a natural being and plays no part in the system of nature'.[17] On the other, he asserts that the 'nature which develops in human history – the genesis of human society – is man's real nature; hence nature as it develops through industry, even though in an estranged form, is true anthropological nature'.[18] It should be underlined that Marx's commitment to the category of nature does not signify his capitulation to a Feuerbachian-style materialism. Nature signifies for Marx the 'double determination' of man; it is the irreducible basis and the constitutive practical arena and means of all human activity and development. Herein lies the substance of Marx's famous charge that Hegel's idealist dialectic confused objectification *(Vergegenständlichung)* and alienation *(Entfremdung)*. Marx considered objectification the essential constitutive activity of the human species through which it formed its own nature in the appropriation and transformation of objects. It could never be *aufgehoben* ('transcended').

The theoretical significance of this distinction lies in Marx's view that the abolition of exploitative forms of social organisation which excluded the vast majority of human beings from the historically created wealth produced by them did not mean the *transcendence of objectification as such*. It implied only the elimination and end to those alienated social forms. The fully realised human being remained completely at home in the activity of objectification. Marx's unqualified affirmation of this category spelt the death of Hegel's theologically inspired idea of spiritual self-estrangement where objectification marks the finitude and dependence of humanity in contrast to the essential self-sufficiency of spirit.

Marx's fusion of historicism and naturalism clearly presupposes a conception of history involving a double dialectic. Both man's interchange with nature and his social interaction with his fellows are concretely inextricably bound together and only analytically separable as two distinguishable aspects of a unified, dynamic historical process.

Totality and teleology

Marx's comprehensive new understanding of humanity as finite subjectivity called into question the very basis of the Hegelian concept of totality. His attack on the confusion of objectification and alienation constituted a break with the Hegelian idea of the identical subject/object. His affirmation of objectification collided with the Hegelian assertion of an all-encompassing spirituality in which nature was reduced to spiritual self-externalisation. This idea of an ultimate philosophico-theological identity, however interpreted, was repugnant to Marx. It signified a definite closure of history and a specific cessation and limit to humanity's self-unfolding.

We have already rehearsed some of the reasons for Marx's objections. His revolutionary call to a future orientated praxis required the repudiation of this theoretical closure of historical perspectives as 'ideological'. Hegel's 'end of history' sanctified many obsolete institutional residues of late feudal society as instantiations of the rational Idea. Futhermore, it restricted philosophy to the contemplative theoretical task of comprehending the world 'cut and dried'. Against all this, the Marxian concept of an objective, historically conditioned, finite subjectivity presupposed a ceaseless historical struggle against the resistances of nature and the previous limits of humanity's historically inherited social institutions, relations and patterns of life. This image of man in a permanent state of toil and historical self-transformation is especially conducive to a theory of open-ended historical totalisation. For all the humanist, dynamic elements of Hegel's vision, he never discharged the theological idea that the human essence was 'all that it will ever be'. For him, this idea of a pre-given, immanent *telos* was indispensible to a meaningful, intelligible account of human experience.

Given Marx's incontestable break with this idealist teleology, it is perhaps surprising to find its disfiguring traces in the 1844 manuscripts marring his realisation of an open-ended conception of history. He may have abandoned an *idealist* teleology but he immediately got caught up in an *anthropological* teleology irreconciliable with a truly open-ended concept of man's self-totalisation. Marx's early vision of communist society is marked by a teleological humanist anthropology that posits the resolution of *all historical oppositions and contradictions*. The explanation of this theoretical lapse is probably quite simple. Marx wanted to sharply contrast the alienated conditions of contemporary bourgeois society with the possibility of a radically alternative socialist future. But this is posited in abstract philosophical terms which frame a completely utopian vision of socialist society conceived as another 'end of history'.

At this stage, Marx understands communism as the 'genuine resolution of the conflict between man and nature, man and man – the true resolution of the strife between existence and essence, between objectification and self-confirmation, between freedom and necessity, between individual and the species'.[19] Ironically, here Marx repeats Hegel's error. In viewing communism as the 'riddle of history solved', he implicitly forecloses the historical process and proclaims an anthropological teleology. Hegel's spiritual essence is simply replaced by a notion of human essence whose historical realisation would signify the reconcilation of all historical tensions (both social and natural), the culmination of the total historical process and the attainment of a universal value perspective from which to judge and condemn all existing social conditions.

It would be grossly unfair not to acknowledge that this Marxian utopian vision was conceived not as the 'end of history' but as its new beginning. The actual realisation of unalienated social relations, a true symbiosis with the natural environment and real creative human freedom unconstrained by limitations imposed on the great majority of the population in the past by the division of labour and social relations of domination. However, Marx's fragmentary comments do not supply a conception of this idea that is consistent with, and adequate to, the radical historicist turn of his own thinking. His residual Hegelian framework still entailed a closed concept of historical totality.

Yet, as the idea of historical becoming was paramount to his thinking, he already differentiated his position from Feuerbach's philosophy of man. This is clearly evident in his unequivocal rejection of the idea of fixed, eternal anthropological traits in favour of a radical historical open-endedness. This tension in Marx's conception is traceable to his reliance upon philosophical abstraction in framing his idea of the future. This final obstacle to a fully consistent radically historicist conception of totalisation was soon eliminated by Marx's own searching self-critique.

The critique of philosophical history

In the opening pages of the German Ideology Marx and Engels declare: 'We know only a single science, the science of history'.[20] This assertion marks a consolidation of Marx's critical reflection on philosophy and a particularly sharp formulation of the emerging new standpoint. Marx was mainly responsible for the exposition of the science of historical materialism. He presents the new science within a running polemic against philosophical abstraction and all forms of teleology. The object of this attack are the 'chimeras' of idealist speculation shared by Hegel, Feuerbach, the Young Hegelians and, until recently, Marx himself.

The science of history is to be empirically based reserving no place for the 'freaks' of philosophical abstraction. Marx ridicules all philosophical history:

> The individuals, who are no longer subject to the division of labour, have been conceived by the philosophers as an ideal, under the name of 'man', and the whole process. . . has been regarded by them as the evolutionary process of 'man', so that at every historical stage 'man' was substituted for the individuals existing hitherto and shown as the motive force of history. The whole process was thus conceived as a process of the self-estrangement of 'man', and this was essentially due to the fact that the average individual of the later age was always foisted on to the earlier stage, and the consciousness of the later age on the individuals of an earlier. Through this inversion, which from the first disregards the actual conditions, it was possible to transform the whole of history into an evolutionary process of consciousness.[21]

Marx argues that once close attention is paid to actual historical conditions of concrete societies, philosophical abstraction is seen as transparently distortive and indirectly apologetic. When replaced by a science of history which restricts itself to the examination of concrete, lived relations and conditions of real individuals in historically specific socio-economic forms, this abstraction loses 'its medium of existence'. This more rigorous standpoint results in a concretisation of Marx's concept of history.

Already implicit in Marx's idea of finite subjectivity was a rejection of the idealist abstraction 'history' and a shift of focus to the objective social practices of representative social actors. In the 1844 manuscripts the discussion of alienation centers on objective, institutionally determined relations between individuals which impose their own independent logic upon the results of individual actions. This tendency is explicitly consolidated in the German Ideology. Marx now declines to speculate on the historical process as 'a whole' and its meaning. Instead of this discredited idealist strategy, his attention turns to the actual material conditions of history. His conception

> does not end by being resolved into 'self consciousness' as 'spirit of the spirit', but that each stage (of history) contains a material result, a sum of productive forces, a historically created relation to nature and of the individuals to one another, which is handed down to each generation from its predecessor; a mass of productive forces, capital funds and circumstance, which on the one hand is modified by a new generation, but, on the other also prescribes for it the conditions of life and give it a definite development, a special character. It shows that circumstances make men just as much as men make circumstances.[22]

This materialist perspective on history drastically modified Marx's concept of totality. The totality of history has no immanent meaning aside from that created and ascribed to it by the practices of living, concrete individuals. History itself cannot act. Only individuals are real historical actors. It was philosophical mystification to impute some autonomous purpose to the collective results of these acts. Marx was not about to deny the existence of supra-individual material and ideal historical structures and processes. His theory of alienation clearly presupposed an awareness of reified social power that sustained a quasi-independence and confronted its human creators

> as an alien power existing outside them, of the origin and goal of which they are ignorant, which they thus are no longer able to control, which on the contrary passes through a peculiar series of phases and stages independent of the will and action of men, nay, even being the prime governor of these.[23]

The whole force of Marx's critique is directed at alienated bourgeois social relations. Therefore, the key to understanding his denial of supra-individual purposes and meanings in history lies elsewhere. It depends upon the *emancipatory idea* implied by the practical self-understanding of the new theory.

Marx assertion of the ideological character of the Hegelian philosophy implied a very general claim about the material determination of all theory. In opposition to Hegel and the philosophical tradition which viewed reason as an impartial faculty and theory as a *mode of representing* an extra-theoretical world, Marx interpreted theory in general as *an expression of living social practices* and his own in particular as an adequate self-consciousness of the proletariat, of the practical needs and necessities of its material situation.[24] This practical understanding of theory had a double meaning. Firstly, Marx saw his own theory as an expression of the interests and needs of the new historically developing class. It was the articulation of this socially determinant perspective on bourgeois society. It clarified why the proletariat was driven to revolutionary activity by the conditions of its practical life situation. Secondly, Marx envisaged his theory *as a practical communication* to this social class as a vital contribution to its members self-clarification and the formation of a truly revolutionary subjectivity.[25]

This practical orientation of Marx's theory had a decisive bearing on his reformulation of the concept of totality. Once he had proposed the revolutionary praxis of the proletariat motivated by its own historically expanding, but socially constrained, needs as the social source of a dynamic, critical perspective, Marx was compelled to fashion a concept of history appropriate to it. From this practical standpoint, history had to be viewed as an *ongoing process of totalisation* in which individuals collectively attempted to transform their common life situation, thereby practically imposing their own ends upon history. The difference between Hegel's idea of totality and Marx's emphasis on the dynamism of practical totalisation is the difference between the *philosophical ascription of a meaning to history as a whole* and the concrete strivings of a class as they modified inherited social institutions and meanings, making conscious, partial, always revocable decisions about, and sense of, their present historical situation from the perspective of its current social possibilities. Marx reinforces precisely this distinction when he claims that while it is always easy to attribute the consciousness of some existing contradiction to the individuals of an earlier age, this need not mean that it actually existed for them.[26] The notion of a total historical process is clearly deflated by Marx's new perspective. It is reduced to the idea of practical, historically circumscribed and conditioned, totalisation carried out by concrete social classes.

This specific idea of practical totalisation is not explicitly elaborated in the German Ideology. Nevertheless, the concept is clearly implied in Marx's critique of the philosophical concept of totality. This presence is confirmed by his talk of communism not as a 'state of affairs' or 'an ideal' but as 'real movement'. Marx was primarily concerned to eliminate the teleological idea of self-unfolding integral to Hegel's metaphysics. His firm conviction, later bolstered by extensive historical studies, was that history was not inherently self-unfolding. What he later called 'extended reproduction' was not automatic and depended upon a number of historically contingent factors; it was only possible after the attainment of a certain level of historical development.

For the Marx of the German Ideology, history is an open synthesis of contingent situations through the socially inter-related activities of historically situated social agents. Behind this conception was his insight into the concrete becoming of world history as a result of the world-wide extension of bourgeois commercial relations and their incorporation into this system of vastly dissimilar cultures and levels of economic development. Marx retained the historically mediated subject/object dialectic which had provided the phenomenological structure of the 1844 manuscripts but with radical modifications. He clearly now recognised concrete needs and practices of differentiated social producers as the real motor of this dialectic. The self-unfolding of history can now only refer the immanent ensemble of bourgeois socio-economic relations and its rapidly expanding world system. Earlier conditions of production periodically are felt as fetters on present activities and needs. Contemporary social actors are led to struggle for their replacement. This understanding of historical contradiction makes explicit the clash of *two existing, concrete realities*. On the one side, the historically attained shape of human subjectivity with its corresponding structure of needs, abilities and aspirations. On the other, the existing institutionalised forms of social organisation invested with the material interests of dominant social classes. Thus, Marx retains Hegel's historical immanentism but in a radically new form implying a *totalising concept of history that is contingent, open, non-automatic and empirically verifiable*.

The concrete idea of social totality

The German Ideology marks a decisive reorientation in Marx's concept of totality. This concept is henceforth stripped of its former philosophical abstraction and provided with a largely new theoretical content and limitation. In this guise it maintains a central place in Marx's conceptual armoury. In all later works it serves to conceptualise the reproduction of bourgeois society.

This revised concept of totality refers to the interlocking ensemble of socio-economic relations and structures which, in the unceasing process of their reproduction, constitute a whole and regulate the material life situation of all social actors in a given society. Contrary to structuralist interpretations of Marx,[27] it should be emphasised that this concretisation of the concept of totality did not mean the abandonment of a diachronic, historical dimension. It is true that Marx was now increasingly concerned with the theoretical task of comprehending relatively stable systems of relations. But he undertook this task from the standpoint of immanent processual revolution. This dictated the primacy of the longer-run perspective of historical discontinuity focusing on the various dimensions of internal destabilisation including the strengthening collective, consciousness amongst the proletartiat.

The requirements of Marx's new task stipulated a double emphasis. A completely adequate theoretical comprehension of real historical societies was not open to a perspective which simply reduced everything to the changing subjective praxis. Against the German ideologists, Marx insisted that existing institutionalised forms of ossified praxis would not collapse before philosophical revolutions. They are relatively stable, self reproducing systems which regularise and codify social activities. Marx clearly realised the necessity to theorise this structural aspect of society as a moment of historical continuity which conditioned all social praxis.[28] However, these structural relations do not reproduce themselves but depend upon the actions of living subjects conditioned by them. They condition an immanent historical force that, in turn, incessantly subjects them to the rigours of practical challenge. This means that theory must grasp both aspects of continuity and discontinuity. A concern for understanding the continuity of reproduction cannot lose a sense of historical transformation and interruption. Marx sees historical discontinuity as a moment of practical incongruence between historically engendered subjective aspirations and needs and resistant, inflexible social relations and institutions forged by powerful material interests. Marx's critical approach demanded that the totality of socio-economic relations be viewed from the dynamic perspective of their immanent future possibilities. Such a perspective could not presuppose a simple, linear notion of social progress. On the contrary, it had to acknowledge historical contradictions and the temporary impasses induced by conflicting social classes motivated by conflicting interests, alternative social visions and values.

Marx's critique of philosophical abstraction articulates, amongst other things already mentioned, his expressive understanding of theory. Critical theory expresses palpable social needs and clarifies the present objective conditions for their possible satisfaction. This means an iron check on the figments of philosophical imagination:

> Thus if millions of proletarians feel by no means contented with their
> living conditions, if their 'being' does not in the least correspond to their
> 'essence', then, according to the passage quoted (out of the Philosophy of
> the Future) this is an unavoidable misfortune, which must be borne
> quietly. These millions of proletarians or communists, however, think
> differently and will prove this in time when they bring their 'being' into
> harmony with their 'essence' in a practical way, by means of revolution.[29]

This rebuke to Feuerbach expresses Marx's utter contempt for the German 'philosophies of essence'. These create 'freaks', abstract from concrete empirical conditions and allocate to philosophy a 'false' autonomy. Yet it should not be concluded from the ferocity of this attack that Marx had himself totally abandoned the concept of essence. His polemic is specifically directed at

Hegelian and Young Hegelian ideas of essence. He particularly rejects the Hegelian concept of a teleological spiritual essence and Feuerbach's naturalistic anthropology presupposing eternal, natural human-species traits. These concepts are not empirically verifiable and preclude historical specification. Ironically, those who usually deny a concept of essence to the mature Marx invariably understand this concept only in the forms denounced by him.

Marx's revolutionary standpoint presupposes a critical, evaluative perspective on existing society. It follows from his historical immanentism that the values directing this critique could not take the form of ethical imperatives. This critique found its orientation from felt empirical needs and concrete social possibilities. Marx's famous Sixth Thesis on Feuerbach says as much when it dispenses with the term 'human essence' in abstraction from concrete history. Feuerbach is criticised for 'abstraction from the real historical process' while the the the 'real human essence' lies in the 'ensemble of social relations'.[30] The real human essence is the 'sum of productive forces, capital funds and social forms of intercourse, which every generation finds in existence as something given'.[31] Given Marx's relentless criticism of existing bourgeois society and its ensemble of socio-economic relations, his ironic demasking of this central philosophical concept can only imply that he viewed existing, historically produced anthropological possibilities fixed in the social and cultural wealth of human objectifications produced under bourgeois relations as the real basis of such notions. Marx therefore abandons a much abused philosophical term but preserves the concept by redefining it in a concrete, immanent way.

These historically generated human possibilities inscribed in the concrete world of social objectifications constitutes for Marx the only non-ascriptive source of critical values. They are existing productive forces denied to the majority of contemporary individuals. Their lack engenders needs that press these individuals to change their situation. From this configuration of realised social wealth and individual deprivation Marx derives the values required for the critique of bourgeois society. The unfulfilled historical potentialities fixed in these productive forces constitute the basis of a perspective on a historically produced human essence. The contemporary practical struggle of the proletariat dictates a view of history that makes it intelligible in terms of the socialist goal of this struggle. This understanding of the concept of human essence does not require the imputation of an essence to history itself. This concept is a theoretical construct which specifies certain historically produced human attributes as essential traits on the basis of which history can be conceived as a developmental sequence and contemporary struggles determine their long-term aims:

> Marx meant, it seems, by 'human essence' primarily those characteristics
> of the real historical existence of mankind which make it possible to
> comprehend history as a continuous unified process that has a
> developmental tendency. The universality of man and his freedom mark

the general direction of the historical progress of humanity, while the characterisation of man as a conscious social being engaged in material productive self-activity refers to those necessary traits, those dimensions of this total developmental process on the basis of which the above historical tendency unfolds and in the sphere of which it becomes manifest.[32]

George Márkus has offered this interpretation of Marx's idea of human essence. These essential attributes are *abstractions of historically produced human capacities and possibilities inscribed in the socially objectified world.* Human essence is not therefore a figment of the philosophical imagination but a sum of historically acquired potentials manifested, positively, in the objective level of existing productive forces, in the skills, capacities and culture of living individuals and, negatively, in the felt needs and suffering of the proletariat. Marx's observations on the character of communist society only reinforce this interpretation. This society represents both the full emancipation and further enhancement of the already objectified, albeit alienated, ensemble of historically accumulated abilities, needs and social possibilities.

The theoretical function of the Marxian concept of human essence was to designate some human traits as *essential, as values in relation to which the present social totality could be inserted within a constructed developmental process.* In this way, the Marxian critique grounded itself in actual, immanent historical possibilities yet still retained its critical relation to existing bourgeois society. Aside from this important theoretical function the concept has an urgent practical meaning. It expresses the massive contemporary suppression of existing human potentials.

The becoming of world history

So far the exposition of the Marxian concept of totality has proceded in mainly negative terms. We have sought to distinguish it from Hegel's version of totality outlined in Chapter One. While it is essential to underline that Marx's turn to the 'science of history' in no way relinguished a critical orientation to history, it is equally important to recognise that he perceived the historical process as *presently crystallised* in a palpable, extensive, modern social reality.

The concept of history presented in the German Ideology with its emphasis on empirical conditions shows Marx's increasing awareness of historical contingency. He states: 'World history didn't always exist; history as world history is a result'.[33] The possibility of conceiving 'world history' presupposes very real empirical conditons and is no mere theoretical construct. Marx presents a very forceful image of its empirical reality – its material, cultural and economic contemporaneity: 'this transformation of history into world history is by no means a mere abstract act of "self-consciouness", the world spirit... but a quite material, empirically verifiable act'.[34] Marx perceived world history all around him, not only in the cosmopolitan manners and tastes of bourgeois society but more importantly in the voracious world commercial system. This system interlinked the fortunes of different nations, cultures and societies in the all-encompassing intercourse of the bourgeois world market. World history is thus conceived as a product of bourgeois society and especially of the extended division of labour and fierce economic competition which motored its rapid expansion and ongoing dynamism. In pre-capitalist epochs, a unification on this scale and to this depth was unimaginable. Not even the *Pax Romana* which established a loose political unification over the then known world and fostered the extension of commerce and trade routes achieved anything like this. The Roman Empire remained precarious and such unification as it realised was only superifical and very limited. It resulted from slow, marginal, accidental influences that waxed and waned with the fragility of trade and the fortunes of conquest.

Compared to the relative isolation and subsistence conditions of pre-capitalist society, capitalism had engendered a commercial activity that in the space of a hundred years engulfed the entire world and incorporated even the remotest areas into a single unified economic system:

> It [large scale industry] produced world history for the first time, insofar as it made all civilised nations and every individual member of them dependent for the satisfaction of their wants on the whole world, thus destroying the former natural exclusiveness of separate nations.[35]

Marx refuses to view world history merely as a theoretically superimposed diachronic process. Empirical observation supplies world history with a spacial and very material dimension. Industrial production and market competition created an 'automatic' system based on world-wide mutual interdependence. This had already been perceived by social critics like Rousseau, in predominantly negative terms, as the chief source of modern decadence and alienation. While not ignoring the brutality of European colonisation and conquest, Marx recognised the progressive aspect of these developments. The incorporation of virtually the whole world into a complex system of interdependence not only dissolved the physical isolation of disparate native populations but also engendered a convergence of histories and historical destinies. The reality of a number of parallel but distinct histories in the pre-capitalist epoch evaporates before a unified world history as independent cultures succumbed to Western penetration and the irreversible disintegration of subsistence economies subject to occidental values and insertion into a single world market.

Marx's concept of progress

Above, it has been argued that Marx's concept of human essence was in large measure *anticipatory*. It implied a unity of history and of humanity at least partially *theoretically superimposed* on empirical conditions. It was *prospective* even if this unity was conceived as immanent to the dynamic tendencies of bourgeois society, as *constitutive of the needs of contemporary struggling social forces.* This anticipatory moment also informed Marx's idea of historical progress. Progress, for Marx, carried a substantial prospective significance derived from a practical historical reflection primarily motivated by an orientation to the future.

Marx's concept of progress hinges on history's real antinomies. Historical progress is uneven and contradictory. Despite the catastrophic destruction of traditional societies, their cultures and the artifically induced poverty created amongst large segments of indigenous populations, he clearly believed the explosive expansion of bourgeois society had offset these costs with a historically unequalled multiplication and diversification of human productive forces. Sharing the confidence of his age, Marx maintained that the victory of bourgeois society generated a whole range of new anthropological possibilities which had never before existed in traditional societies. Capitalism had created the objective conditions that made a truly human existence *possible.* Yet, this objective achievement had not mitigated the fundamental contradiction of all previous historical development between species wealth and individual deprivation. This basic contradiction between real contemporary human possibilities and the stifling general life conditions in which the great majority of population were compelled to live was the basis of Marx's ambivalence towards capitalism.

This ambivalence was constitutive for Marx's understanding of historical progress. On the one hand, he presents an emphatic objectivist interpretation of progress supported by an empirical overview of contemporary 'world historical' conditions stressing the unsurpassed level of productive forces sustained by bourgeois society. On the other hand, his unrelenting criticism of the bourgeois form of this 'progress' leaves little doubt that Marx regards assertions of historical 'progress' as definitely only *provisional or prospective.* The achievements of capitalism are such *only from the viewpoint of the possible fulfilment and continued enhancement of the complex structure of already historically attained human needs and capacities.*

On the empirical side, Marx maintained two indices of progress. Firstly, he speaks of man's evergrowing mastery of nature:

> The bourgeois, during its rule of scarce one hundred years, has created
> more masssive and more colossal productive forces than have all the
> preceding generations together.[36]

Marx viewed this burgeoning technical mastery over nature as an unambiguous human achievement. To this technical and scientific progress he added the extension of social co-operation as expressed in the bourgeois division of labour and its sophisticated system of exchange and markets. Yet, his praise was heavily qualified as he attributed most of the contemporary human degradation and alienation to this same modern, more socially mediated, system of socio-economic organisation. His stress again fell on the contradictions of this 'progress':

> The modern labourer. . . instead of rising with the progress of industry, sinks deeper and deeper below the conditions of existence of its own class. He becomes a pauper and pauperism develops more rapidly than population and wealth.[37]

Within Marx's immanentist understanding of historical development, this recognition of 'uneven' progress played a crucial theoretical role. The pauperisation of the proletariat explained the practical necessity of the historical emergence of the totalising perspective theoretically expressed in critical theory. How did Marx understand the material condition of the proletariat as the basis of a dynamic totalising perspective?

Until the early 1850s when Marx, under the pressure of improved economic conditions and rising wages, reassessed his initial theory of wages, his view of the proletariat had not fundamentally changed since he first recognised the link between theory and praxis in1843. Then he had asserted that the proletariat was a class of bourgeois society which, paradoxically, was at the same time not a class of this society. He meant by this that although the proletariat was a product of this form of social organisation, had its material life situation within it and played an indispensible productive role in the bourgeois division of labour, it was, nevertheless, still deprived of all civil and political rights and excluded from virtually all benefits of the wealth and culture accruing to the dominant classes. The workers were potentially bearers of 'universality' because they lacked particuliar rights and interests within the bourgeois framework of society.[38] Their emancipation required a *social revolution* that would abolish all classes and thus liberate not just the proletariat but all members of society.

Marx's understanding of the proletariat did, however, undergo some change in the intervening years. In the German Ideology, it is no longer 'the total loss of humanity' and 'its total redemption' in Hegelian terms of a teleological return of humanity to its essence. Futhermore, by this time Marx has sharpened his sociological definition of the proletariat which now refers explicitly to that class of individuals condemned to depend upon the new industrial organisation of production. But despite these refinements, he still argues that the proletariat is capable of comprehending the totality of bourgeois society only because *it stands completely outside this society* thereby engendering a transcendent, revolutionary historical perspective. Despite the clarity of Marx's argument, clearly one of the difficulties with his position here is the question of how an immanent historical force, one constituted by the economic relations of bourgeois society can achieve a transcendent perspective? The subsequent history of the workers movement in Europe and elswhere – particularly the reformist direction of social democracy – was repeatedly to pose this question on the practical level of working-class politics.

The failure of the 1848 revolutions, the return of economic prosperity and the relative stabilisation of bourgeois society thereafter caused Marx to revise his initial pauperisation thesis regarding the material conditions of the proletariat. The theme of the reproduction of capitalist relations already foreshadowed in the German Ideology now takes prominence as Marx turned to the problem of the *'logic' of capitalist reproduction* and attempted a deeper understanding of its economic structures. Out of this critical science of history focused on existing empirical conditions emerges a *negativist* concept of totality. He treats the interlocking ensemble of bourgeois socio-economic relations as *a whole in process to be comprehended only fully from the perspective of its own immanent negation*. For Marx, this negation was not to be the result of a 'higher' speculative view but a consequence of the immanent future presently manifest in contemporary structural dysfunctions and social contradictions within bourgeois society.

The priority of the logical over the historical

From the early 1850s, Marx's work shows a further concretisation of the concept of totality in response to these new theoretical demands. In these works of which the most famous are the Grundrisse and Capital, the theme of alienation and the independent character of bourgeois economic processes is translated into a concerted programme to discover the logic of capitalist reproduction. This line of inquiry anticipates a perspective that becomes more pronounced as the nineteenth century wore on. Marx views capitalism in terms of its *systemic reproductive process* which imposes its own necessities and requirements regardless of the will of isolated individuals as long as they accept this framework of societal instititutions as 'natural'. His conditional rider 'as long as' reinforces, however, the emancipatory intentions that shape Marx's conceptualisation. Yet, with the weakening of radical socio-political opposition, with the incorporation of the workers into the bourgeois order, a bleaker, more pessimistic vision soon emerges. Thinkers like Simmel and Weber will repeat Marx's criticism of the quasi-objective, autonomous character of bourgeois social processes but they are not revolutionaries. They cannot perceive radical emancipatory possibilities in any of these processes. Their critique will be *cultural:* concerned with processes that are described in almost purely negative terms as oppressive, alien, increasingly meaningless and outside of human control.

Marx's new concerns are reflected in his methodological statements from the 1850s. He argues that the scientific understanding of bourgeois society requires that priority be accorded to these self-reproducing, processual socio-economic totalities. Without a genuine analytical understanding of the 'logic' of these systems, historical explanation amounts to little more than a contingent series of historical events lacking any real necessity.[39] Moreover, Marx argued that while capitalist production is historically mediated, its present foundations were not to be found in these historical origins. On the contrary, the specificity of the existing capitalist system consists in it producing its own conditions of existence and this is evidence of it becoming an 'automatically' self-reproducing, dynamic system:

> It must be kept in mind that the new forces of production and relations of production do not develop out of nothing, nor drop from the sky, nor from the womb of the self-positing Idea; but from within and in antithesis to the existing development of production and the inherited, traditional relations of property. While in the completed bourgeois system every economic relation presupposes every other in its bourgeois form, and everything posited is thus also a presupposition, this is the case with every organic system. This organic system itself, as a totality, has its presuppositions, and its development to its totality consists precisely in creating out of it the organs which it still lacks. This is historically how it becomes a totality. The process of becoming this totality forms a moment of its process, of its development.[40]

The apparent automaticity of the capitalist system is a necessary illusion having its real basis in the development of a world encompassing network which mechanically reproduces or provides the required socio-productive relations. But this illusion could not be simply ignored or wished away. Marx insists that critical theory must provide a unified understanding of this self-reproducing totality by indicating the necessary unity of its partial systems and, simultaneously, revealing its determination by a set of contradictory, historically contingent, relations which are themselves subject to immanent change in the very process of their reproduction and open to conscious intervention on the part of a collective social subject.

Marx achieves this double aim in establishing that all the constitutive elements of the world capitalist system – production, distribution, exchange, consumption – are not merely related parts but subordinate moments of a self-reproducing, concrete, social totality. He demonstrates the systematic inter-dependence and inter-relation of all the elements in the process of self-maintenance and self-expansion of the whole. Crucial to this demonstration was the logical unfolding as these relations and their categories. But despite this new emphasis, the question of historicity, of historical genesis and historical transcendence remains. It has merely been displaced onto another level and incorporated into the analysis of the immanent antitheses and contradictions of the dynamic bourgeois social totality.

This immanent critical method is viewed by Marx as the sole scientific manner of ascertaining the real basis of historical dynamism within capitialist society. Yet, he clearly does not equate historical dynamism with the mere self-reproduction of existing capitalist relations. He underlines the *contradictory features of capitalist reproduction*. Particularly, he shows how these contradictions prefigure the demise of bourgeois relations and open up an alternative future perspective:

In order to develop true laws of bourgeois economy, therefore, it is not necessary to write the real history of the relations of production. But the correct observation and deduction of these laws, as having themselves become in history, always leads to primary equations – like the empirical numbers e.g. in natural science – which point towards a past lying behind this system. The indications [Andeutungen], together with a grasp of the present, also offers the key to the understanding of the past. . . . This correct view likewise leads at the same time to the points at which the suspension of the present form of productive relations give signs of its becoming – foreshadowings of the future. Just as, on the one side the pre-bourgeois phases appear as merely historical, i.e. suspended presuppositions, so do the contemporary conditions of production likewise appear as engaged in suspending themselves and hence in positing the historical presuppositions of a new state of society.[41]

This and many similar passages illustrate the continuing emancipatory emphasis in Marx's later works. The attempt to theorise capitalist reproduction is undertaken from the perspective of historical discontinuity and the emancipatory potentials of existing social contradictions. At the same time, this passage reinforces the point that Marx is not primarily concerned with the historical genesis of bourgeois commodity relations. The later economic manuscripts show his preoccupation with the problem of a critical presentation of the totality of these relations. Central was the question of an appropriate theoretical beginning to logically order all elements of the totality so they assume their rightful place in the critical exposition. Marx struggled with this difficulty for over a decade in which time his views did change. The question of a logic of presentation is resolved differently in the Grundrisse and Capital. Yet, the concept of totality presupposed by his critical, immanent method which conceptualised capitalism as a *self-reproducing, dynamic and contradictory* system remained constant in these efforts.

Open-ended historical totalisation and socialism

Marx's critical method involved the insertion of the dynamic, self-reproducing bourgeois totality into the open-ended stream of empirical history. The dynamism of history is intimated in the internal contradictions and emerging historical possibilities of the capitalist system. Our assessment of the adequacy of Marx's reformulation of the concept of totality largely depends upon the consistency of this critical vision of history. It should be remembered that he castigated Hegel for his abstraction from real history and his ideological closure of the historical process. Does Marx's own concept of history avoid these failings? Can his advocacy of an immanent critical method and an empirical, open-ended concept of history be reconciled with his anticipation, and conceptualisation, of socialism as the end of pre-history?

Marx's understanding of the spectrum of historical possibilities engendered by the immanent contradictions of capitialism varied considerably over time. In the Grundrisse he posits socialism as the successor to the existing, contradictory social arrangement: 'The alien and independent character in which it (the objective bond) presently exists *vis-à-vis* individuals proves only that the latter are still engaged in the creation of the conditions of their social life, and that they have not yet begun, on the basis of these conditions, to live it'.[42] The values associated with this immanent socialist society are those implied by his concept of human essence. Characteristically, Marx argues that present conditions of alienation and reification are 'a necessary result of the fact that the point of departure is not the free social individual'.[43] The values endorsed in this vision of a 'universally developed', 'free', 'social individual' who 'exercises social control' over his/her own social relations, are identical to those found in Marx's concept of human essence'.[44] Yet, despite this continuity of general orientating values, his concrete assessment of the real historical possibilities varied between the Grundrisse and Capital.

In the Grundrisse, Marx presents a radical utopian view of socialism based on the extrapolation of the massive technological progress occasioned by the recruitment of science as a major productive force.[45] He envisages complete automation, and as a collorary, the growth of de-stabilising radical needs amongst workers who in prosperous times participate in cultural activities and move towards acquisition of conscious subjectivity. Such an optimistic scernario is significantly modified in Capital.

In the third volume of Capital Marx explicitly retracts the idea that the law of value could be undermined by capitalist technological development. He categorically asserts the supra-historical status of the generalised content of the law of value:

> Secondly, after the abolition of the capitalist mode of production, but still
> retaining social production, the determination of value continues to
> prevail in the sense that the regulation of labour time and the distribution
> of social labour among the various production groups, ultimately the
> book-keeping encompassing all this, becomes more essential than ever.[46]

In Capital, the dissolution of the boundary between freedom and necessity which was the basis of Marx's more optimistic forecasts in the Grundrisse, is repudiated for a different view which upholds an organisational separation of these two spheres in socialist society. In a famous formulation, Marx argued that 'the realm of necessity' was *the necessary basis* for the blossoming forth of human freedom.[47]

The 'basic prerequisite' for this envisaged separation of the spheres of necessary labour and free time in socialist society was the fragmentation and scientific simplication of the operations of industrial labour enabling a shortening of the working day. This represented a clear narrowing of Marx's earlier views of the objective possibilities engendered by capitalism.This more sober revision is accompanied by a shift of focus to the objective dysfunctionalities of the system. This interest centres on commercial disequalibriums which devalorise capital and endanger the traditional living standards of workers.[48] Corresponding to this changed diagnosis of present possibilities is *a transformation of Marx's view of socialist society.*

Marx's earliest view of socialism was marred by the teleological framework inherited from Hegel which dictated a concept of history as 'the riddle of history solved '. In keeping with this idea of historical closure, his concrete vision of socialism was formulated along romantic lines as an organic, unmediated totality. So, despite a radical historicism that from the outset underscored Marx's idea of humanity, his initial concept of socialism posited a utopian reconciliation of all historical antagonisms and contradictions – between man and man, man and nature, individual and species, freedom and necessity. This idea of socialism did not survive the German Ideology's programme for a concrete, empirical science of history. Marx stripped his idea of socialism of its most utopian excesses and already in the Poverty of Philosophy he was concerning himself with the question of the most economically efficient organisation of production. He settled for the centrally planned allocation of tasks within the framework of the earlier repudiated social division of labour.[49]

The Grundrisse represents a resurgence of utopianism in Marx's thinking. Although these fragments hardly amount to a wholly consistent vision, his interest in radical automation again indicates an elimination of the division of labour. The drastic extension of free time in this vision of socialism provides for the individual acquisition of the totality of historically created human possibilities as a social goal.[50] Making the individual the overriding end of social activity posits the reconcilation of freedom and necessity. Marx did not go so far as to maintain that work should become play:

> But as living labour loses its immediate, individual character whether
> subjective or entirely external, as individual activity becomes directly
> general or social, the objective elements of production lose this form of
> alienation. They are produced as property, as the organic social body in
> which individuals are reproduced as individuals, but as social
> individuals.[51]

Even in this utopian mood, Marx never returned to his initial view of socialism as the complete resolution of all historical oppositions. He particularly emphasised the dynamic character of socialist society. Any idea of a reconcilatory end of history was simply abandoned along with the organic notion of social organisation. Marx stresses the prospect of infinite human 'becoming' and individual development. Obviously this had consequences for his ideas of the historical process and of the future. This radically progressivist concept of socialism was tied to Marx's belief that the capitalist system universalised human needs and allowed even the proletariat, in times of prosperity, to share in the technical and culture achievements of this universalisation. History is viewed as a profound unfolding of human potentialities and this emancipatory dynamic colours the future. Radical new needs are posited as a major source of capitalist instability in the future. However, this was only a momentary stage on the way to Marx's more guarded and pessimistic assessment of contemporary trends in Capital.

To explain this narrowing of Marx's vision of future possibilities, Márkus has pointed to the impact of bourgeois stabilisation after 1848, working class quietism in the following decade, and Marx's intense immersion in political economy.[52] Whatever it causes, this transformation is clearly evident in Marx's comparison of pre-history and history in Capital. Not only does he now display a greater historical realism concerning the technical possibilities created by capitialist production but there is also a noticeable displacement of his emancipatory emphasis away from subjective development and destabilising needs towards a concentration on objective factors like over-production, systems disequilibrium and the revolutionary development of the means of production.[53]

While in Capital Marx's revolutionary goal continues to be the free, self-development of social individuality, a discrepancy emerges between this posited historical goal and his description of the immanent dynamics of capitialism. Marx no longer emphasises the expanding forces of production (in the Grundrisse humanity's greatest fixed capital) in the form of expanded needs. He even rehabilitates the law of value as a trans-historical principle. In the context of capitalism this law signified the necessary maintenance of wages around a subsistence level except for marginal and only temporary improvements exacted through successful class struggles. This scenario undercut Marx's earlier anticipation of a developing broadly-based, conscious, revolutionary subjectivity. The analysis now pointed to the danger of the collapse of Western civilisation due to the dysfunctionalities of capitalist development but the idea that a truly emancipated socialist society could emerge out of this crisis was sustained *only by Marx's revolutionary faith.*[54]

This dissonance between Marx's posited historical goal and his concrete analysis of the immanent tendencies of the capitalist system was accompanied in Capital by a disquieting resurrection of Hegel's teleological terminology. In Volume 3, Marx specifies the 'historical task' and 'historical mission' of capitalism and also speaks of the socialist revolution as the 'negation of the negation'.[55] More than a mere terminological regression, these phrases are symptomatic of a historical finalism which permeates this last idea of socialism. Socialism now signifies a break in the false continuity of history which allows social development to assume a completely new form. This 'realm of freedom', the beginning of 'true history' means the end of history as it had been. But now the universalistic values of socialism forfeit their dynamic, 'becoming' dimension from the Grundrisse and take on a finalistic appearance. Socialism appears to signify the complete cessation of history in so far as concerns the immanent development of new social forms.

This reversion to an unconscious historical teleology in <u>Capital</u> invites the conclusion that Marx ultimately succumbed to precisely the failings he had criticised in Hegel and the other Young Hegelians. Some commentators have interpreted these residues as evidence of a concealed theological impulse in Marxism. While the existence of this and other serious tensions in Marx's work cannot be denied, they hardly dull Marx's real theoretical achievements. His understanding of totality represents a great advance in the critical, immanent interpretation of history and in the development of a practical immanentist notion of critique. He preserved the humanist, emancipatory impulses of Hegel's philosophy of history by initially concentrating all his attention on the question of *practical realisation*. Out of this orientation came his revolutionary new understanding of theory. Critical theory, as all other culture, is now viewed by Marx as an *expression of the perspective of real social interests*. At the same time, this theoretically articulated consciousness is a crucial agent in the process of revolutionary social change as a *communicative clarification of the proletariat's self-understanding*.

On the theoretical level, Marx's new perspective called for a rigorous attack on the remnants of philosophical abstraction in historical understanding. With this polemic against idealism came a new emphasis on the historical significance of human production. Here Marx made his greatest philosophical contribution with the paradigm of production as a new materialist mode of understanding human historical self-creation.[56]

From the <u>German Ideology</u> Marx emphatically repudiated all historiosophic teleologies. He consciously limited his enquiries to the examination of specific concrete social forms understood as socio-economic ensembles in the dynamic process of their own contradictory self-reproduction. Marx preserved Hegel's progressive understanding of history not by smuggling in concealed teleological notions but by viewing the totality of bourgeois relations as the bearer of a 'human essence' fixed in its social and cultural objectifications: as a sum of productive forces bequested to contemporaries as a legacy of humanity's historical development and continuity. For Marx, these accumulated powers and values represented the possibility of unalienated human progress. Despite the theoretical shortcomings and final tensions in his realisation of this programme, this concept of history was empirical, immanent, open-ended and emancipatory.

Even if we acknowledge these theoretical gains, how is Marx's own relapse into a hidden teleology to be interpreted? Clearly it signifies a valiant attempt to *synthesise an immanentist understanding of history* with the *practical demand for the radical transcendence of the present*. Marx's final analysis of the immanent forces of the capitalist system did not sustain his hopes for radical transcendence. The unacknowledged, unconscious return of a conceptual teleology signifies his commitment to the practical goal of radical transcendence at the same time as his honesty compelled him to recognise theoretically the increasing obstacles to its contemporary realisation.

The retreat into the antonomies of cultural pessimism

Chapter Three

The *Geisteswissenschaften:* the rise of a negative concept of totality

To understand the further evolution of the concept of totality it is necessary to explore a new era of post-Hegelian cultural reflection in Germany. The Marxian concept of totality elaborated in the preceding chapter had no impact on these political and cultural discussions. While the increasing political strength of German social democracy in the last decades of the nineteenth century generated some interest and sympathy amongst academics and forced leading contemporary thinkers to engage with Marxism, they responded to the popularised orthodoxy disseminated by Engels and the leading theoreticians of the German party. This reading viewed Marx as the founder of a new materialist *Weltanschauung* and a truly 'scientific' evolutionary theory of history.

The orthodox reception of Marx's thought resulted from a combination of factors. There were theoretical tensions in Marx's later *oeuvre* which encouraged a scientistic reading. Several important manuscripts remained unpublished until well into the twentieth century. But probably most decisive was the intellectual climate of the last quarter of the nineteenth century dominated by the triumphs of modern science and the inroads of positivism. To appreciate this radically changed cultural ambience it is essential to briefly recall the profound historical transformation which overtook Germany in the last quarter of the nineteenth century and its cultural impact. The stabilisation of bourgeois society after 1848 and the subsequent rapid industrialisation that followed completely reshaped the experience, socio-political expectations and cultural horizons of German society. These changes infiltrated every sphere of modern life. In the light of such a momentous historical upheaval it is hardly surprising that changed perspectives gave rise to a new understanding of the concept of totality.

In 1883, the year of Marx's death, Wilhelm Dilthey published his *Einleitung in der Geisteswissenschaften* (Introduction to the Human Sciences). This very influential work claimed to establish the foundations and methodology for the autonomous treatment of the historical sciences. Dilthey adopted the German translation of J. S. Mill's term 'moral sciences' to describe the traditional humanities disciplines. Dilthey's initiative[1] was part of a late cultural push to defend the *Geisteswissenschaften* and its cultural values against the inroads of positivism and bourgeois, scientific-materialist culture. The following chapter will analyse the intellectual and cultural needs which fostered this development and elaborate the new concept of totality to which it gave rise through the work of some of most outstanding thinkers of the *Geisteswissenschaften*. A survey of the work of Dilthey, Simmel and Weber also provides an indispensible introduction to the cultural problematics that shaped the early thought of Georg Lukács. As mentioned, Lukács is crucial to the history of the totality concept because he resurrected the Hegelian-Marxian version of the concept at a time of renewed revolutionary social impulses after the First World War.

However, before embarking on this survey it is necessary to set the historical scene by outlining some of the major elements of the new cultural configuration in Germany in the second half of the nineteenth century.

Industrial modernisation and the threat of positivism

The failed revolution of 1848 marks a watershed not only in German politics but also in German culture. The political failure of the liberal oppposition signified the collapse of democractic reform and the accomodation of the bourgeois to political subordination. The political optimism that had characterised Hegel's diagnosis of modernity dissolved under the impact of historical events and political disappointments. Germany was modernised under the auspices of Bismarck's authoritarian Prussian regime.

A major cultural index of the gathering socio-economic crisis which precipitated the revolutionary outbreak was the internal dissolution of Hegelianism, the radicalisation of its left wing in the early 1840s and its subsequent rapid fall from cultural supremacy. The first signs of disaffection with Hegelian metaphysics signified an imminent culture shift. Hegelianism was superceded as Germany entered a new historical era. As Thomas Willey has concluded, this decline was irrevocable: 'it was as inevitable as any intellectual response can be that the convergence of empirical science, industrial progress and political disillusionment would provoke the repudiation of a speculative philosophy seemingly so out of joint with the changing times'.[2]

Hegelianism was overtaken by a process of cultural secularisation accompanying rapid social and economic modernisation. Initially, the resulting cultural vacuum was partially made good by German historicism. Historicism had roots in Hegel's epoch with the Romantics and the Historical School of law and jurispudence. Nevertheless, it shared important features with the newly emerging positivist programme taking its lead from the triumphant natural sciences. In Germany the historians had led the opposition against Hegel's speculative concept of science and opposed their exhaustive empirical investigations of 'real' history to Hegel's philosophy of history.[3] While affirming some of Hegel's theological presuppositions,[4] men like Ranke and Droysen denied the speculative idea of an immanent historical *Begriff* ('concept'). To them, this philosophy of history was nothing more than a subjective, a priori construction. Hegel had merely marshalled the real historical facts into it by a procedure of simplification and distortion. To Hegel's purported revelation of the essential rational meaning of universal history, the historicists opposed a call for painstaking empirical research. Such a rigorous approach assumed a 'value-free' investigation of individual historical 'facts' without the imposition of a priori rational schemas. This ideal of historical science received its most famous formulation in Ranke's programme to narrate the course of historical events 'just as they happpened'.

The great virtue of historicism lay in its affirmation of the old classical cultural values. While it demonstrated a new concern for historical individuality and an awareness of the immense diversity of cultures, these insights only reinforced a theological interpretation of history. The idea of a rich historical panorama confirmed the historicists' Christian belief in human freedom. Ranke's famous idea that every society was 'equally close to God' for some time obscured the problem of historical relativism. Only later when the inroads of secularisation had thrown into question the entire ensemble of traditional values was the historicist's repudiation of Hegel's belief in the rational unity of history and historical progress perceived as an acute problem.

The leading historicists manifested a religious resignation before the incomprehensible 'whole' of history. They were typically conservative but not virulently so. Unlike the late Romantics' opposition to the French Revolution, their conservatism involved no expressly reactionary political commitments nor nostalgia for the past. It was merely a consequence of their positivist methodology. Their positivist acceptance of the historical 'facts' implicitly required a conservative submission to the powers of the past. They unwittingly raised the partial moments of the historical process to the *de facto* status of sole bearer of objective norms.[5] Despite the potential tensions that in Dilthey's time flared to antagonism, there was initially a close affinity between historicism and scientific positivism.

Nineteenth-century positivism does not admit an easy characterisation. The founder of the doctrine, Auguste Comte (1798-1857) relied on a comprehensive philosophy of history designed to vindicate the progress of science. Paradoxically, the main thrust of the popularised doctrine was a wholesale critique of traditional metaphysics and philosophical history. Positivists proposed to abandon the old philosophical questions concerning the nature of being and restrict the scope of theoretical inquiry to empirical knowledge accessible to observation and testing. But as positivism was associated in the public mind with the recent achievements of the natural sciences it easily succumbed to interpretation as a total explanation. It was popularly identified with the crude materialisms that flowered in the wake of scientific triumphs and the decline of Hegelian idealism. These were characterised by the naturalist assumption of an objective world of 'facts', a mechanistic and determinist conception of the natural sciences and a leaning to associationist psychology. As part of its anti-metaphysical, anti-idealist campaign, positivism discarded the epistemological idea of subjective synthesis in favour of the specialist compartmentalisation of knowledge into spheres of factual expertise.[6] This ensemble of ideas became widely disseminated in the general culture of the age and created an environment in which philosophy was thrown completely on the defensive. Even the question of the rationale for its continued independent existence was often posed.

In the increasingly positivist climate of the second half of the nineteenth century the philosophical return of Kant was another complex phenomenon. Initially the 'back to Kant' movement was also polemically anti-speculative and aimed at the metaphysical excesses of classical German Idealism. Kant's critical strictures were easily interpreted along the lines of positivism as a sharp rebuke against metaphysical questioning and the containment of philosophy to viable terrain: mapping out the boundaries of human knowledge and clarifying the conditions of its possibility. The writings of Lange and others in the first generation of neo-Kantians manifested a general sympathy for the pervasive positivist and materialist trends of the time and demonstrated their co-operation by viewing the Kantian categories in non-transcendental, psychologistic and anthropological terms. This apparent theoretical convergence was, however, only ever partial and with a changed perception of cultural dangers – particularly a growing sense of cultural crisis in a rapidly modernising society – hardly survived into the next generation.

The last decades of the century witnessed a growing cultural backlash against positivist ideas. Many intellectuals became increasingly disturbed by the apparent trends of the 'materialist age'. They began to challenge the crude belief in the unquestioned virtue of the new 'self-sustaining' economic, technological and scientific 'progress'. H. S. Hughes aptly described this European wide reaction as a 'revolt against positivism'.[7] Owing to the unique configuration of historical factors mentioned before, this reaction was particularly acute in Germany. The accelerated pace of Germany's industrialisation accentuated the pains required by such a massive socio-economic transformation. At the same time the new age represented a challenge to the esteemed cultural position of intellectuals in Germany.[8] Here culture was perceived by the intellectual elite as the very basis of a free, humane society. This conviction and enormous cultural expectations had been fuelled by the very considerable role played by culture in the gestation and flourishing of German national feeling at the end of the eighteenth and beginning of the nineteenth century. In Germany, the heroic illusions of the Enlightenment regarding the future had primarily culturalist manifestations. In the face of such cultural expectations, the prosaic reality of late nineteenth-century bourgeois society was a profound disappointment for many. Moreover, the advance of scientific culture represented a threat to both traditional intellectual's esteemed social status and cherished cultural ideals.

The second generation of neo-Kantians represented a moderate defence of the old cultural values in a context of bourgeois society's new scientific culture and the strident claims of positivism. This stance was expressed in their deep concern for the autonomy of philosophy and other historical disciplines and their resistence to the encroachments of scientism into these areas. Some of the most significant intellectual figures from late Wilhelmian Germany were to be more or less affiliated to this generation of neo-Kantianism. Dilthey, Simmel and Weber all contributed to a powerful, but resigned, critique of culture which expressed an emerging, widely felt, disquiet even amongst political moderates over the apparent immanent directions of capitalist society and its real contradictions.

Wilhelm Dilthey: a hermeneutical concept of totality

The work of Wilhelm Dilthey (1833-1911) represents a unique crystallisation of the competing intellectual trends of the late nineteenth century. The project of his *Einleitung in der Geisteswissenschaften* was to reconcile the contemporary demand for scientificity with the preservation of the perceived achievements of historicism. As a student of Ranke, Dilthey was committed to both the ideal of exhaustive empirical research and to the representation of historical events in all their full particularly and diversity. Yet he acknowledged the Historical School were hard pressed to defend their programme against a mounting wave of sceptical positivist criticism. They failed to provide a convincing epistemological justification for their method. Encouraged by the works of Comte, Mill and Buckle, other positivists insisted that the only legitimate form of rational understanding involved the subsumption of particular events to universal laws. From this perspective, the procedures of the historicists were open to charges of subjective arbitariness. Futhermore, the radical historicisation of all values opened up an epistemological relativism that if followed logically could not recoil from questioning the value of science. Once history was raised to highest principle and all phenomena viewed as culturally and historically variable, a yawning relativism appeared to follow. Dilthey accepted the substance of these criticisms and assigned himself the mediating epistemological task of securing an autonomous method and solid foundation for the historical sciences. He proposed to rescue the claims of scientific history to objectivity by clearly defining its own boundaries with a Kantian-style methodological self-reflection. This was the only way of preserving the value of the pursuit of rational scientific knowledge to which Dilthey was committed.

This clear theoretical programme also had a more practical cultural significance. Since the demise of Hegelian metaphysics no alternative comprehensive worldview had arisen capable of providing a synthesising interpretation of the world of experience. Despite its popularisation, positivism was never really equipped to fit this role. The heart of the doctrine was the renunciation of all efforts to understand the world in its totality and the restriction of theoretical explanation to appearances in accordance with the natural scientific model of uniform and universal laws. For the positivist, knowing was an instrumental activity which provided no meaningful orientation in the world. The concepts of science were hypothetical constructs whose sole utility lay in potential control over natural processes.

The situation with historicism was rather different. With the dissolution of Hegelianism, it had usurped the traditional cultivating role belonging to philosophy. As mentioned earlier, it became the upholder of the classical cultural values.[9] Its intermediate position somewhere between philosophical idealism and methodological empiricism fitted it for this role.[10] Despite Ranke's dedication to exhaustive empirical research, his view of history as a narrative of the scenes of human freedom retained theological impulses. While he rejected the idea that the divine meaning of history was expressed in rational concepts, he went along with Hegel in presupposing the unity and full self-transparency of history. Here the historicists clearly parted ways with positivism. The view of history as the arena of human freedom and spontaneity could never be reconciled with the overriding determinism of the positivists. They expunged meaningful human action and therefore eliminated that which constituted the real essence of history for the historicists. At the back of Dilthey's project to secure the knowledge and experience accumulated by the historical sciences was the sure recognition that the growing influence of positivism in the culture of the late nineteenth century signified a threat to all those cultural values tied to the idea of human freedom.

Dilthey struggled with this self-appointed task the rest of his life without ever coming to an entirely satisfactory conclusion. The details of this odyssey need not concern us here. Of more immediate interest is the way in which he rethought and reformulated the concept of totality within his project to found a hermeneutics of the historical sciences.

The concept of understanding *(Verstehen)* was the focal point of Dilthey's efforts to vindicate the autonomy and validity of the methods of the historical sciences. To him, understanding constituted the methodological foundation of all interpretation in these sciences. Until the nineteenth century engendered a radical break with the experience of historical tradition, the importance of understanding had been overlooked due to the overwhelming continuity of cultural values. Metaphysical notions like the Hegelian spirit expressed this sense of indestructable identity and continuity amidst increasing historical diversity and distance between historians and their subjects. With the final collapse of such unifying conceptions under the weight of all the pressures of modernisation, the full theoretical implications of historical and cultural diversity had to be faced. Responsive to this dilemma, Dilthey sought to establish an *alternative basis* to ensure the continuous meaningfulness of human reality across time and space.

Kant's renewed popularity in this increasingly secular and anti-metaphysical climate has already been noted. His programme to ground scientific knowledge in the transcendental conditions of experience attracted Dilthey. Yet, after Marx, Feuerbach and historicism it was no longer possible to simply revive Kant's antiquated, abstract Enlightenment view of human reason. Dilthey responded by replacing the Kantian transcendental subject with the 'whole man', the real subject. 'Wholeness' here signified all dimensions of experience and all aspects of socio-historical conditioning. He viewed reason and consciousness as eminently historical.

Effectively, Dilthey overturned the Kantian natural scientific paradigm of experience. Cognition and perception were relativised as partial dimensions, albeit very important ones, within a greater sum of subjective experience. He promoted a richer, more qualitiative notion which did not efface feeling, desire nor subjective temporality. The Kantian *Erfahrung* ('experience') gave way to the more qualitiative *Erlebnis*. For Dilthey, the experience of the 'whole man' was itself an immediate 'whole':

> Consciousness of experience is one with its content just as subjectivity is
> one with its subject; experience [*Erlebnis*] is not an object which
> confronts the person who has it, its existence for me cannot be
> distinguished from what is present to me.[11]

Initially Dilthey construed the role of understanding as the penetration of the inner mental states of historical subjects using an empathetic technique of re-experiencing. By the time of his late hermeneutics, however, he had abandoned this psychologistic framework of understanding which depended so much on the problematic area of individual mental states. He then emphasised expressions *(Ausdruckë)*. He eventually realised the problem with all attempts to report mental states. While their very immediacy appears to recommend them as sure foundations for knowledge, they simply escape unadulterated description. The description of an inner state involves the rearrangement of the mental contents out of their immediate, lived fluidity into a fixed organisation of reportable unities. Attention to these mental states constitutes another component of consciousness which both transforms the original configuration and presupposes another attentive act to capture it.[12] It was this problem of the vicious circle of psychologism which led Dilthey to concentrate on the objective domain of expressions. These were actually 'given' to the historical sciences and reorientation in this direction avoided the difficulties of mental states and psychologism. His final conception settled on a triadic framework of understanding revolving around the circuit – *Erlebnis, Ausdruck* and *Verstehen*.

This later emphasis on expression clearly implied far more weight on the category of objective spirit.[13] Dilthey insisted that the immediate intelligibility of *Erlebnisse* presupposed prior social conditioning which constantly determined all human comprehension:

The fundamental relation between experience and understanding at which we now arrive is that of mutual dependence. More closely defined, it is one of gradual elucidation through the constant interaction of the two classes of truth. The obscurity of experience is illuminated, the mistakes which arise from narrow comprehension of the subject are corrected, experience itself is widened and completed, by our understanding of other people – just as other people are understood through our own experience.[14]

From this perspective, inter-subjectivity assumes a central interpretative significance. The individual's experience presupposes a shared social world. The intelligibility of this world presupposes a process of gradual initiation into the shared inter-subjective world of meanings, rules and practices which constantly mediate the individual's life. Recognition of the social contextualisation of meaning forced Dilthey to redirect his attention towards the objective field of relations and conventions which make meaningful subjective experience possible.

Fragmentation of totality

The preceding short sketch of Dilthey's major concerns and theoretical framework provides the basis for a reconstruction of the several versions of the totality concept to be found in his mature thought.

Biography served Dilthey initially as a model for his most simple understanding of totality. Conscious life was readily characterised as a dynamic, totalising process. Self-understanding involves a totalising fusion of memory, understanding and expectation. Consciousness signifies a unity and continuity amidst perpetual processuality:

> Life and its course form a pattern which develops through the constant
> absorption of new experiences on the basis of the older ones: I call this
> the acquired mental structure. The way this process takes place allows for
> the structure continuing even while change is going on. This fact, which
> can be demonstrated in all mental life, I refer to in terms of the category
> of essence.[15]

The mind performs an ongoing internal structuration of experiential moments guided by its own immanent, open-ended *telos*. This structuration is constantly in flux as new experiences require renewed synthesis and revision in fusing past, present and future into a meaningful totality. Dilthey upheld this idea of open-endedness maintaining that consciousness was inherently dynamic ceasing only in the moment of death.

After Dilthey's objectivist turn this first version of totality diminishes in importance. Once his attention was turned to language and other inter-subjective modes of objectification it simply lost its paradigmatic significance. The later

Dilthey generally treated meaning in terms of effects which he called 'expressions of life' (*Lebensaüsserungen*).[16] These refer to concepts, judgments, other linguistic structures and emotive expressions. The principal bearers of these meanings are the great social and cultural institutions which perpetuate and continuously reinvigorate these ideal discourses. Like Simmel and Weber who will be discussed shortly, Dilthey was concerned about the increasing relative autonomy of these massive systems within society as a whole. Nevertheless, he never thematised this development as a problem and thus never went as far as they in establishing its cultural consequences.

Dilthey clearly viewed these systems of cultural objectification as ultimately the products of collective social activity. Previously formed objects were transformed by the actions and words of contemporaries who passed away leaving only these enduring expression of their lives and purposes. This historicising point is underlined with his assertion that every 'fact' is man-made and therefore historical.[17]

The category of historical objectification indicates the presence of another concept of totality in Dilthey's work. Collective contributions to these systems of culture amount to acts of historical totalisation. Objectification is the source of a historical dynamic which constantly engenders transformed, revised and freshly created human objects:

> Only through the idea of the objectification of life do we gain insight into
> the nature of the historical. Here everything arose from spiritual action
> [*geistig Tun*] and therefore bears the hallmark of historicity. It is
> interwoven into the world of the senses as a product of history.[18]

Typically, Dilthey repudiates all metaphysical connotations attached to this idea, especially the Hegelian option of ascribing an essential spiritual meaning to the historical process. He prefers to view history as open-ended, irrational and essentially self-renewing.[19] Notwithstanding qualms with Hegel's teleology of history, he was not inclined to reduce history to a chaos of creation and destruction. In line with his early historical optimism, his middle course was a secular version of the 'ruse of reason'. History possesses a purposeful coherence shaped by the contemporary form of objective spirit. For Dilthey, spirit was an ideal social medium which conditioned the thoughts and actions of each and every individual within a given society. He attributed this purposeful coherence to the functional interlocking of the varied systems of social activity which produced a systematic coherence (*Wirkungszusammenhang*).[20] This inter-articulated system of socio-cultural institutions and practices formed the conditioning medium which historicism had raised to metaphysical proportions as the 'spirit of a people'. Dilthey viewed these transistory epochal spirits as supra-individual subjects of historical totalisation. Like Hegel he maintained it was impossible for a historian to escape the influence of this native medium but against him he insisted that this precluded *supra-historical* objectivity in the historical sciences:

Thus an epoch is centred on itself in a new sense. The common practices of an epoch become the norm for the activities of individuals who live in it. The society of an epoch has a pattern of interactions which has uniform features. There is an inner affinity in the comprehension of objects. The ways of feeling, the emotions and the impulses which arise from them, are similar to each other. The will, too, choses uniform goals, strives for related goods and finds itself committed in a similar way. . . . Thus, every action, every thought, every common activity, in short, every part of the historical whole, has its significance through its relationship to the whole of the epoch or age.[21]

How could a science of history which presupposed objectivity cope with the manifest relativity of understanding and its all too evident historical fracture? This problem represented a potential obstacle to Dilthey's programme. He recognised the prevalence of misunderstanding even within a shared culture but excluded the problem of such dissonances as *practical difficulties outside the concerns of historical hermeneutics*. This primary interest in the contemplative understanding of the past indicates the limits of his concept of historical totalisation. Unlike Marx, who understood historical totalisation in terms of the practico-social project of contemporary revolutionary politics and employed his theory of class struggle to problematise the whole question of present social misunderstanding, Dilthey was unable to perceive the *contemporary practical implications* of the category of historical totalisation.

However, even within Dilthey's chosen domain of historical reflection he was confronted by the theoretical problem of a break in, or distortion of, understanding across cultures and historical distances. Having discarded the traditional idea of a unified inter-subjective reality as presupposed with the Hegelian concept of spirit, he resolved upon another, albeit problematic, solution. Inter-subjectivity was guaranteed by a *common human nature* which allowed the individual to transcend the bounds of his/her own unique experience. 'The identity of human nature and individuality ... is the presupposition of the understanding'.[22] In a seeming paradox, the unconcealed admirer of historicism and its critique of the Enlightenment had recourse to the 'abstract' idea of a common human nature. Closer inspection soon reveals, however, that Dilthey's solution was less a return to the past than a surrender to strengthening contemporary cultural currents. Dilthey's idea of common human nature was influenced by the vitalist doctrines (*Lebensphilosophie*) which became very popular around the turn of the century in Germany and elsewhere.

Dilthey's version of human nature was fundamentally shaped by Romantic organic notions of life. Its basis tenent was that all life constitutes a whole which manifests itself concretely in irreducible diversity. Each organ of the individual plays a functional role in the reproduction of the organism and the individual is subordinate to the continuity of the species. Under the pervasive influence of evolutionary theory, it was commonly believed that these naturally occuring teleological processes could provide values and goals applicable to the conceptualisation of social reality.[23]

This idea of the fundamental unity of life amidst apparent multiplicity served as a neat theoretical solution to the problem of historical discontinuity and cultural diversity. The attraction of the idea was already evident in the early Dilthey. He was enthusiastic about the inexhaustibility of life and anchored understanding in a universal participation in life shared by all historical individuals. Despite his allegiance to the task of scientific comprehension he was prepared to acknowledge the limits of intelligience in the face of this phenomenon.[24] The dangers of an unconscious revival of metaphysics are clearly present in Dilthey's later use of the concept of life. Whereas the idealist Hegel viewed *life as a particular, inferior mode of spirit,* the vitalist Dilthey *inverted this subsumption, seeing spirit as only a particular within the greater totality of life.*[25]

The privilege accorded to the concept of life signifies not only a third understanding of the concept of totality but also a debilitating tension in Dilthey's work as a whole. Life is understood as an inexhaustible and irrational whole for which there can be *only approximate understanding and no comprehensive reduction to logical categories*:

> We can only reach an approximate understanding of life; it lies in the
> nature of both understanding and life that the latter reveals quite different
> sides to us according to the point of view from which we consider its
> course in time.[26]

Life is an irrational totality. The concept which in Hegel's system was quintessentially rationalist, here takes on the entirely opposite meaning; *spirit is overturned in favour of irrational life.* Unfortunately, reason is not the only casualty in Dilthey's acquiescence to *Lebensphilosophie.* He also characterised the historical process as irrational. This is no mere slip of the pen although he equally denies that history is a chaos. The tension between these two ultimately irreconcilable views is resolved unconsciously in favour of *a radical de-historicisation of the concept of totality.* Once life is perceived as everchanging yet always the same, a view of history as *potential emancipation,* which Dilthey came close to comprehending with his idea of historical totalisation, recedes before the vitalist tide.

This accusation of the unconscious erosion of historicity in his thought finds weighty confirmation in Dilthey's scepticism towards the idea of historical progress. His historicist education revolted against the theory of progress found in the classical philosophies of history. He relentlessly criticised both Hegelian teleology and Comte's positivism. While this criticism was undoubtedly justified, without some concept of historical progress Dilthey's own idea of historical totalisation collapsed into *a process of mere change.* Occasional early formulations suggest the possibility that history had an immanent 'single direction'.[27] This probably followed from his almost exclusively culturalist account of the emancipation of reason from metaphysics and religion. However, this optimistic theme remained theoretically unsubstantiated and ran counter to all his later explicit reflections on the question of progress. While his insights into the provisional character of all historical judgments and his open-ended conception of historical meaning were sound, his vitalist presuppositions completely dehistoricised his general theoretical standpoint by subordinating history to an irrational concept of life.

Although Dilthey perceived the mounting signs of historical crisis, he remained receptive to the idea of a possible reconciliation between science, subjectivity and tradition. As Gadamer has argued,[28] the fundamental impulse of his mature ideal of historical consciousness was the subjective effort to transcend all historically conditioned limitations and the belief that only conscious recognition of historical conditionedness could undermine prejudice and dogma:

> The historical consciousness of the finitude of every historical
> phenomenon, every human or social state, of the relativity of every sort of
> belief, is the last step towards the liberation of man. With it, man attains
> the sovereign power to wring from every experience its content, to
> surrender wholly to it, without prepossession.[29]

Precisely in this advocacy of subjective cultivation, however well-intentioned, one senses a retreat from the crisis of contemporary history into individual interiority. Dilthey's diagnosis of contemporary historical possibilities was shaped by disillusionment with industrial society and a rising pessimism:

> Present-day reflection upon human existence fills us with the feeling of
> the fragility of all life, the power of dark instinct, of human suffering
> because of dark forces and illusions, and the finitude of all life – even
> there where the highest attainments of social and cultural life arise.[30]

Cultivation in the form of historical consciousness signified a broadening of the subject's humanity and a resigned respect for all other manifestations of life threatened by the contemporary 'progress' of modern industrial civilisation.

Simmel: the tragedy of culture

The vitalist currents unveiled in Dilthey's work assume a much stronger and more explicit form in the philosophy of Georg Simmel (1858-1918). Though his thought underwent a number of major philosophical shifts,[31] it never strayed far from the problem of culture. Not only is culture arguably the central focus of an extraordinarily diverse *corpus* of writings, it provides an excellent starting-point to explore Simmel's concept of totality.

Simmel's theory of culture was underpinned by his own idea of culture (*Kultur*). His major work, Philosophy of Money (1900) emphatically rejected the idea that culture consisted in a 'body of objective knowledge and behaviour patterns'. Such an understanding was a relatively new product of the nineteenth century. In striking contrast, Simmel maintained that the true idea of culture pertained *only to subjects*.[32] This authentic idea of culture involved two indispensible concepts: 'soul' and 'objectification'.

For Simmel, the soul signified a latent potentiality existing naturally in the individual which could only attain complete realisation through a *process* of cultivation. According to Simmel, the human subject was the only being known to possess an inherent a priori demand for perfection.[33] At the core of Simmel's concept of subjective culture was the ideal of a unique perfection inscribed in the soul as an immanent *telos*. This perfection was anything but a mere 'specialist expertise'; it was the realisation of some original inner promise. All aspects of the individual's life had to be harmonised into a unified whole. The soul is the profound inner impulse which shapes the contents of life into an organic unity by the imposition of its own personal stamp.[34] On this view, culture is rooted in an inner soulish teleology.

This idea of culture certainly involves an organic unfolding of the personality and talents of the subject. It does not, however, imply that this 'unfolding' can be completely internal or self-sufficient. Simmel even argues that purely instinctive development or inner self-improvement – such as religious enrichment – cannot be considered as cultural achievements in the true sense. Such purely internal efforts simply lack real objectification. This category, which has already been met in Hegel, Marx and Dilthey, remained central also to Simmel's thinking about culture.

Simmel maintained that culture necessarily required the employment of external means in the process. Culture was essentially *a value augmenting process* involving a 'unique teleological interweaving of subject and object' achieved through the transformative interaction of these two correlates.[35] While this understanding of culture has a very Hegelian ring, Simmel claimed no ontological significance for this idea. It was, in Kantian terms, a 'metaphysical presupposition of our practical and emotional essence'.

The heavy subjectivist emphasis of this concept of culture yields a pronounced subjectivist accent in Simmel's interpretation of totality. The tendency towards interior retreat already indicated in Dilthey is here supplied with a much stronger philosophical articulation. For Simmel, self-cultivation is the ultimate goal of historical development. The sum of human social objectifications amounts to little more than a reservoir of *accumulated means* subject to the arbitary and sporadic whims of self-cultivation.

Andrew Arato maintains that Simmel viewed the human species as only an abstract correlate of this rapidly expanding fund of social products. He recognised no possibility of mediation between the species and concrete individuals.[36] Without a concept of collective subjectivity, Simmel excluded the possibility of understanding historical totalisation as an emancipatory or unified process. This reluctance contributed to his very pessimistic diagnosis of modernity and introduced a peculiar antinomy into his interpretation of objectification. This antinomy emerges with Simmel's ideas of the 'paradox', and ultimately, the 'tragedy' of culture:

> It is the paradox of culture that subjective life which we feel in its continual streams and which presses from itself out towards its consummation [*Vollendung*], viewed from the idea of culture, cannot attain this perfection out of itself but only by means of those forms which have now become alien, crystallised to self-sufficient closure [*Abgeschlossenheit*]. Culture emerges – and this is decisive for its understanding – when two elements come together of which neither contains it separately: the subjective soul and the objective spiritual product.[37]

Vitalism is clearly at the heart of these notions of tragedy. Both life and the world of objects are incomplete and deficient. Each pole of this opposition is dependent upon the other. Subjective life is inexhaustibly vital and flowing but lacks form. Only the imposition of form supplies this amorphous flow and fecundity with direction and shape.[38] Subjective life is therefore only a material and one constitutive moment of life. Without form it would be shapeless chaos, an incessant flow.

By contrast, form means definition, limitation and rigidity; it inhibits the perpetual, immanent flow of life. Form imposes order and resists flow. Formed objects are self-sufficienct in virtue of their own internal 'logics'. Simmel perceived form as both necessary and, consistent with his vitalist leanings, a real threat to culture under modern social conditions. It results in an inevitable calcification, the formation of alien, impersonal, mechanical processes of 'objective' totalisation. Max Weber coined the term 'rationalisation' to exemplify the same phenomenon. These processes transcended the true *telos* of culture (as Simmel saw it), lacked soul and escaped human control. They stood as an obstacle, inhibiting the living organic ends of subjective totalisation. This increasingly more aggravated opposition between life and form was the crux of Simmel's idea of the paradox of culture. The enhancement of life required a means that quickly ossified into a stultifying force.

From the perspective of vitalism, however, this seemingly threatening paradox was open to a positive interpretation. The opposition between form and life was an invariant tension which periodically exploded. Obsolete forms are overthrown and the cataclysm engenders fresh unities as opposition momentarily subsides before complementarity.[39] From this moment of harmony, Simmel derived the criteria which distinguished vital, authentic life forms from those grown redundant and inappropriate. Culture implied this harmony: the affinity between soul and form.

The other side of this tension was the inevitable alienation of forms: their every increasing autonomy and distance from their original creators. Objectification freezes life but such harmonious perfection is only transistory and repels life. Once detached from its life's blood, form becomes something more than life. Form is the actualisation of immanent potentials and creative energy but, at the same time, it is also immoveable, rigid and lifeless. Paradoxically, form is a dimension of life utterly indifferent to the meanings of subjective life. Forms follow their own independent logics and trajectories.

The upshot of this train of thought was that Simmel offered no guarantees that the metaphysical postulate of subjective synthesis would be met. Indeed, his historico-sociological analyses suggested that this postulate had been rendered unrealisable by the progress of modern objective culture. In the Philosophy of Money Simmel argued that historical development generated an increasing multiplicity of forms both symbolic and technical. This increasing multiplicity was aggravated by the accentuated automaticity and independence of their logics of development. In the face of this empirical trend, the prospects for subjective assimilation were endangered by the sheer growing weight of objective products.

Culture enriches life but its products are detachable and 'betray' the original creative subject. They participate in a multitude of ideal worlds – social, ethical, scientific, erotic. Each world contains an infinite number of possible developmental trajectories.[40] Simmel cites law as a clear example of a human objectification possessed of its own immanent logic and autonomy. In modern civilisation, the objective dynamics of culture had exponentially amplified this tendency amounting to an automatic, detached totalisation indifferent to the needs of living culture.

Here Simmel's argument undoubtedly introduces another dimension of the totality concept into his theory of culture. The 'objective', almost automatic totalisation of modern cultural processes is essentially devoid of human freedom, subjective significance or value. This is an extremely pessimistic idea which turns Hegel's and Marx's humanist reading of the concept of totality on its head. Simmel has taken the concept of alienation and detached it from an emancipatory dialectic. He shared Weber's resigned trepidation before the inexorability of objective totalisation.

In Simmel's cultural disgnosis of modernity the stress fell on the *increasing preponderance of cultural objects over subjects*. This trend developed in consort with the modern division of labour. Borrowing from themes in the sociology of Ferdinand Tönnies,[41] he maintained that the fragmentation of the modern production process effected a complete dislocation between the wills of producers and their products. The de-subjectivisation of the production process required a fracture of the traditionally skilled artisan-worker who could no longer be the sole creator of a whole unified object. Skilled work was devalorised in an organisation of production based on industrial technology and a demand for simple one-sided skills. Simple abilities were more readily inserted into the new complex, objectively organised and fragmented processes of manufacture. Simmel also analysed wage labour along Marxian lines. But for him wage labour was *just one instance of an underlying historical trend* associated with the modern division of labour.

Simmel refused to ascribe any particular weight to the specific crisis of contemporary bourgeois society. Marxian theory served only to corroborate his 'metaphysical' vitalist interpretation of culture.[42] Present social contradictions could not be eliminated. Culture continued only because the infinite possibilities and energies of life could not be contained in any finite ensemble of forms. This inexhaustibility was the source and stimulus of the perpetual opposition and dynamism apparent in cultural transformation. Simmel shared Dilthey's view that the totality of life could not be rationally encompassed. With this vitalist framework he hoped to construct 'a new storey beneath historical materialism'.[43] His later philosophy worked to realise such a programme. Alienation was interpreted in terms of the universal dynamic of life and form. In sympathy with this tendency, Simmel indicated little interest in the contemporary historical basis of alienation and resigned himself to its perpetuation.

Instead, contemporary alienation was magnified into a 'universal fate' which Simmel termed the 'tragedy of culture'. 'Tragedy' designated the fact that the massive weight of objective culture, originally the product of subjective aspirations and toil, threatened to overwhelm its creators. The same process whereby individuals were to attain perfect self-realisation also bore within it the seeds of soulless indifference and human negation. The individual was simply unable to keep pace with a culture expanding in geometric proportions. The capacities of individuals to assimilate developments were too limited. Simmel noted the increasing imbalance and the pervasive perception that the great technological advances of modern civilisation were intimidating, meaningless and alien.

He was mesmerised by the strange inversion that transformed means into their own self-serving and self-perpetuating ends. Rather than relieving humans of slavish labour, industrial technology posited men as complete slaves. They became slaves of both the machines and the products they produced. Simmel viewed this development as a 'revolt of the products' in which 'the complicated precision of machines, products and the supra-individual organisations of contemporary culture' had become the 'true masters of modern life and the real bearers of its significance and intellectual potential'. This was symptomatic of the 'tragic phase' into which contemporary culture had entered. He held out no promise for the alleviation of this tragedy and its antinomies. In fact, he quite cynically viewed these contradictions as the very lifeblood of culture and assumed that somehow Life would finally regain the initiative and triumph over the accumulated dead weight of objective culture. Specific practical policies might ameliorate but never reverse nor set contemporary discrepancies into balance:

> No cultural policy can eliminate the tragic discrepancy between objective culture, with its unlimited capacity for growth, and subjective culture,

which can only grow slowly. But it can work towards reducing this discrepency by enabling the individual to make better use and more rapid use of objective culture in our lives as the raw material of subjective culture, which, when all is said and done, is the only thing that gives the former any real value.[44]

The mood of this diagnosis sums up Simmel's view of the prospects confronting modern bourgeois society in the early decades of the twentieth century. From it can be extracted three decisive connotations of the concept of totality. Firstly, Simmel viewed subjective totalisation as the only real value to be derived from the historical accumulation of cultural objects. This subjectivisation of the concept has already been met with in Dilthey's work. Although Simmel also allocated a central place to the category of objectification in his theory, its significance for the understanding of history was undermined by his vitalist framework and repetition of the Hegelian conflation of objectification and alienation. Simmel reasoned that as objects obey their own inscribed 'logics' and lack the fluidity of life, the opposition between life and form was inevitable and, in principle, untranscendable. Again as in Dilthey the amorphous *totality of life* has theoretical priority over historical praxis. In Simmel this is the dominant understanding of totality. Life is permanently in struggle with its own ossified forms. Simmel shares with Dilthey the idea of the totality of life as timeless, inexhaustible and irrational. As a result of the priority accorded to life, *the essential historicity of real concrete subjectivity is unconsciously devalued.* History becomes the constant struggle of life against itself, of formation against form. The contemporary crisis of objective culture is considered irresolvable. The question of a rational reconstruction of social organisation and cultural vitality is therefore prematurely closed. Simmel contemplated in resignation the uncontrolled acceleration of objective totalisation; a process devoid of meaning and threatening to what passed for contemporary freedom. He gained some respite from this third grim image of totality only through an absorption in, and fascination with, the diversity of life forms and the presentiment of life's eventual liberation from the restraints of these frozen forms. But this reflective consolation hardly disguises the unmistakeable narrowing of perspectives for social reform and the loss of the emancipatory, critical standpoint which, only decades before, had constituted the main theoretical bite and real cultural significance of the concept of totality.

The 'iron cage' of history

The work of Max Weber (1864-1920) represents probably the most impressive attempt to articulate and confront the new felt sense of crisis pervading German society at the turn of the century. In his hands there is also a continuation and sharpening of the process of philosophical transformation undergone by the concept of totality. As with Simmel, the extent and diversity of his output make it difficult to characterise but several commentators have viewed 'rationalisation' as a thread which unifies much of it. This interpretation is well supported by many passages in Weber's work. In a late Introduction to the collected essays on the sociology of religion he states that the central task of universal history is the characterisation and explanation of the unique rationalism of modern civilisation.[45] His own comparative studies appear to be unified by just such a universal historical perspective focused on 'this specific and peculiar rationalism'. This theme is especially worth pursuing as it permits the reconstruction of Weber's implicit critique of the classical Hegelian-Marxian historicist concept of totality.

While Weber attributed universal significance to the phenomenon of 'rationalisation', he refused to view it as the basis of a new philosophical interpretation of history. His critique of such immanentist concepts of history was the foundation of his own methodological reflections. Even more importantly, Weber simply did not believe that the phenomenon of rationalisation could be construed as a single process. On the contrary, he viewed it as a number of *historically contingent* yet, in western civilisation, *ultimately interlocked processes*. Weber maintained, however, that despite disparate historical sources, rates of development in various spheres of life, the diversity of interests and values they fostered, these processes did share common features. He mentions de-personalisation of social relations, the refinement of techniques of calculation, the enhanced importance of specialisation, the intellectualisation of all realms of culture and the extension of rational control over both natural and social processes. In various studies of the economy, law, administration, religions and culture, Weber ventured to explicate these commonalities and explore how they had completely transformed the lifeworld of modern western society.

He ultimately asserted that behind these multiple processes of cultural change was a unifying rationalistic principle that *it was possible to master all things by calculation and comprehensively understand all aspects of life.*[46] The impact of these processes on the traditional lifeworld was summed up in his notion of 'disenchantment':

> As intellectualism suppresses belief in magic, the world's processes
> become disenchanted, lose their magical significance and henceforth
> simply 'are' and 'happen' but no longer signify anything. As a
> consequence, there is a growing demand that the world and the total
> pattern of life be subject to an order that is significant and meaningful.[47]

In traditional societies, magic and religion supplied experience with meaning and circumscribed the sanctified ends of all action. Rationalisation had eliminated the meaningfulness of experience, at least in the universal, ultimate sense furnished by the great world religions, without being able to quench the thirst for it. Disenchantment signified an experience stripped of ultimate meaning, one exposed to infinitely many possible attitudes and value stances towards the world of which none was sanctified or above intellectual dismemberment.

For Weber, the consequences of rationalisation were summarised in his diagnosis of modernity: both a 'loss of meaning' and a 'loss of freedom'. The former is explicated in the idea of disenchantment. The erosion of traditionally legitimated hierarchies engender a crisis of subjective experience. Here Weber was specifically concerned with the domain of ideologies and religious *Weltanschauugen* ('world views'). Obviously, however, the processes of rationalisation also enroached into and transformed organisations, institutions and other material practices such as the economy, law and public administration. All, according to Weber, evidenced the increasing incursion of a totally impersonal, objective rationality which constrained human freedom of action. His vision of modernity implied this 'loss of freedom' as an impending threat to modern civilisation.

Specifically, Weber drew attention to the gradual elimination of charismatic authority and the personalised character of most earlier forms of social relations. He also underlined the increasing subordination of all institutions and action to assessment in terms of the instrumental principle of 'goal rationality'. These trends jeopardised the nascent individual freedoms only recently secured with the emergence of bourgeois civil society. Weber viewed them as ominous signs of an increasingly de-personalised world of objective processes which had progressively excoriated human meaning and disengaged itself from subjective needs. The autonomy of many of these processes from human control and subjective needs was evident with the imposition of their own 'objective logics' upon the growing mass of individuals subordinated to them.

Implied in this interpretation of rationalisation and its impact on modernity is a new understanding of the category of totality. More correctly it suggests a fragmentation of the Hegelian-Marxian concept into a *number of different concepts of totality which then acquire both positive and negative value connotations*. This fragmentation is most clearly evident in the first dimension of Weber's two-dimensional diagnosis of modernity: the 'loss of meaning'. This phase signified the collapse of the traditional Christian cosmology which hypostasised a fixed, hierarchical, harmonised metaphysical concept of totality. This traditional concept, whose last great philosophical representative had been Hegel, was synomous with a unified holistic interpretation of the world. In its traditional context it had enabled individuals to make sense of their experience in categories and values secured by historical tradition and the weight of collective social practices. While Weber was far from viewing the destruction of traditional cosmologies in solely negative terms (indeed, on balance, he always underscored the challenge of potential individual liberation in terms of ethical autonomy) none the less he honestly confronted the *predicament* arising from it. The modern individual was thrown adrift and experience was robbed of its former security. The processes of rationalisation were virtually irreversible and the collapse of the old ideologies engendered an epochal crisis manifest in the breakdown of authoritative traditions and *Weltanschauungen*.

These obsolete traditional cosmologies and metaphysics provide a first version of the totality concept in Weber. Such interpretations has been historically surpassed and were now intellectually untenable. They survived as an option only for those individuals who chose to abandon the complexities of contemporary ethical responsibility in the face of the dynamics of rationalisation.[48]

Weber was by no means alone in recognising the irreversible loss of the traditional idea of totality. Both Dilthey and Simmel also noted this disintegration of the old religio-metaphysical version of totality with a resigned stoicism. Yet, it was Weber alone who placed this modern dilemma at the centre of his methodological considerations and his substantive diagnosis of modernity.

In a passage from 'Religious Rejections of the World and Their Directions', he detailed the most important objective consequence of the march of rationalisation:

> The rationalization and the conscious sublimation of man's relations to
> the various spheres of value, external and internal, religious and worldly,
> have pressed towards making conscious the internal and lawful autonomy
> [*Eigengesetzlichkeit*] of the individual spheres, thereby letting them drift
> into tensions which remain hidden to the original naïve naturalness of
> man's relation to the external world.[49]

To fully appreciate the rationale of Weber's repudiation and transformation of the traditional metaphysical concept of totality, it is necessary to closely analyse this argument. Modernity, for Weber, was characterised by the disappearance of a harmonised hierarchy of values. Science, art, religion, politics, the economy, in sum, all the various spheres of cultural value now asserted a real autonomy and resisted subordination within a religiously ordained hierarchy. These autonomous value spheres were set on independent courses determined only by their own internal structure and the logic of their specific forms of action. Each patterned an aspect of life in accordance with its own immanent prescriptions. Even more decisive for Weber's ultimate diagnosis was the fact that each value sphere also made universalistic claims and insisted upon its own validity as an absolute schema of interpretation.

Modern experience clearly contradicted these hyperbolic claims. It was plagued with perpetual conflict and competition between the advocates of the different value spheres on contested terrain. Moreover, no single value by itself could encompass and order the totality of modern experience. None could infuse modern experience with unified meaning.

From this evidence of unconstrained autonomy and the disappearance of a universally recognised sphere of absolute validity, Weber concluded that hierarchisation, outside of a personal subjective choice of 'fate', was impossible. Johann Arnason has reformulated Weber's 'loss of meaning' as 'parcellisation of meaning' obviously to underline the *multiplication of value spheres in modernity, their increasing divergence and incompatibility*.[50] If the breakdown of the old concept of totality signified the collapse of monism, modernity had given rise to a new era of polytheism.

The subjectivisation of totality

Weber's contemporary individual confronted a world stripped of inherent human significance. In their efforts to explain the world in terms of impersonal, objective laws, natural scientists had extinguished the human subject. The disappearance of a secured objective meaning for the world left the modern subject before a surfeit of competing values and potential meanings between which he/she was required to choose. The challenge of this unique historical situation was accepted by Weber and he endeavoured to unequivocally draw out its existential consequences.

He saw the modern individual set before an arduous task. But one that held out the prospect of liberation from the age-old straightjacket of 'received' self-definition and world order. The attraction of this liberation lay in the potential realisation of a new ethical dignity forged in radical autonomy. This was nothing like a rosy vision of the future but a diagnosis that provided the historico-sociological foundations of Weber's ethics of responsibility. It signified a robust wager on ethical subjectivity as the principal bulwark against the increasing power of the impersonal processes of rationalisation. It was a view of ethics which *radicalised the element of choice* in social action but also emphasised the weight of these choices by driving home the fact of *individual responsibility* for the foreseeable consequences of self-chosen actions. The individual was enjoined to make rational choices which took real account of the individual's location within a complex configuration of intersecting social and cultural processes.

No sphere of activity was exempt from the grim recognition of the weight of individual choice and responsibility. Nowhere was this more true than in science: Weber regularly insisted that science was incapable of answering life's most fundamental questions:

> The fate of an epoch which has eaten of the tree of knowledge is that it must know that it cannot learn the meaning of the world from the results of its analysis, be it ever so perfect; it must rather be in a position to create this meaning itself. It must recognise that general views of life and the universe can never be products of increasing empirical knowledge, and that the highest ideals, which move us forcefully, are always formed only in the struggle with other ideals which are just as sacred to others as ours are to us.[51]

Recognising the limits of science, Weber was prepared to problematise even the value of intellectual activity itself. Unable, as it had in the past, to show men 'how to act rightly in life and, above all, how to act as a citizen of the state', rational analysis had to be silent before the ultimate questions of human meaning and direction. Whether intellectual activity enriched life or became an end in itself was a matter of individual choice.

The emancipatory, ethical dimensions of this understanding of the modern individual's predicament are obvious. But we can also discern in this interpretation another version of the new emphasis on subjective totalisation already outlined in Dilthey and Simmel. According to Weber, the individual must create his/her own meaning by choosing a particular value and living to the full its realisation with responsibility and consciousness. Despite the great strain this placed on the psychical resources of the individual, he believed it revealed the essence of the true personality. The true personality consciously affirmed his/her choice as a 'calling' (*Beruf*) and organised his/her life around it as an integral, self-created coherence. Repeatedly, Weber argued that the unique meaning of a truly human life consisted in this self-constructed unification and harmonisation of individual action in accordance with elected values:

> The freer the action. . . i.e. the less it has the character of a natural event, the more the concept of personality comes into play. The essence of personality lies in the constancy of its inner relation to certain ultimate values and life-meanings, which, in the course of action, turn into purposes and are thus translated into teleologically rational action.[52]

This radically subjectivised understanding of totality was the only version of the concept that preserved the original emancipatory and critical meaning of the category found in Hegel and Marx. For Weber, this was the only version of totalisation he could positively affirm in the historico-cultural conditions of the early twentieth century. He *reduced the initial historical and inter-subjective dimensions of 'totality' to the mere totalisation of an individual life* integrally expressive of the integrity, inner coherence and significance of the personality alone.

Weber never discounted the risks and possible contradictions accompanying this emphatic subjectivisation of meaning and value. He was aware that such individual commitment could take the form of a 'demonic' possession in leading to the annihilation of other cherished values. One of the starkest instances of this was Weber's own relentless espousal of German imperialist interests.[53] While he saw no rational way of resolving the question of value choice, his emphasis on responsibility signified the attempt to synthesise adherence to ultimate values with a conscious recognition and evaluation of their likely consequences in the sphere of action. Despite its problems, Weber viewed this conception as the true instantiation of the Kantian ideal of ethical autonomy in a world devoid of universal principles. In modernity, this ideal required the individual to assume the task of self-creation through the adoption and realisation of subjective values.

This extreme subjectivist stance also disposed of theoretical inadequacies that Weber had highlighted in his own methodological writings. In keeping with the pervasive anti-metaphysical and positivist spirit of the epoch, he ruthlessly exposed any trace of comforting illusions. In the essay 'Roscher and Knies' (1903-5), he joined the polemic against all 'emanatist' notions of history. This attitude carried over into his later interpretative sociology which roundly condemned all quasi-Hegelian ideas of supra-individual substance. He argued that all such metaphysical residues had no place in a critical, sober, scientific outlook. Not content with this prescription, he maintained that even concrete supra-individual structures like the state required theoretical reduction in order to become scientifically accessible in terms of the predictablility of certain types of individual action:

> Interpretative sociology considers the individual and his actions as the basic unit, as its 'atom' – if the disputable comparison for once may be permitted. In this approach, the individual is also the upper limit and the sole carrier of meaningful conduct. . . . In general, for sociology, such concepts as 'state', 'association', 'feudalism', and the like, designate certain categories of human interaction. Hence it is the task of sociology to reduce these concepts to 'understandable' action, that is without exception, to the actions of the participating individual men.[54]

Weber insisted that all supra-individual meaning be reduced to the level of the personality for which there existed a possibility of understanding. This extreme move was dictated by his conviction that the categories of *telos* and totality were only legitimately applicable when referred to the inner unity, coherence and meaning of an individual life.

Totalisation without the totaliser

Weber maintained few illusions concerning the obstacles which modernity had already placed in the way of his ideal of responsible, self-conscious subjectivity. Subjective totalisation was threatened on all fronts by the increasing subordination/enslavement of subjects to the impersonal 'logics' of the autonomous value spheres and their distinctive developmental trajectories. In the famous passage from The Protestant Ethic and the Spirit of Capitalism, Weber described the 'fate' of modernity as an 'iron cage' acknowledging the irresistible power of the modern industrial economic order and the threat it posed to individual freedom:

> This order is now bound to the technical and economic conditions of machine production which today determine the lives of all the individuals who are born into this mechanism, not only those directly concerned with economic acquisition, with irresistible force.[55]

Though he remained wary of outright historical predictions, Weber viewed this 'objective mechanism' with its attendant broader social and cultural manifestations as a grave danger to the ultimate survival of subjective autonomy and totalisation.

This presentiment of an impending 'loss of freedom' was the other side of Weber's diagnosis of modernity. The material fate of vast populations now depended upon the increasingly bureaucratised mechanisms of private capitalism. He ridiculed as completely utopian all thoughts that these vast systems could be eliminated.[56] Large economic organisations demanded the further refinement of specialisation within bureaucracy. The increasing universality of these tendencies signified the rapid encroachment of rational 'discipline' into all private and public relations of authority.[57] Such organisational imperatives gave rise to the professional expert and greatly restricted the role of individually differentiated conduct and charisma. The personality type of the 'specialist without spirit' epitomised for Weber all the dangers of present trends towards organisational regimentation prescribed by rational principles. Both the specialist and the bureaucrat were servants of a totally impersonal order. Each was required to subordinate personality to impersonal, objective rules and functions. They were prisoners of the 'chain of command' which reduced them to mere cogs in the vast mechanism obeying prescriptions laid down from above. They had to meet functional requirements for the optimal performance of the system according to calculable rules.

Weber clearly viewed the modern development of a vast economic, political and social mechanism as a new hybrid form of historical totalisation which threatened to detach itself from any human project for real social emancipation and endangered freedom and meaningful life. This autonomous systemic monster increasingly operated according to its own purely functional requirements and followed an objective course that very often negated the needs of contemporary populations. Such an objective, impersonal form of totalisation was the great modern threat to subjective totalisation. Weber's call for the full realisation of ethical responsibility and subjective emancipation has to be seen in the context of this portent of a likely future dominated by the 'iron cage': humanity's subordination to the purely objective requirements of an 'automatically' self-totalising socio-economic system.

This negative utopia encapsulates Weber's understanding of the concept of totality. His historical diagnosis of modernity in terms of these processes of rationalisation amounts in most important respects to a reversal of the cultural meaning of the totality concept bequeathed by the immediately preceding revolutionary epoch of Hegel and Marx. It is true that both these earlier thinkers anticipated the threat inherent in the unregulated dynamics of the bourgeois market. They still maintained, however, a predominately optimistic vision of modernity based on their distinctive understandings of its contradictory, but ultimately progressive, emancipatory historical dynamics. Weber's negative version of totality discarded what he believed to be the partially 'illusory' idea of emancipatory historico-social potential inherent to the objective dynamics of capitalism. The glimmer of hope in his picture was the aforementioned possibility of authentic subjective totalisation. Yet even this very deflated, albeit important, positive conception of totalisation was constantly endangered by the increasing pervasiveness of the ever-encroaching, impersonal processes of the complex, soulless mechanisms of modernity.

At this point it is worthwhile to briefly recapitulate the results of the analysis so far. In Weber, the totality concept is fragmented into three constitutive moments each of which receives a different accent and evaluation. Firstly, Weber declares the historical obsolescence of the traditional religious and metaphysical images of totality as a result of the contemporary confluence of the multiple processes of rationalisation. In its place he adumbrates two other mutually hostile images of totalisation. The modern socio-economic-cultural system driven by its own contradictory, impersonal logics becomes his negative image of objective, mechanical totalisation which increasingly threatens to stultify and even annihilate the only positive version of totalisation he can still endorse: that of authentic, subjective totalisation. This sharp opposition of two antagonistic images of totality with its pessimistic assessment of the real prospects of the human subject opposed to the ever-expanding power and reach of objective socio-cultural forces illustrates that Weber's analysis is not unlike that of his friend Simmel. The great difference between the two is that Simmel ultimately opted to transcend this opposition with a third vitalist inspired concept of totality. That of the irrational forces of life which allowed him to sustain a curious faith in the eventual reassertion of life itself. Weber was unwilling to countenance such comforting 'metaphysical' solutions to the dilemmas of modernity. He left the destructive opposition unresolved and pinned his hopes on the radical subjectivisation of the totality concept.

To consider the philosophical implication of Weber's radical subjectivisation of the totality concept it is necessary to take a close look at his solution to the dispute over values that raged amongst his contemporaries. His answer discloses some of the internal strains in his reinterpretation of the category of totality.

Rickert and Weber on values

A comparison between Weber and the neo-Kantian Heinrich Rickert brings into sharp relief the deeper philosophical presuppositions of Weber's reformulation of the totality concept. Weber's approach to the value question was both *culturalist and subjectivist.* He explicitly emphasised the culturally specific and subjective status of all values. Rickert only partially shared this view. While he insisted that historical cultures were *the only real source* for the study of values, this did not inhibit him from arguing very emphatically that values themselves were *supra-historical.* His version of the Heidelberg neo-Kantian 'two-world theory' maintained that values could be valid (*gilt*) without this entailing their actual existence. The 'two-world theory' was a philosophical dualism involving the distinction between validity and existence. Rickert also maintained that values could be hierachically ordered into a system although he never actually made good this claim by himself realising the programmatic system. However, this stance clearly conflicted with Weber who consistently argued that modernity had undermined all objective hierarchies. Moreover, he deduced from his close analysis of the dissolution of the traditional value hierachies the endemic conflict of value choices and their purely historico-cultural determination.

This comparison makes clear that while Weber did borrow important elements from Rickert's neo-Kantian philosophical arsenal[58] (and in one respect these are vital), his position was in other respects quite idiosyncratic. This is evident in his interpretation of the transcendental presuppositions of the natural and social sciences. He consciously abandoned the orthodox neo-Kantian universal claim:

> The transcendental presuppositions of every cultural science lies not in
> our finding a certain cultural or any 'culture' in general to be valuable but
> rather in the fact that we are cultural beings, endowed with the capacity
> and the will to take a deliberate attitude towards the world and to lend it
> significance.[59]

Weber very elequently underlines his historico-cultural interpretation of values. F. H. Tenbruck has drawn attention to precisely this aspect of his thought: that, for Weber, human reality was a cultural web.[60] Weber's culturalism was responsible for the abandonment of the orthodox neo-Kantian absolutist 'transcendental' grounding of objectivity in favour of a recognition of the cultural specificity of modern occidential science.

As mentioned, not even the scientific value of truth was excluded from Weber's relativist insight into the limited historico-cultural significance and value of *all* value orientations. Reinforcing this point, he referred to the fact that members of non-western cultures find the fundamental occidential values like 'rationality' incomprehensible.[61] As if to underscore the tenuous historical basis of such values, he did not rule out the possibility of a 'Chinese ossification' of the quest for knowledge.

Such observations were probably also intended to shake western intellectual arrogance and forcefully illustrate that the scientific worldview was by no means universal nor incontestable. Weber viewed it as a culturally conditioned image. The scientific value of truth was valid only 'for those who seek the truth'.[62] He persisted with this strong culturalist interpretation of values despite the clear indications of his own analysis that the occidental system of values – especially that of objective truth – had attained an almost universal significance in modernity. They were the only values with the prospect of universality and, independently of their specific historical origin, potentially obligatory for all. In Weber's thought this potential universality is a paradox requiring unravelling.

At this stage of the analysis the main point is that in Weber's account culturalism was ultimately reducible to subjectivism. In the context of modernity, he maintained that every objective basis for the validity of values – including that of cultural unity – had dissolved. In this situation, the ultimate ground of valorisation was confined to the subjective convictions of the individual. Thus, Weber's emphasis on cultural determination was overlayed by an extreme subjectivism or decisionism. Judgments of validity became matters of faith falling outside the province of science altogether: value judgments were irrational and therefore lacked an objective basis.[63]

Weber's ethics are grounded in precisely this cultural condition. The emancipatory overtones and ethical implications of this celebration of subjective totalisation resound in his description of personal dignity. The dignity of Weber's individual lay in the fact that for he/she 'there exists values about which he/she organises his/her life'; self-realisation consists in the wholehearted pursuit of 'those interests' around which his/her life was orientated and for which he/she claimed universal validity.[64]

Philosophical roots of Weber's subjectivism

Even sympathetic critics of Weber's work have questioned the necessity of his methodological retreat into extreme subjectivism. Karl Löwith, for instance, perceived in it merely a theoretical abstraction from the isolated conditions of modern individuality in the contemporary bourgeois state.[65] The individual subject who defined his /her own reality and created his/her own meaning was nothing less than a product of these modern socio-historical conditions. The question raises itself: why should these specific conditions be elevated to the status of the sole paradigm and pre-condition of scientific interpretability for all meaningful action? Weber's resolution of the value question does provide an answer but it also reveals a problematic conception of the subject/object relation at the core of his radical subjectivism.

Weber's 'resolution' of the problem of values involves a syncretism. His radical culturalist interpretation of values presupposed that they were cultural products of the activities of *concrete social communities*. Many times Weber made this point when he argued that individuals were conditioned by the social institutions and the 'cultural web' in which they developed to consciousness.[66] Weber might have concluded from his recognition of the conditionedness of human subjectivity that, at least in the first instance, *individuals were incapable of actually creating values*. In fact, they merely found them already existing as either, in traditional social contexts, unchangeable 'givens' to be internalised, or, in modernity, as an array of choices to be affirmed, denied or transformed, depending upon the character of existing historical subjectivity and its practical options.

Clearly this particular culturalist dimension of thought was swamped by Weber's adherence to the idea of the transcendental epistemological subject taken over from Rickert. The notion of a transcendental epistemological subject entailed the image of an isolated creator, forming an infinite, amorphous, unformed 'reality'. Deceived by this image, Weber *underplayed the inter-subjective, social construction of historical objectivity and, accordingly, the values embodied in it* to which he had elsewhere frequently drawn attention.

Seyla Benhabib has offered a very cogent explanation of this damaging tension in Weber's methodological thought. She contends that his theoretical elimination of the inter-subjective dimension of the creation of values was tied to his defence of the neo-Kantian theory of moral autonomy. Like the neo-Kantians, he contested the view that valid moral imperatives could be derived from the objective course and logic of historical and social developments.[67] This stance signifies his commendable refusal to countenance any theoretical proposal which would subordinate individual moral autonomy to objective forces and processes. His position is especially understandable in view of his characterisation of these objective forces as the bearer of an alien, impersonal totalisation increasingly detached from the concern for human freedom and meaning.

Yet, however explicible was Weber's reasoning, it plainly involved a confusion. To summarise Benhabib's conclusion, he wrongly bestowed upon the neo-Kantian *normative proposition regarding autonomy an epistemological significance* that rightly belonged to the insight that values are constituted in a social world by the deliberate attitude of human beings towards a finite segment of the infinite world sequence.[68] The result of this confusion between the normative and epistemological aspects of the neo-Kantian value theory was the perpetration of a systematic distortion in presenting 'social contexts of interpretation and interaction as if they were the intentional choices of individual actors'.[69] This distortion betrayed a fundamental shortcoming in Weber's theory of meaning and its limitation to the idea of subjective totalisation. The constitution of the social world through collective human activity, which had been the cornerstone of, and emancipatory cultural meaning behind, the Hegelian-Marxian revolutionary theoretical idea of historical totalisation, could not really be articulated within the Weberian paradigm of a subjective imposition of meaning. Actually meaning is always already inscribed in the material objects of the man-made world and the inherited socio-cultural environment constructed through the activities of past social praxis.[70]

Weber's conscious reduction of the inter-subjective dimension of historical totalisation to the paradigm of subjective totalisation rendered him incapable of articulating a viable concept of social praxis. This theoretical move had some justification in the context of contemporary debates. He warned against the illusory character of immanentist versions of the historical process. His scepticism has lost none of its bite when we reflect on the subsequent utopian readings of history amongst the early Western Marxists. Weber's attack on 'immanentist history' was a timely reminder of the overblown claims of philosophical mythology. Lukács' idea of the proletariat as the collective, subject/object of history, soon to be examined, perpetrated precisely this error. Yet, Weber's unheeded remedy was hardly better than the distortion he hoped to eradicate. His radical subjectivisation of the totality concept deformed his view of history. It eliminated an essential historical dimension from his understanding of the subject/object relation in history. The practical problem of rationalisation only seemed more intractable once he had *theoretically excluded* consideration of social praxis. The exclusion of an analysis of social relations and contexts of social interaction from Weber's account elevated his contemporary asssessment of the priority of personal choices and subjective action to a trans-historical, transcendental aspect of the human condition. Despite his genuine protests against determinist and teleological views of history, his denial of, and conscious theoretical elimination of any form of inter-subjective, historical dimension of the totality concept transformed his provisional diagnosis of modernity into an irrevocable 'fate' which supposedly revealed the true existential basis of all human history. This *existential basis was the subjective necessity of creating and imposing meaning on the meaningless, resistant world*. Weber could easily affirm the unique role of occidental culture in world history and acknowledge its potential universality because his masked transcendentalism ultimately presupposed its instrumental rationality.

Practically, Weber's deflation of the historical, practico-emancipatory dimension of the totality concept reflected his scepticism regarding radical socio-political projects. From his perspective of the isolated subject, the practical goal of radical social action fashioned from collective debate and driven by a pragmatic teleology towards the realisation of radical reform could neither be articulated nor theorised. In the absence of such a practical concept of social praxis, Weber's view of the future was overshadowed by the impending victory of impersonal, objective cultural processes. In this vision, totalisation was dehumanised and automatic. Processes follow their own inscribed 'logics' and functional requirements. Nothing remains of the humanist and emancipatory spirit infusing the radical historicist understanding of totality.

Weber's reduction of the positive cultural meaning of the concept of totality to its mere subjective dimension was problematic even in its own terms. Its status as a real option soon dissolves before one's eyes. How could the autonomous personality be sustained amidst the pervasive processes of rationalisation. The insidious triumph of instrumental rationality slowly infiltrates every sphere and aspect of life. Even personal commitment to ultimate values was endangered, according to Weber, by the gradual instrumentalisation of thinking and its reduction to a species of calculation. So-called rational considerations would soon reveal that such values were unrealisable and therefore dispensable. The impending fate of modernity ensured that the interlocking processes of economic and political rationalisation placed increasing restraints on every facet of autonomous individuality. Weber's prophetic negative utopia of the 'iron cage' encapsulates this powerful, but exceedingly pessimistic, vision of the socio-cultural trends of modernity.

Weber prided himself on his robust political realism and sober, scientific objectivity. His late assessments of the Russian Revolution manifest this caution. He viewed all emancipatory hopes as so much wishful thinking when not sustained by cold scientific judgment. This was the basis of his unremitting critique of previous versions of totality and his preference for a very deflated and narrow subjectivist understanding of the limits of totalisation. His stance was a resigned response engendered by historical conditions unfavourable to a project of socio-political experimentation. Weber failed to recognise the conditionedness of his own perspective. His diagnosis went further and eliminated all hope of modernity vitalising new emancipatory social potentials. With the metaphysical residues and mythological exaggerations of the philosophy of history, Weber also discarded all other notions of historical totalisation based on the dynamics of contemporary social praxis. This lack of theoretical discrimination was an important omission in Weber's radical subjectivisation of the concept of totality. But to fully appreciate the persuasiveness of the Weberian diagnosis of modernity it is illuminating to consider Georg Lukács' early struggles with it. Weber's subjectivist resolution of the totality question represented a great challenge to Lukács' own youthful cultural ideals. His pre-Marxist writings evidence a concerted theoretical attempt to break out of Weber's 'iron cage'.

Chapter Four

The pre-Marxist Lukács: the longing for totality

Georg Lukács (1885-1971) was the son of a well-to-do Hungarian, Jewish bourgeois family. He received his early tertiary education at the University of Budapest and immediately became involved in the cultural life of Budapest through his co-foundership of the Thalia Theatre. This attempt to lift the standard of the national theatre in Hungary, to introduce modern Western plays and bring performances to working class and provincial audiences indicates his critical attitude to official Hungarian culture.[1] This initial dissatisfaction with Hungarian cultural life was instrumental in turning Lukács to German thought and the contemporary work of the thinkers discussed in the last chapter.

While Lukács was convinced of the backwardness and meaninglessness of contemporary official Hungarian culture, he saw no immediate prospects of radical change to the existing order and considered any struggle against it hopeless. He was also out of sympathy with the positivist spirit endorsed by the leading oppositional journals of the day concerned to import the ideas of the more advanced liberal-democratic nations. He advocated modernisation but was not attracted to the culture of western civilisation. After the closure of the Thalia venture in 1904 Lukács periodically travelled through Germany and began to immerse himself in its classical literature and philosophy. During the next ten years he studied at Berlin and Heidelberg, acquainting himself with the work of Dilthey, Simmel and Weber. With the latter two men he developed quite close friendships. The attraction of these thinkers was their penetrating insight into the deep problems of modern culture. All Lukács' writings over the next decade represent an exploration, dialogue and critique of the interpretations of contemporary cultural crisis proffered by these leading thinkers of the *Geisteswissenschaften*.

While Lukács was deeply influenced by these older thinkers, his own early writings cannot simply be assimilated to their standpoint; they are neither a 'typical product' nor a 'brilliant synthesis' of borrowed ideas.[2] His first formulations of his own concept of totality clearly evidence the originality of his earliest writings. It is true, however, that in this early phase Lukács was never able to provide a comprehensive or even a completely consistent answer to the problem of contemporary cultural crisis. Nevertheless, the value of these early works lie in Lukács' relentless exposure of the antinomies of all proposed solutions, his perserverance in the pursuit of an adequate solution even when this effort appeared hopeless. The intensity of this resolve bestowes on his early pre-Marxist thought an insight into the deepest dimensions of the modern crisis of culture that more than balances the lack of a fully coherent theory.

The problem of culture

The problem of cultural crisis stands at the centre of Lukács' earliest writings. In his 1909 appreciation of the work of the Hungarian poet Endre Ady he endorses the poet's 'revolutionary spirit' and expresses his utter disillusionment with Hungarian cultural life:

> Everywhere, the Hungarians are the 'most modern'. In a lamentably grotesque way they are in the most radical forefronts of every new artistic and philosophical movement. . . . Because there is no Hungarian culture in which they could join, and because the old European culture is meaningless in this respect, only the distant future could bring forth for them the dreamed of community. . . . Endre Ady's Hungarian poems are of this world of the revolutionary spirit deprived of revolution.[3]

As mentioned, Lukács was not only in opposition to the stagnant official culture but also to 'progressivist' efforts to superimpose modern liberal individualist culture on a 'backward' society. The pivot of Lukács' ideal of culture was the *idea of community* and the individualism of western bourgeois society was absolutely destructive of it.

Lukács specifically elaborated his concept of culture in another essay published in 1913:

> Culture. . . is the unity of life, the life-enhancing, life-enriching power of unity. . . . All culture is the conquest of life, the unifying of all life's phenomena with a single force. . . so that whatever part of the totality of life you look at, you always see, in its innermost depths, the same thing. In an authentic culture, everything becomes symbolic.[4]

For Lukács, culture signified something far more encompassing than the relatively modern idea of 'high culture'. He identified culture with meaningful life. For life to be meaningful, both it and the world in which it was lived had to be interpretable according to a coherent set of ideas of values. True culture presupposed the harmonious unity of subject and object; it required the integration of life and world. The possibility of such integration depended upon a *common meaningful interpretation of life and world enabling mutual understanding*. Lukács' own analyses of the social conditions which engendered the great classical tragedies underlined that meaningful life was attained only in relations with others.[5] Without the existence of a shared sensibility and community, the quest for individual fulfilment necessarily led to conflict, atomisation and social dissonance. Culture presupposed that experience was suffused with shared emotions and values which engendered a harmonious, collective interpretation of the world.

Paul Honigsheim recalls a conversation with Max Weber that illustrates the depth of Lukács' commitment to this collectivist understanding of authentic culture. Weber allegedly remarked:

> One thing became evident to Lukács when he looked at the paintings of Cimabue (who painted at the beginning of the Italian Renaissance, but who had a closer relation to the Middle Ages than to the Renaissance), and this was that culture can exist only in conjunction with collectivist values.[6]

Clearly, Lukács believed that only a common interpretation of the world supplied individual acts with an unproblematical significance and meaning while allowing the world to be viewed as a unified, coherent whole. Throughout Lukács' early work he resurrected a number of historical instances of integrated cultures which served as normative ideals. During the Heidelberg phase recalled by Honigsheim, he had turned to the natural–organic communities of the Russian peasantry depicted in the works of Tolstoy and Dostoevsky. They appeared to Lukács to promise a renewal of communal sensibility and the possibility of a great new culture. This recurring theme indicates his continuing preoccupation with the question of culture, its pre-conditions and contemporary possibility.

In Lukács' pre-Marxist works the concept of totality was equated primarily with this ideal notion of an authentic, unified culture. Even while many of his writings in this period question the contemporary possibility of authentic culture in this totalising sense, the ideal of totality remained as an ever present normative standpoint in all his reflections on the alienation of modern life and the crisis of its culture. Not even the very powerful sceptical arguments of Simmel and Weber could dent Lukács ideal of culture. While he accepted the force of these arguments demonstrating the disintegration of homogeneous cultural unity he could not abandon the ideal.

This unwavering commitment to the idea of authentic, unified culture explains Lukács' restless dissatisfaction with the theoretical and practical alternatives offered in the works of his older contemporaries. Their resigned subjectivist responses to the loss of cultural unity, however empirically forceful, were incompatible with his deepest understanding of the meaning of culture. Even during his most pessimistic phase when he abandoned all hope of cultural renewal, his theoretical writings consistently opposed the leveling of the Hegelian idea of absolute spirit to that of objective spirit. Against all attempts to eliminate the former idea as a metaphysical residue of the Hegelian theory of culture, Lukács upheld the distinction on the grounds that the absolute sphere represented a guarantee of the metaphysical existence of a 'common home'. In the essay entitled 'Aesthetic Culture', he insisted that 'it belongs to the essence of culture that it is the common treasure of men'.[7] The domain of high culture signified a 'longing for community' as a deepest human need. Against contemporary trends to historicise and subjectivise cultural values, Lukács saw a guarantee of the communal essence of culture in this historically produced but eternally valid realm.

The last chapter argued that Dilthey, Simmel and Weber shared a tendency to *reduce the concept of totality to a subjectivised notion of individual totalisation*. In an epoch of social stabilisation and rapid industrial development of bourgeois society, the former practical and historically emancipatory dimensions of the concept were lost and replaced by a subjectivist emphasis on inner cultivation. While Dilthey retained the Hegelian concept of objective spirit it served merely a hermeneutical purpose orientating theoretical interpretation of the past. Interest in history became detached from a practical programme for radical socio-political reconstruction. In Simmel and Weber the subjectivist option was even more forcefully and consistently paraded. Recall the concept of 'subjective culture' in Simmel and Weber's idea of personality. In both these cases, the stock of historically accumulated cultural objectivations served merely as a reservoir of means to be selected by present subjects. At best, the resulting subjective meanings could be exemplary and inspire others. Yet, in this scenario the traditional collective basis of culture was minimised and viewed as a casuality of irreversible historical disintergration.

Under the impact of tragic personal events Lukács was also to seriously explore the subjectivist option.[8] Yet, his earliest analyses of the problem of cultural crisis had *already* revealed the antinomies and limitations of this form of response. In 'Aesthetic Culture' Lukács mounted a concerted attack on the very idea of subjective cultivation. The aesthete, who Lukács took as the typical representative of the goal of subjective cultivation, was a product of those processes of historico-cultural fragmentation highlighted by Simmel and Weber under the heading 'intellectualisation/rationalisation'. Like Weber's typical specialist, he was devoted to the specialised cultivation of inner life. This goal demanded the sacrifice of the *whole of life* to *one of its partial possibilities*.[9] Whereas both Simmel and Weber accepted this narrowing of life's possibilities as the inevitable cost of modern achievements and the only meaningful option left to the modern individual, Lukács pressed his analysis further and examined the *necessary outcome* of the aesthete's choice. The refinement of the inner self implied a cult of the atomised subject and his passing moods. Fixation on the inner self engendered an isolation from culture as a whole and with it the separation from other men:

the development of a general culture which engages men only at one point and never touches the whole of their humanity tends to weaken the human in men.[10]

Subjective atomisation and the refined pursuit of personal fancy and enjoyment undermined the communality at the root of real culture. The unifying principle of aesthetical culture was that nothing rises beyond the merely individual.[11] The passive surrender to subjective sensation and inclination involved the dissolution of the ego generated by active creation and self-creation. The art of the aesthete was, for Lukács, a dilettantism resting only on the shifting grounds of subjective impression and lacking a formed, unified direction. The aesthete was a specialist pandering only to other specialists. Engrossed in his own interiority, he abandoned the common problems of life that unified the artist with his public and embraced esoteric values incompatible with a broad cultural impact.[12]

The problem of perspectives

The great difficulty with interpreting Lukács' pre-Marxist *oeuvre* lies in the fact that while he tenaciously held on to the ideal of a unified cultural totality, his assessment of the historical viability of this ideal waxed and waned with changing circumstance and evolving perspectives. At best this ideal led a precarious existence as an exemplary past symbolising a cultural condition to be realised anew in more favourable conditions. However, Lukács was unable to show how a meaningful, harmonious cultural totality could be reconstituted under modern conditions. He was confined to theorising its contemporary absence and contemplating the prospects of a future return. The volatility of this standpoint presents an interpretative difficulty.

Lukács' early views cannot be assimilated to a single perspective because he never satisfied himself with a fully coherent theory; instead, these works constantly explore alternatives. One may speak of development but it is essential to recognise the underlying fluidity and the real breadth of theoretical perspectives to be found in his pre-Marxist phase. It is necessary therefore to supplement Lucien Goldmann's pathbreaking reconstruction of this period with a more complicated picture. For Goldmann, the early Lukács' originality lay in his anticipation of existential ontology.[13] Recent studies have draw attention to the neglected early Hungarian works and essays to highlight the presence of an equally important stream of socio-historical analysis that is less obvious in the better known writings.[14] A tentative full reconstruction is characterised by György Márkus in the following analysis of the physiognomy of the early period:

> In Lukács' diagnosis during this period one can detect two parallel forms of analysis, one metaphysical and existential, the other historical. The two processes, or levels of analysis, change from work to work, often merging within one and the same work to such an extent that any sharp distinction

101

or opposition can, in a certain sense, only be a construct imposed for the purposes of interpretation. With almost periodic regularity Lukács himself tried to clarify their relationship both in principle and methodologically. However, between these two types of analysis there remained, at least implicitly, unresolved yet fruitful contradictions, relating not only to questions of methodology. . . . For underlying this problem of methodological 'parallelism' is a deeper problem, a philosophical dilemma (although the two are not identical nor can one be reduced to the other). The issue is whether the condition of the age in which he lived was an expression of the existential and ontological tragedy of culture or of an historical crisis from which recovery was possible.[15]

For the sake of an exposition that presents the full complexity of Lukács' early thought, it is necessary to reconstruct the significance of the concept of totality within both types of analysis and orientations to modern culture. As each mode of analysis radically transformed the precise meaning of Lukács' diagnosis of modernity, the result was a different interpretation of the possibility of authentic culture. It needs to be underlined, however, that this neat separation of the early *oeuvre* into two distinct modes of analysis is merely a methodological aid to presentation and somewhat artificial. In reality, both approaches and perspectives are *inter-dispersed throughout Lukács' early thought* in a way that manifests his own inability to arrive at a completely consistent theory.

The sociology of crisis

Until fairly recently Lukács' pre-Marxist relation to Marx had not been fully investigated. A close examination of all the early works demonstrates not only that Marxian sociology played a major role in this period but it also corroborates the view of Lukács as an independent thinker. Lukács initially discovered Marx under the auspices of Simmel's sociology. He then studied him assiduously in laying down the sociological groundwork of his first major theoretical work, the History of the Development of Modern Drama (written between 1906-9 but only fully published in Hungarian in 1911).[16] He was greatly impressed by Marx's sociological finesse in revealing the concrete social basis and contents of specific ideal forms, concepts and values.

This aspect of Marx is clearly evident in the originality of Lukács' appropriation of him. While Simmel had also heavily borrowed from Marxist sources in elaborating his theory of the tragedy of culture, he moved increasingly towards an ahistorical, metaphysical interpretation of contemporary cultural crisis as an inevitable contradiction in the process of Life. Lukács did not follow Simmel along this path. His theory of modern drama, on the contrary, clearly propounded the thesis that great tragic drama was always the cultural expression of a class in the process of decline. The historical decline of a class was a sociological pre-condition for the immanent crisis of values and valuations making tragedy the appropriate and plausible representation of life for the class in question.[17] While Lukács maintained that the modern decline of the bourgeoisie created the formal possibility of modern tragic drama, he thought it too early to determine whether this possibility would be realised. In modern conditions, the problem of aesthetic realisation was intensified by the development of an objective culture resistant to symbolic expression.[18] This analysis shows that Lukács at a very early stage already grasped the historically determinate character of modern cultural crisis and, more broadly, the ideological class basis of all cultural forms.[19] In particular, he related the characteristics of contemporary objective culture to the qualitative change in the structure of alienation with the emergence of capitalist society and bourgeois class struggle.

This striking departure from the typical 'tragic' view of culture maintained by his elder contemporaries potentially opened a more optimistic perspective on modern cultural crisis. A historico-social posing of the problem of cultural disintegration allowed for *a possible historical solution* in terms of a radical historical transformation of society. The early essays make tentative suggestions as to a number of possible historical scenarios,[20] but, on the whole, Lukács' analyses remained pessimistic regarding the immediate prospects of the historical overcoming of the crisis.

In spite of this very perceptive appropriation of Marx, it would be a mistake to identify the early Lukács too closely with an authentic Marxian approach to culture. On some issues his elder contemporaries were much truer to Marx than he. Nowhere was this more glaring than in Lukács' refusal to abandon the Absolute and pare down the historical process to an immanent dialectic of finite subjectivity and objectivity. In a relativist intellectual climate suspicious of all universal values, he was unable to sacrifice the universal and timeless validity of the great cultural objectivations.

Lukács' insistence on this point constituted a major objection to the contemporary Marxian interpretation of culture. This was spelt out in a 1915 review article of Croce's Theory and History of Historiography. While defending the merits of Marxian sociology as a method of clarifying the socio-historical determination of cultural products,[21] he mounted a vigorous defence of the autonomy of literature and a concerted attack on the orthodox Marxian view which reduced its status to that of a sociologically bound ideology. He was prepared to acknowledge the historicity of the genesis and reception of significant works of culture but argued strongly that this recognition be reconciled with the appreciation of their timeless validity. The crux of Lukács' argument was against a crude reductionist version of Marxism with a vindication of the autonomy of superstructural phenomena. In an earlier essay 'Towards a Theory of Literary History' (1910) Lukács argued that 'the pure great forms are separated from all communities, they become ahistorical and asocial, beyond all space and time'.[22] The means of communication, modes of reception, language, etc., are socio-historically determined. These aspects of form are 'the truly social in Literature'.[23] At the same time, however, the paramount disassociative, universal element in the great literary forms which was the basis of their timeless appeal and validity could not be eliminated.

The function of the Hegelian Absolute in Lukács' early thinking was not simply to serve as a bulwark against relativism. The affirmation of the timeless validity of the great cultural forms *also, and more importantly, provided him with a locus for the possible resolution of the aggravated contemporary antinomy between subject and object.* In the existing conditions of cultural crisis where the individual was increasingly more alienated from a growing array of meaningless objective processes, the sphere of the Absolute offered Lukács, if not the prospect of immediate reintegration, at least the hope of an ultimate metaphysical unity and community.

Having considered Lukács' general relation to Marxist theory, the analysis is better placed to elucidate the central elements of his historico-sociological approach to the crisis of culture and the manner of its articulation of the ideal of cultural totality.

The normative function of history

Lukács' view of modernity was premised on the reigning pessimistic assessment of contemporary culture. He largely took over the diagnoses presented by Simmel and Weber. Objective cultural processes – especially the irrational relations of the bourgeois market – had assumed a lawfulness and autonomy detached from either subjective meanings or collective cultural aspirations. Objective culture was increasingly bereft of living human significance. Lukács did, however, go further than his predecessors in maintaining that this objective situation *eluded all attempts at subjective synthesis and resolution.* The lone individual creator faced an impossible task. The project of inner cultivation ultimately succumbed to a senseless pursuit of authentic experience. Severed from a common *Weltanschauung* and sensibility for the world, the subject retreated from action and its own unified will dissolved through passivity and resignation.

Lukács frequently resorted to Kantian philosophy as an expression of his own diagnosis of modernity. Kant clearly captured and articulated the modern conditions of cultural fracture and individual fragmentation. Typically, Lukács underlined the Kantian emphasis on the incommensurability of human faculties and the autonomy of their forms:

> Science affects us by its contents, art by its forms; science offers us facts
> and the relationship between facts, but art offers us souls and destinies.
> Here the ways part; here there is no replacement and no transition. In
> primitive as yet undifferentiated epochs, science and art (and religion and
> ethics and politics) are integrated, they form a single whole; but as soon

as science has become separate and independent, everything that has led up to it loses its value.[24]

In affirming the *contemporary* truth of Kantian philosophy it is noticeable that Lukács assumes a historical perspective. Although at times inclined to treat this historical development as a Weberian 'fate', as an existential condition of modern experience, he also regularly considered the problem of cultural crisis as a specific historical condition. The latter view at least localised the crisis and allowed his ideal of an integrated, harmonious culture to be historically concretised even while acknowledging its irretrievability.

The very structure of Lukács' historico-sociological mode of analysis provides an immanent normative significance. It enables him to both characterise and condemn bourgeois modernity by comparing its life-enervating, antagonistic social conditions compared with those of archaic, organic societies possessed of collective cohesion and cultural unity. *The basic framework of this comparative mode of diagnosis was the contrast between the dynamic, open societies of western modernity with the more stable, closed traditional ones.* The former progressively undermined and destroyed cultural integration while the latter rested upon, and constantly fortified, precisely those integrative, organic features. In the two major works where this approach dominated – History of the Development of Modern Drama (1911) and Theory of the Novel (1916) – the comparative mode provided both a glimpse of a historically lost, unified, cultural totality and a norm underscoring the degree of decline and cultural dissolution.

In both works Lukács lauded the unsurpassed cultural achievement of the Greeks. Central to this was a common sensibility and value hierarchy which found its finest expression in the total identification with the *polis*. The phases of this unique culture served Lukács as exemplary models in the shape of the literary forms which were the immediate objects of the studies. The Homeric age represented the quintessence of cultural integration and community. These were the 'happy ages'; individuals were in immediate harmony with the natural powers through a collective interpretation that securely embedded them in a communal world which was familiar and meaningful.[25] In this world the essence of life was immanent to experience. As Lukács put it, in the epic the Greeks answered the question of life's essence before it had ripened into a matter of philosophical reflection.[26] Meaning was here sensuously present in everyday life and there was never any need to delve beyond appearances. Compared to modernity, the cosmos of the epic was limited and naïve. Yet this was the real source of its perfection and the contentment of its inhabitants:

> For totality as the formative prime reality of every individual phenomena
> implies the something closed within itself can be completed; completed
> because everything occurs within it, nothing is excluded from it and
> nothing points at a higher reality outside it; completed because everything
> within it ripens to its own perfection and, by attaining it, submits to

limitation. Totality of being is possible only where everything is already homogeneous before it has been contained by forms; where forms are not a constraint but only the becoming conscious, the coming to the surface of everything that has been lying dormant as a vague longing in the inner-most depths of that which had to be given form; where knowledge is virtue and virtue is happiness, where beauty is the meaning of the world made visible.[27]

The Homeric world is governed by a natural *telos* in which every individual phenomenon has its rightful place know to all. This empirical reality is given and complete. Therefore the contemplative gaze reveals an essence only in need of illumination.[28]

Subjectivity is never problematised in the world of the epic; the individual is too secure within the order of things. In striking contrast to the novel, the subject is subordinated to a hierarchy of values embodied in the visible world and sanctified by tradition.This perfect balance and unity between subject and object encouraged Lukács to submit *that the epic hero was never actually an individual at all but a representative of the fate of the entire community.*[29] Unlike the typical hero of the novel, the epic hero never ventured to find himself. His was not the precarious voyage through his interiority in order to discover his essence. The internal and external security of the epic lifeworld simply excluded adventure in the modern sense.The events of the epic had a quantitive weight measured in terms of their significance for the family or the community.[30] There could never be any real question of the epic hero failing his tests because at the most fundamental level, he was profoundly passive. His adventures merely provided the opportunity for the forms of the 'objective and extensive totality of the world' around him to unfold themselves.[31]

For Lukács, the immediate harmony and homogeneity of the Homeric epic constituted an 'ideal type' against which the uncertainty, loneliness and alienation of contemporary culture were brought sharply into focus. The artistry of the depiction was not intended to evoke nostalgia for the past. Like Hegel and Weber, he recognised that modern individuality could not 'breathe in a closed world'. Once dissolved, the historico-social limitations which had generated organic cultures could not be artificially re-imposed. The perfect balance and security of the 'closed world' could not make up for the lack of freedom integral to the self-understanding of contemporary authentic subjectivity. In the Theory of the Novel, Lukács does not propose a return to a lost past but tentatively postures towards a future cultural regeneration. More will be said about his future utopia shortly.

Lukács' understanding of the sociological pre-conditions of Greek culture is most clearly elaborated in his early work on the development of modern drama. There he argued that the pinnacle of Greek drama was only attained after everyday life had ceased to be 'a home' for the Greeks. This assertion conforms with the broader thesis of the work that great tragedy is an expression of a social class in decline. In fifth century Athens, drama expressed the emergent contradictions between the old and new values in a culture whose essential core of collective social experience had not yet been completely eroded:

> For the Greeks, the fact that life ceased to be the home of meaning merely transferred the mutual closeness, the kinship of human beings, to another sphere, but it did not destroy it: every figure in the Greek drama is at the same distance from the all-sustaining essence and, therefore, is related at the deepest roots to every other figure; all understand one another, be it as mortal enemies, for all are striving in the same way towards the same centre, and all move at the same level of an existence which is essentially the same.[32]

The embeddedness of all acts and events in a traditional web of meanings and common evaluations in an organic culture bestowed a real security upon life. While the Greeks could never be sure of 'fate', their existential security engendered confidence and the capacity to form life. The drama book constantly traces the essential aesthetical qualities of classical tragedy to its nourishment within a homogeneous culture, to its unique integration within the broad cultural life of the *polis*.

This claim was substantiated by detailing the connection between the aesthetical forms and communal significance of ancient tragedy and its origins in the traditional religious ceremonies of the *polis* community. Born from religious observances and celebrations in which the entire community expressed its deepest felt life problems, these tragedies shared the sole ethic of the people. Their aesthetical power was not impaired by the ideological and value struggles which provided a resistant material for modern dramatic creation and reception. The dramatic stage was a public institution tied to public religions and communal festivals; public performance and popular reception was at its heart.[33] Lukács underlined that this intimate relation between drama and a common religious experience, obscure to us, was the key to the now lost integration of culture. In stark contrast, the inability of modern drama to win a mass public, its separation at birth from the stage and performance, are indicative of the increasing isolation of culture from its erstwhile source of life in the community and the resulting cultural crisis.

Lukács perceived the consequences of this diremption between culture and community life in the aesthetical forms themselves. The emotional power and poetic immediacy of tragic verse was explained by the embeddedness of ancient drama within vital popular institutions. This verse drew directly on the sensous imagery of religious myth. Myths were a ready-made source of concrete images crystallising the innumerable life feelings and communal interpretations passed down through many ages.[34] They retained an authority bound up with the weight of a timeless tradition that was still familiar and vital enough to absorb new social experience. At the same time, both tradition-bound and flexible, the images of the mythic fables produced their symbolic-poetic effects. They carried their tragic poetic weight naïvely and without consciousness because they were still vital and familiar although steeped in the mist of timeless authority.[35]

The result of this integration of art within the other life practices and communal forms was enhanced artistic consequences. Lukács reinforces this point by adumbrating the non-religious origins and inspirations of modern drama. The loss of a living religious *Weltanschauung* shared by all deprived the poetic images of modern drama of the power of immediacy. As products of *intellectual reflection* these images were characterised by abstraction and disengagement from the immediacy of sensuous experience. The everyday sensuous images that sustained classical tragic verse could no longer provide the symbols of life's meaning in the more complex modern world. Lukács maintained that the abstract, intellectualised quality of modern dramatic language, like other formal and structural characteristics of modern tragedy, was rooted in the specific fragmented and alienated conditions of modern bourgeois life.

Dynamic, bourgeois society

While Lukács was clearly concerned with the aesthetic difficulties of modern drama, they were only ostensibly the main topic which allowed him to indirectly canvass the deeper problem behind them. Consistently in his treatment of aesthetical issues, he returned to the fundamental, intransigent life problems inherent in the conditions of modern bourgeois culture. He formulated this necessary relation between historical conditions and the character of its art quite unambiguously in the following terms; 'Life as a material is no longer dramatic'.[36] Unspoken was his conviction that there could be no *purely artistic solution* to the problem of bourgeois existence.

Lukács' philosophical treatment of modernity in Theory of the Novel revealed the contradictory features of its immanent dynamism and expansionism. Whereas the integrated societies depended upon an unconscious *limitation and harmony*, modernity was characterised by dynamism and the increasing autonomy of its constitutive social, cultural and economic processes. The totality of modern experience could *never be a category of empirical life*. In this expanding and increasingly unfamiliar world, meaning and substance were no longer open to the empirical gaze and seemed always more illusive, never quite tangible. The pervading sense of estrangement from a complex, foreign and increasingly meaningless world Lukács expressed in the idea that form was no longer a coming to consciousness of all that lay dormant as a vague longing but rather a conscious, creative subjective imposition of form on an orderless, recalcitrant world.[37]

The experience of modernity was brilliantly captured in Kant's philosophical dualism. An unbridgeable abyss separated subjective aspirations and intentions from the soulless, independent powers and processes of mechanical, lawful objectivity. Unable to perceive its essence in the surrounding world, modern subjectivity was set upon a course of endless striving never to attain satisfaction nor completion. As with Kant, essence becomes a postulate: a command to continue the search without any prospect or hope of attaining its goal. Lukács conceded that the modern 'infinite' world was 'richer in gifts' than the ancient closed cosmos but, for all that, it lacked any stable meaning that was more than a momentary approximation.[38] The Kantian distinction between the phenomenal world of external, lawful appearances and the noumenal world of the autonomous, intentional soul perfectly expressed this modern diremption of experience. The good intentions of the modern individual regularly went amiss in an empirical world of immanent laws beyond the subject's control. The scope of authentic action was now drastically narrowed while the domain of reified, formally free, but accidental activities expanded immensely. Paradoxically, modernity was characterised both by *an increasing search and feeling for personality* and the commensurate danger *of intensified de-personalisation and loss of authentic selfhood.*

Lukács perceived all these characteristic trends and features of modern alienation in the world of the novel. Just as the contemporary subject still *postulates* the idea of essence, so too, the modern epoch 'still thinks in terms of totality'. This, however, was no longer the extensive totality of immediate empirical life.[39] Having lost the 'natural' and naïve integration of cultural values, art in modernity had assumed its own autonomy and abandoned representation of the given empirical world.[40] Totality not being given in the modern world, the author was compelled to *construct* the totality of the novel. Lacking this sensuous, organic quality, this constructed totality could only be a system of abstract terms and concepts without the poetic and aesthetic qualities immediately suitable for form-giving.[41]

The dissonance of modern experience which required the fragile, constructivist form of the novel was reproduced in the dilemmas confronting the novel's heroes and heroines. Lukács insisted that the hero/heroine was invariably *a seeker* whose adventures were always life determining quests for meaning. In a clearly Weberian formulation, he suggested that the novel was 'the artform of virile maturity'. It was an acceptance of the existential-ethical challenge posed by a fragile, hostile and meaningless world. Deprived of the collectively significant mythical 'histories' expressed in the storyteller's tale, the modern novelist had to creatively *select and construct* the hero/heroine's quest for self-recognition and self-discovery out of the infinite multitude of possible events. As dissonance was irremediable, the novel remained a problematic form appearing always 'in the process of becoming'.[42] Subjective creativity may solve this formal problem of the novel's 'bad infinity' but it could not disguise the absence of real reconciliation and the fact that 'a mere glimpse of meaning' was 'the highest that life has to offer':

After such self-recognition has been attained, the ideal thus formed irradiates the individual's life as its immanent meaning; but the conflict between what is and what should be has not been abolished in the sphere wherein these events take place – the life sphere of the novel; only a maximum conciliation- the profound and intensive irradiation of a man by his life's meaning – is attainable.[43]

Lukács could have well substituted real empirical life for 'the life's sphere of the novel'. Art was unable to transcend the dissonances of life. In the modern world, 'is' and 'ought', subject and object were opposed and the contemporary individual, like the hero/heroine of the novel, pursued his/her own subjective meaning alone. For Lukács, this condition was a symptom of crisis. The subjectivist stance adopted by Weber, Simmel and Dilthey was not a real remedy to the dissolution of authentic culture.

In his work on the evolution of modern drama Lukács had underlined the key historico-social processes underlying the contemporary predicament of culture. In analysing these objective processes he drew heavily on a Simmelian interpretation of Marx. He accounted for the great cultural transformations of modernity in terms of the extended bourgeois division of labour. This represented a complete overthrow of the non-rationalistic methods and productive relations of the guilds. He tied this whole development to a qualitative change in the character of alienation:

> The essence of the modern division of labour is, seen from the standpoint of the individual, that it severs labour from the always irrational and thus qualitative capacities of the worker, and places it under the objective, goal orientated criteria which stand outside and have no relation to his personality. The main economic tendency of capitalism is this same objectification of production, its separation from the personality of the producers. Through the development of the capitalist economy, an objective abstraction, capital, becomes the real producer and capital has no organic connection even to those who happen to own it. Indeed, it is increasingly superfluous whether the owners are personalities at all (as is the case of joint stock companies).[44]

Lukács' emphasis falls here on the tendency towards de-personalisation inherent to the modern bourgeois division of labour. Individual, qualitative capacities and personal relations were systematically displaced by uniform, quantitative operations and impersonal, calculable contractualisation. Bourgeois society emancipated both production and consumption from earlier socially imposed restraints. This erosion of former organic ties, however, was brought about 'automatically' by the logic of the market and division of labour. All traces of individuality, the qualitative and irrational were gradually eliminated through the processes of uniformisation and de-personalisation. But a free enterprise economy and its transformation into a function and field of individual achievement did not, Lukács maintained, result in a real progress in individuation. On the contrary, the necessary development of a whole network of abstract, intricate bonds narrowing the scope of individual action, the imposition of impersonal, uniform rules and patterns of operation *actually thwarted individual expression and conduct.* For Lukács, the modern preoccupation with individuality was a *symptom of crisis.* The ideology of the individual only masked the disappearance of individuality from everyday life.[45]

Imperceptibly in Lukács' reception of Marxian sociology occurs a subtle fusion between the theory of alienation and the *Geisteswissenschaften's* critique of culture. Marx's own analysis of alienation had been anchored in his interpretation of capitalist production and its impact on the wage labourer. He had not explicitly drawn the cultural consequences that are largely already implicit in his own analysis. Without knowing of this unpublished theory, Lukács focused on the de-personalisation inherent to the new productive processes and showed how they generated an intensified search for identity as formerly artisan work lost its immanent meaning. Once the organic connection between the labourer and his object was broken, the object no longer immediately satisfying and meaningful to the producer, the problem of meaningfulness arises as an index of alienation. It was natural that Lukács' preoccupations with the broad question of culture as meaningful life context would lead to a culturalist interpretation of Marx's analysis of wage labour. He invariably drew attention to the correspondences between fundamental transformations of basic economic processes and their cultural consequences. In his analysis of the distinctive features of modern drama he remarked that this drama was bourgeois 'because the cultural forms of contemporary life are bourgeois and because the forms of every expression of life today is determined by those forms'.[46] Anticipating his later pathbreaking general theory of reification, he was already drawn to view cultural problems as manifestations of a form of alienation penetrating every aspect of bourgeois life.

The future of culture

Lukács' account of the antinomies of dynamic, bourgeois societies is extremely pessimistic. Like Simmel and Weber, he derived no solace from modern historical development. Social 'progress' meant only increasing de-personalisation and the growing autonomy of all socio-cultural processes. This objective totality of mutually conflicting processes and values offered no real prospect of cultural renewal. Yet, in principle, the historico-sociological methodological orientation he adopted to the problem provided at least the open possibility of other futures, however unlikely they appeared from a contemporary perspective.

Lukács certainly had canvassed other scenarios for cultural renewal. Given his interest in Marxism and the existence of a strong social democratic movement in Germany, the worker's movement was an obvious candidate. Before the First World War, several scattered comments reveal that he had contemplated and explored socialism as a future historical alternative. Because socialism represented the ideal of collectivism and was opposed to the rampant and fruitless individualism engendered by bourgeois society, it loomed large in his early discussions of future cultural prospects.

His image of socialism at that time had little to do with the real social democratic movement and its contemporary ideology. Paul Honigsheim's reminiscences from the Heidelberg period[47] testify to the fact that by then Lukács was quite contemptuous of this movement whose politics was limited to parliamentary reformism and whose ideology was plainly positivist relying on an unquestioning faith in the deterministic forces of history. In spite of this scathing critique of existing social democracy, Lukács did perceive the very radical potentialities expressed in Marxian theory:

> The system of socialism and its world view, Marxism, is a synthesis. It is the most cruel and strict synthesis since medieval Catholicism. To express it, when the time comes to express it artistically, only that form will be adequate which is strictly comparable to Catholicism's true art (Giotto and Dante in the first place).[48]

Lukács believed that the cultural significance of this synthesis had hardly been recognised. Marxian theory rejected all superficial ideas of culture limited to subjectivity, its whims and moods, and located the real determination of culture at the deepest level of the total social process. Reformist social democracy would never realise the cultural potential of this Marxism which lay in the idea of a revolutionary socio-cultural transformation. Such a revolutionary action by the proletariat was one of the possible scenarios considered in his History of the Development of Modern Drama as a means for the preservation of art and culture. Lukács envisaged an anonymous-collective 'socialist babarism' destroying the over-refinement of bourgeois culture and recreating 'the sole ethic' which had typified the medieval Catholic or Shakespearian world.[49]

Clearly this was a fanciful vision, a world away from the existing movement's capitulation to a passive faith in the power of objective historical forces. Lukács' refusal to see this socialism as a real politico-cultural alternative to bourgeois society was confirmed by its compliance with war sentiments at the outbreak of the First World War in 1914. This disastrous turn of events compounded Lukács' despair coming as it did soon after the death of Leo Popper and Irma Seidler. Prompted by this mood, he experimented with a purely subjectivist reading of the intolerable external situation. His resistance to the complete alienation of bourgeois society expressed itself in a profoundly tragic existentialist-metaphysical reinterpretation of the existing crisis of culture. Shortly this alternative perspective will be examined more closely.

For the moment, it is enough to stress that Lukács' vacillation between perspectives continually generated a resurgence of utopian elements despite his generally pessimistic diagnosis of bourgeois society. Such elements resurfaced again in the more open historico-sociological perspective that shaped Theory of the Novel (written in 1916). Although this work presents an especially barren depiction of modern alienation, it closes with a brief utopian vision of a future Dostoevskian society.[50] During this period probably under the influence of his first wife, the Russian anarchist Yelena Grabenko, he became very interested in the ideology of the Russian anarchists and the social conditions which gave rise to the novels of Tolstoy and Dostoevski.

In the final pages of Theory of the Novel Lukács asserted the curious view that Dostoevski did not write novels. According to Lukács, his heroes were not of the paradigmatic problematic type forging a meaning for their world through a series of lonely adventures. In contrast, Dostoevski's central figures inhabited a 'new world' which Lukács associated with the surviving organic social conditions of the Russian peasantry. Dostoevski's works foretold of a world of true human brotherhood and authentic communication between souls. Actually these few lines indicate only a glimpse of what was to be a much larger work on Dostoevski of which Theory of the Novel remained the only completed part. However, Lukács' notes reveal that an important part of the envisaged work treated the radical new social form anticipated by Dostoevski.[51] This utopian positing of a unified social totality in the form of a future mystical community of freedom and authenticity enabled Lukács to project his historical framework beyond the 'absolutely sinful' present into the visionary future prefigured solely in art.

In the context of European military engulfment in a catastrophic war, the contemporary domination of an irrational objective system and what Lukács perceived as cultural disintegration, he was driven to look to the East for a model of cultural integration capable of sustaining his own ideal. Out of profound despair came messianic hope. Within a historico-sociological perspective, this hope was expressed in the form of a visionary historical utopia.

However as mentioned, Lukács' perspective vacillated and during this same period – especially between 1911 and 1914 – his despair over contemporary conditions led to a much more pessimistic interpretation. In order to give some idea of the full breadth of his early work and analyse the features of his subjectivist interpretation of the crisis of culture, it is essential to give an account of this very different approach.

The metaphysics of tragedy

Lukács' alternative existential-ontological approach to the crisis of culture fomulated most clearly in his unfinished Philosophy of Art (1912-14), and some other major essays, produced a fundamental reformulation of the problem itself. It involved the interpretation of modern alienation in existential terms as a trans-historical problem of the individual subject's life. A tragic account of culture has already been outlined in Simmel. But more than Simmel or any of his contemporaries, Lukács fully explored the real antinomies of this tragic world view. He achieved this by laying bare its ontological presuppositions.

In the tragic perspective, the ideal of a cultural totality recedes and is transmogrified into a shadowy metaphysical faith. Futhermore, Lukács poses the dilemmas of life solely in ethical terms in conditions of isolation and estrangement. He does not completely neglect the problem of inter-subjectivity as objectification is still central to his understanding of authenticity, however, his main emphasis falls on the achievement of authenticity in a world of inescapable loneliness and chaos.

This reformulation of the problem requires a new set of ethical and metaphysical categories. Lukács adopts the Simmelian terms 'soul' and 'form'. The main distinction in this purely philosophical treatment of the problem is that between 'soul life' or 'real life' and 'ordinary, everyday life'. This is the tragic opposition permeating all human experience. On this view, the catastrophic antinomy between subject and object underscored in his historico-sociological analysis is *hardened into an outright dualist interpretation of reality*. In contrast to the *essentiality of value* attributed to 'soul life' by Lukács, he views 'everyday life' as a sphere devoid of value and charged with an ineradicable loneliness. This dualist interpretation emphasised the value of 'soul life' without going so far as to dissolve the everyday into illusion. Lukács' metaphysics turned on the question of *value* and his intepretation of everyday life concentrated solely on this question. For him, the soul was the founding, generative principle of all essential, authentic human self-expression. It was the deepest core of every individual personality and the fundamental source of all evaluation. In a letter to Paul Ernst, he wrote, 'And yet, only the soul has a metaphysical reality'.[52] He equated the soul with the creative essence of all valuable human activity.

In comparison to value *enhancing* soul activity, empirical life simply lacked real purposeful coherence and necessity. It was governed merely by a multitude of external determinations and never directed to a determinant end.[53] The everday was equivalent to the domain of mechancial processes and forms which Lukács' sociological analysis contended had lost their essential meaning and grown alien and merely conventional. He went so far as to conceive these two spheres as mutually exclusive and mutually negating:

> Life is an anarchy of light and dark: nothing is ever completely fulfilled in life (everyday life), nothing ever quite ends; new, confusing voices always mingle with the chorus of those that have been heard before. Everything flows, everything merges into a another thing, and the mixture is un-controlled and impure; everything is destroyed, everything is smashed, nothing ever flowers into real life (soul life). To live is to live something through to the end; but life means that nothing is ever fully and completely lived through to the end. Life is the most unreal and unliving of all conceivable existences. . . . Real life is always unreal, always impossible, in the midst of empirical life.[54]

Lukács' description of the distinction between the two life spheres amounted to a complete transfiguration of experience. Although, strictly speaking, he was concerned only with their *relative value*, his account of the irruption of real life into the everyday depicts a supernatural awakening that abolishes the categories of space and time and eternalises the moment of the individual's discovery of his/her essential meaning. Yet, Lukács admitted that it was not possible to live the whole of life at this peak of intensity. Life involved the tragic recognition that the 'eternal moments' were elusive and that the individual always, in some sense, returned to the alien, valueless world of meaningless convention and lifeless objectivity.

At a philosophical level, Lukács' conceptualisation and framing of the problem involved a double-fronted struggle against both Hegelian metaphysics and contemporary vitalism. While he enthusiastically endorsed Kierkegaard's espousal of the 'truth of subjectivity' against the Hegelian idea of a supra-individual spirit, he steadfastly refused to celebrate the immediate, irrational stream of experience.[55] Against contemporary vitalism, Lukács' concept of the soul was informed by deep ethical motivations; it signified a calling for the greatest possible realisation of the individual's personal human potentialies. This was an imperative for the complete unfolding of all unique powers and energies of will. The soul represented the untapped personal vocation residing in latent capacities; therefore it was an *inner power,* in principle able to supply direction and create meaning.

For Lukács, a life directed by the soul was equivalent to the realisation of individual authenticity. Authenticity demanded the *translation of capacities into deeds* and *the moulding of life in a personally chosen direction with a unique shape*. In an explicit rebuttal of the value of cultivated interiority, Lukács dismissed an easy contentment with subjective intentions and/or introspection. His idea of personal actualisation demanded a choice amongst existing universal values and their resolute imposition on the world. The fact that the individual choses between existing values meant that authentic objectification transcended mere subjective inwardness. These objectifications were not exhausted in individual meanings but *possessed a general human relevance*. In deeds and works the products of soul life entered a realm of objectivity and therefore assumed normative significance for others. The same idea underpins Lukács' idea of tragic selfhood:

> The final tension of selfhood overleaps everything that is merely
> individual. Its force elevates all things to the status of destiny, but its great
> struggle with the self-created destiny makes of it something supra-
> personal, a symbol of some ultimate fate relationship.[56]

While the antagonism and opposition between the spheres of life could never be transcended, authentic self-actualisation required their mediation.

Form fulfilled this necessary task of mediation. In its broadest meaning, 'form' designated the organising activity of the soul allowing for the objectification of latent potentialities. Thereby, the chaotic material of everyday life was marshalled into a meaningful structure underpinned by a value system. Lukács perceived form as the link between authentic subjectivity and the realm of inter-subjectivity.[57] Each form signified a particular a priori through which the soul concentrated on a single value. Rejecting the all-encompassing Hegelian Absolute as 'unprovable' and accepting the neo-Kantian verdict concerning the irreducible autonomy on the value spheres, Lukács viewed form as the only guarantee of a supra-individual, inter-subjective plurality of meanings. The concept of form allowed him to connect genuine authenticity and supra-individual value. Form *both homogenised the soul and substantiated the regulative idea of universal values*: it was 'the only pure relevation of experience'[58] and 'the ideal outside the self'.[59]

Within this conception of a metaphysically diremped existence Lukács explored its ethical dilemmas. This analysis gravitated around the question of how to live an authentic, meaningful life and how such a life could become an everyday actuality. Clearly there are links here with the socio-historical question of the possibility of cultural renewal with which it was very often interwoven. Nevertheless, episodically Lukács' view assumed an especially pessimistic and tragic shape. At these moments, he even came to doubt the possibility of any authentic human communication.

The prison house of subjectivity

The first chapter of Lukács' unfinished Heidelberg Philosophy of Art (1912-14) provides a general theory of communication for his aesthetics. This theory is of particular interest because it articulates a most extreme formulation of the dilemma of contemporary alienation and loneliness. It departs from the rather familiar vitalist idea that the personal and qualitative dimensions of pure subjective experience could not be authentically transmitted by rational communication:

> As a consequence the necessary opposition (*Gegensatz*) between the qualitative, incomparibility of pure experience and any sort of conceivable expression of it, which, if it is to be an expression already presupposes something in common between the two subjects of the mutual communication, is established and recognised as an essential characteristic of this sphere.[60]

According to this theory, language involved an abstraction from the sheer qualitative experience of the subject into the universal categories of speech. The universality of the concept rendered it an inadequate tool for the task of transmitting the full qualitative richness of subjective experience. A moment's reflection on this inadequacy exposed doubts both about everyday communication and the possibility of anything more intimate, pure and authentic. Everyday pragmatics usually concealed the limits of language as a means of mutual understanding. As action and consequences are more important in the pragmatic domain than motives and subjective meanings, abstract and banal concepts sufficed to ensure practical success and the impression of being understood.[61] Besides, normally individuals rely not just on the abstract, universal schemas of speech but also call into play a whole range of personal gestures and accentuations that provide elasticity and sublety to the conveyance of meaning. Lukács insisted, however, that the widespread *impression* of being understood, even the endemic use of these personal unfixed adjuncts to speech, did not eliminate the fundamental dilemma. There was no proof that one person's interpretation of personal signals or universal schemas matched their intended meaning.[62]

This analysis justified a radical *ontologisation* of the contemporary perceptions of individual isolation and loneliness. It represented a truly tragic view of the human situation. Implied was that every individual inhabited a totally insulated, lonely world of their own interiority. Despite the deeply felt need to communicate innermost feelings, the very means of communication rendered this desire irredeemable:

> This is the profound misery and ineradicable loneliness of men of the
> world of experience; any approach to something 'general' in expression
> makes it impossible from the very beginning, and what is really his 'own'
> is given, through the fact of expression, a form independent of, and
> separated from the communicating subject, from his will and essence, a
> form which possesses its own dialectics, its own independent factors of
> efficacy and, in addition, an inpenetrable immanence. For the crucial and
> insidious trick of this form is precisely to press the urge for communi-
> cation towards the greatest intensity in what is purely qualitative,
> bestowing on the latter the ravishing and alluring power of immediate
> effect; but the form never allows the effect, the effecter and the effected to
> achieve a commuion and a genuine fufilment – precisely as a result of the
> vehicle of the effect, the incomparable nature of the qualitative – but
> rather leaves it to languish in the perpetual chiaroscuro of the not-quite.[63]

On this interpretation, even the principle means of inter-personal understanding, of communicating our innermost subjectivity is rendered impotent and perceived as just another manifestation of a universal antinomy between subjects and objectifications. Like the other cultural products similarly interpreted by Simmel and Weber, the schemas of human expression possess an inhuman autonomy, an 'inpenetrable immanence' and follow an estranging dynamic.

The tragedy implied by this analysis is of the most radical kind; it has nothing to do with the nature of cultural development nor the immanent movement of life. Lukács locates tragedy in the contradiction at the very heart of human existence: in the communicative act itself and the illusory desire for communion. Prisoners of our own subjectivity, there is no prospect of any relief from alienation. It is inscribed in the ontological condition of humanity.

Art and redemption

Characteristically, Lukács refused to capitulate to the logic and tragic consequences of his own analysis. His systematic aesthetics explored the redemptive possibilities of art and enquired how works of universal significance and meaning could be constructed out of the isolation and chaos of everyday life. In the period of his own personal tragedies and crises, art came to signify a realm of perfection transcending the estrangement of the everyday and an enclave for authentic self-expression.

It is easy to understand why Lukács rejected the contemporary trend to conflate the two Hegelian spheres of Absolute and objective spirit. In his radically dualist view of human existence, only the perfect cultural creations enabled a momentary escape from meaningless conventionality and estranged objective processess. In the sphere of great culture, humans transcended their own tortured isolation and participated in a timeless world of humanity and value:

> The great need men feel for communication, which is only a lessened
> form of their more profound longing for community and unity with one
> another, here (in works of art) finds an abiding fulfilment in life and a
> positive confirmation of it. And in this brotherhood of men with all other
> men, this answer given to the questions he asks of his world, of every man
> and the whole of nature, breaks through the limitations imposed on him in
> space and time; he is freed from his sociological, national and historical
> isolation, from his banishment to the world into which he was born, given
> to him as immediate experience. This human self-evidence of art thereby
> achieves an exalted meaning which goes far beyond the self-evidence
> itself: the possibility of the general and complete communicability of all
> that is human becomes manifested in art and is assured through its
> existence.[64]

The universality of art represents a guarantee of the possibility of authentic human communication and a metaphysical brotherhood. The notion of 'the work' (*Das Werk*) holds a central place in this theory because Lukács viewed the act of artistic creation as an expression of subjective authenticity. In creation the artist fashions the chaos of everyday experience into a meaningful whole and produces a homogeneous, self-enclosed world by selectively ordering just a few of life's infinite possibilities. This aesthetic perfection signified for Lukács the purification of the creator's experience, a transcendence of alienation and transience into an atemporal world of universal significance.[65]

Such great works embodied an unambiguous interpretation of life. The uniqueness of the aesthetic realm lay in this homogenising effect. The other normative spheres allowed dissonance. Science continually expanded to absorb unmastered contents while ethics also systematically included antagonistic contents as a necessary opposite pole: evil.[66] However, the very possibility of the work of art, for Lukács, depended upon the elimination of dissonance and the realisation of a perfect harmony between form and content.[67] The work of art realised the Hegelian idea of concrete totality. This was not an abstract universality but one of perfect integration between structural schemas and the material of life with no sense of dissonance. The form of the work effected the birth of a new microcosm of life invested with the immanent power to evoke new experience.

Lukács explained the universal significance and 'eternal' validity of great works of art in terms of form rather than subjective experiential content. Form – the perfect harmony issuing from the immanent relation of constitutive elements – generated an irresistible evocative power capitivating every receptor with its vision. Lukács cautioned, however, that the potential redemptive power of art was largely illusory. The artist was no more able to escape from universal estrangement than anyone else. Art enabled a *momentary transcendence* of this world but could not abolish it. The promise of real communion between individual souls inherent to great art was a utopia resulting only from its radical separation and detachment from the world of alienation which produced it. Lukács spoke of the 'immorality of art' because the artist created perfection only to sink back into the chaotic mire of everyday life. Pouring his/her innermost subjectivity into the work as a communication of authentic feeling, the artist collapsed back into eternal isolation only to see the work become a foreign entity with an alien life of its own and without really fufilling the aspiration to communion.[68]

For Lukács, this Luciferian quality of art undermined the appearance of art as a vehicle of inter-personal communication. Against this illusory appearance and its deceptive promise, he maintained that art could not transmit authentic subjective experience. Not only did the artist lose the work to its own autonomous realm but also it was only the forms and not the subjective content which generated cathartic impact and evocative power. Form crystallised a compelling vision that in virtue of its own immanent power evoked *the receptor's own, equally subjective, experience*. The aesthetical effect resulted not from a genuine communication of the artist's experience but from a 'misunderstanding' facilitated by the universality of the forms of the work which were equally open and reconcilable with the dissimilar and incomparable subjective experience of each potential receptor. This argument amounted to the strong claim that such 'misunderstanding' was *constitutive of all aesthetic experience*.[69] Thus the impression of interpersonal resonance and communication encountered in aesthetic experience was *merely an illusion* engendered by the universality of the forms which allowed the work to reflect the subjectivity of all receptors.[70]

While this searching analysis supplied Lukács with a theory of aesthetical reception, it annihilated the existential hopes he had initially placed in the redemptive possibilities of art. Art could not alleviate the alienation of everyday life nor supply a medium for authentic communication between souls. Even its redemptive promise was *a danger because it accommodated individuals to unbearable conditions while neither redeeming them nor changing the conditions themselves.* In the diary entries of Lukács' friend Béla Balázs around this time, he mentions that Lukács had become dissatisfied with the immoral, seductive power of art and was appraising an ethical resolution of the existential tragedy of the human condition.[71]

Ethics and redemption

Balazs also recorded that Lukács' 'switch to ethics' involved a new philosophy of messianism along the lines of an ethics of solidarity. The utopian communal brotherhood glimpsed at the conclusion of Theory of the Novel was an expression of this 'new ethics' liberated from Kantian abstract formalism and embodied in the thought of the Jewish mystics and Russian anarchists. Prince Mishkin and Alexi Karamazov were models of the new human type; they transcended the formal realm of duties and out of an immediate soulish imperative abased themselves for the sake of others.

Lukács' new 'ethics of solidarity' was a response to the questions of practice posed by the First World War. Imperceptibly, he was drawn to a more activist view of ethics. In the struggle between duty to the law and the ethics of terrorism, he increasingly favoured the latter. Conscious rebellion against the law could be justified as a heroic sacrifice of the soul for the sake of its own imperatives.[72] The problem of ethics and violence led Lukács to a reconsideration of the politics of Marxism. However, to grasp all the considerations involved in this gradual transformation, the ethical dilemmas posed by the metaphysical-existential account of modern alienation must be examined.

Lukács had never been completely satisfied with his adherence to Kant. While there is evidence that he saw some value in bourgeois professional ethics as a organising principle of life which also promoted a set of communal values centred on the idea of useful work,[73] he more usually viewed the ethics of universal obligation *as just another of the powers of alienation.* The formal universality of Kantian ethics coercively abstracted from the real personal needs of both actors and those with whom they were engaged. This abstraction suppressed genuine individuality in the name of more particularistic or formal-universal duties. Formal ethics simply failed at the most decisive moments of life when understanding and aiding other individuals was far more important than doing one's formal duty.

Lukács' dissatisfaction found its most poignant expression in the short dialogue 'On the Poverty of the Spirit' which loosely fictionalised his own personal crisis after the suicide of Irma Seidler in 1911. This piece focused on the contradictions arising from the mere observance of formal duties. Closely mirroring the Lukács/Seidler real life tragedy, the dialogue explored the self-recrimination of a man feeling morally responsible for a woman's suicide. Speaking with a mutual friend acting as interlocutor the man bemoans the fact that he had not helped the woman in the hour of her desperation despite fulfilling all his formal obligations to her. Observance of formal duties had stifled authentic communication. Too rigid to assimilate the concrete issues and life situations of specific individuals, abstract formal ethics were empty and oppressive. Just like the universal schemas of language which possesses their own immanent autonomy, formal ethics is characterised by a universality that renders it independent of the concrete lives of the individuals who act as its bearers. The radical detachment of abstract universality eliminates the possibility of open, immediate communion and ethics based on 'direct relations'. Lukács characterised ethical duty as:

> a bridge that separates;a bridge upon which we go back and forth, always
> coming upon ourselves, but never meeting anyone else.[74]

The formal ethics of everyday life offered no support or assistance in a situation of isolation and alienation; they were, instead, a power of that alien world, 'one of the powers of alienation'.

In the context of his critique of formal Kantian ethics Lukács did review other possibilities. He rehearses the antinomies of an ethics of creative form considered in the last section only to conclude that artistic creation provides no redemption from the everyday world. More significantly for his future direction, he also hints at the possibility of 'direct relations' open to those individuals blessed with grace. Clearly, Lukács momentarily flirted with a very elitist ethics based on a theory of castes and the idea of predestination.[75] The caste of 'the good' were blessed with capacity to 'read the soul' of others just as they 'read their own'.[76]

Such empathetic communion 'from soul to soul' transcended the limitations imposed by the universal forms of ethics and language; it enabled a direct intuitive knowledge 'wherein subject and object collapsed into one another'.[77] 'Goodness' was simply a gift of grace neither to be willed nor won, nor concerned with the consequences of its actions. Escaping from the world of everyday necessity, 'the good' operated in a realm of complete freedom:

> Goodness is madness, it is not mild, not refined, not quietistic; it is wild,
> terrible, blind and adventurous.The soul of the good man has become
> empty of all psychological content, of grounds and consequences; it has
> become a pure white slate, upon which fate writes its absurd command
> and this command will be followed blindly, rashly and fiercely to the end.
> That this impossibility becomes fact, this blindness becomes clear-
> sightedness, this fierceness becomes Goodness – that is the miracle, the
> grace.[78]

The similarities between this concept of goodness and the Dostoevskian world of truly human brotherhood and direct communication between souls anticipated by Lukács a few years later are clear. Both models were inspired by a practical impulse to overcome a merely formal ethics. That Lukács quickly abandoned the theory of castes and moved away from the explicitly mystical elements of intuition indicate that the earlier model was soon seen by him as a dead end. The suicide of the protagonist suggested that within this framework there was no escape from humanity's ontological tragedy. Once Lukács again turned his attention to underlying social conditions and, inspired by Tolstoy and Dostoevski, posed the question of individual redemption as one of social transformation, he was on the road that would lead to his rapproachement with Marx. At this stage, he was not yet able to articulate the idea of a concrete social transformation but he had emerged from his pan-tragic phase and was more actively seeking an alternative social future.

Kantianism and the problem of totality

The foregoing analysis has shown the presence of *two alternating and regularly intermixed perspectives on one fundamental problem* within the pre-Marxist works. The young Lukács was dissatisfied with bourgeois society and the increasing socio-cultural fragmentation wrought by its modernising processes. He remained captivated by an unrealisable ideal of integrated culture characterised by communal harmony and individual authenticity.

This ideal surreptitiously found it way into both modes of Lukács' analysis. Whether by allusion to by-gone ages or by anticipation of a 'new ethics' foretelling a mystical-messianic overcoming of the 'eternal antinomies' of everyday life, this ideal supplied Lukács with *a normative standard against which he condemned the alienation of bourgeois society*. Even when it became existentially impossible to integrate this ideal, Lukács managed to reaffirm the sphere of the Absolute *as a guarantee of metaphysical reconciliation and human brotherhood*. In these times of despair, his ideal underwent a metamorphosis: it retreated and was reduced to the status of a metaphysical faith.

Lucien Goldmann once suggested that the originality of Lukács' pre-Marxist works lay in the resurrection of the problematic of classical German Idealist philosophy. Goldmann maintained that the heart of this problematic was 'the question of the relation between human life and absolute values'.[79] The determination with which Lukács resisted the contemporary philosophical fashion to eliminate the Hegelian sphere of the Absolute is evidence in favour of Goldmann's contention.

Yet, despite waverings, at this juncture Lukács' primary philosophical commitment was Kantian. While the influence of Hegel progressively strengthened, he derived his philosophic *Weltanschauung* from Kant. In Kant's pluralist conception of the ultimate principles of consciousness, he found philosophical corroboration of the contemporary sociological diagnosis of modernity. This sociological argument for a historical tendency towards the increasing autonomy of value-spheres was clearly compatible with the Kantian idea of the irreducible plurality of values. Kant had provided an argument for the ultimate incommensurability of these spheres. This was decisive for Lukács. Why it was decisive becomes clear on examination of his first serious theoretical confrontation with the Hegelian system.

Lukács was encouraged to reconsider Hegel by Ernst Bloch during their Heidelberg friendship. In the final chapter of his second incompleted attempt to construct a systematic aesthetics for presentation as a *Habilitationshift* – the so-called Heidelberg Aesthetics (1916-18) – he evaluated the Hegelian challenge to his own Kantian standpoint. Lukács maintained that Hegel's great merit lay precisely in his attempt to surpass Kant's pluralism. In his analysis, he assessed the consequences of this Hegelian programme for his jealously defended idea of an autonomous aesthetics. Lukács' concern was clearly motivated by his view of the work of art as a utopia of value; as something which was harmonious and perfectly self-enclosed in stark contrast to the oppositions which rendered everyday life meaningless. Moreover, unlike the theoretical and ethical spheres where this opposition was constitutive, the aesthetical presupposed the transcendence of the antithesis between subject and object, form and content.[80]

Lukács maintained that at first sight Hegel's more concrete understanding of form appeared to offer a great deal. The incorporation of all abstract oppositions as moments within an immanently developing totality provided a more aesthetic concept. The subsumption of all the partially enclosed, particular totalities within a *single concept of a universal, historically unfolding totality understood as rational progress* seemed to achieve the aesthetic unity posited as the utopian goal of the whole critical philosophy. Hegel attained this unity immanently by the processual movement of self-reflective thought.[81]

Lukács showed, however, that the Hegelian realisation of this programme failed in two related ways. Firstly, the system culminated *in the denial of the autonomy of the value spheres.* Hegel's pan-logism implied a value loss as it resulted in the logicisation of the aesthetic and the relativisation of its validity within an all-encompassing logical system:

> differentiations like art or religion conceived as a priori determinations of
> *sui generis* objectivities, contrasted to, and separated from each other,
> cannot exist at all for the Hegelian system if it is consistently thought
> through. They possess a common essential content [*den wesentlich
> Gehalt*] and throughout, with Hegel, content has to determine over the
> forms of appearance, The differences of contents here could be dependent
> on nothing other than upon the stage which spirit has just attained; each
> stage has a determined, pregnantly predominant quality of substantiality,
> objectivity, etc., and corresponding structure of form. Because, however,
> each stage is spirit in its determined, unified, concrete-fulfilled totality,
> this category of the stage (thus, for example, sensuous contemplation,

representation, concept) has to be the sole authoritative, constitutive category of the region for the whole totality of spirit realised at this stage.[82]

In Hegel, theory ultimately devoured the autonomy of the aesthical sphere. This followed from the superiority of conceptual truth which achieved a higher plane and brought the totality to its final unity and closure. Such a conclusion was anathema to Lukács who maintained the absolute value of art to be 'the only possible proof' of an undemonstrable metaphysical unity.

Secondly, Hegel's systematic attainment of unity implied a theoretical reconciliation with a sinful reality. In a criticism which unknowingly reproduces Marx's own critique of the Hegelian philosophy, Lukács asserted that Hegel's contemplative stance involved a tacit aestheticisation of existing socio-historical reality. For him, it was a capitulation to a modern alienated society he felt to be 'absolute sinfulness'. Even at this early stage, Lukács rejected 'reified' contemplation of 'totality' in favour of the Kantian assertion of irreducible value spheres. In modernity only the unadulterated, irreducible sphere of aesthetic value represented a focus for individual authenticity and a guarantee of a metaphysical brotherhood of men.

Clearly Lukács' perseverance with Kant was not without ambivalences. His critique of Kantian ethical doctrines has already been considered. As practical considerations moved further to the forefront of his mind, ethical dilemmas began to turn the tide towards radical politicisation. The historical dissolution of the previously secure late nineteenth century bourgeois society only accelerated the reappraisal of his initial pessimistic view of modern culture. As a willing participant in the forthcoming beginnings of real social transformation, he reassessed his earlier negative judgement of Hegel within the context of a rediscovery of the philosophical meaning of Marxism. The key to this review was changed historical circumstances and his new-found capacity to perceive the present as history.

The irruption of history

Chapter Five

The Marxist Lukács: 'totality' – principle of revolution

Lukács' <u>History and Class Consciousness</u> deserves a central place in this study of the radical, historicist concept of totality. In this work Lukács resurrected and reinterpreted the Hegelian origins of Marxian thought placing the concept of totality at the very centre of Marx's thought:

> The whole system of Marxism stands or falls with the principle that revolution is a product of the point of view in which the category of totality is dominant.[1]

<u>History and Class Consciousness</u> was a powerful synthesis that, despite its very real theoretical tensions, fused together some of the most important elements of the *Geisteswissenschaften's* critique of culture with its novel re-interpretation of Marx. As a result, the various connotations of the totality concept examined in previous chapters were marshalled into a forceful single vision. Lukács demolished the cultural pessimism of his own pre-Marxist phase and elaborated a revised, potentially emancipatory, view of the dynamics of bourgeois society. He preserved the *Geisteswissenschaften's* new insights into the dehumanising potential of these processes but, simultaneously, *critically relativised them as a subordinate moment in his primary concept of the total historical process.* His pre-Marxist ideal of an integrated cultural totality was re-interpreted as the immanent goal of real contemporary social struggles. In the form of a humble re-interpretation, Lukács proposed a radical theoretical unification of the two historically preceding understandings of totality that gave renewed precedence to the *critical, humanist, emancipatory moments* which *predominated in Marx* . However, more than a renewal, he revitalised this positive vision *while taking into account radically changed historical circumstances.* In this chapter, this famous, yet exceedingly problematic, synthesis will be examined more closely.

The irruption of history

In December 1918 Lukács joined the Hungarian Communist Party and became a Marxist. Although the biographical details of this remarkable personal transformation lie ouside the scope of this study,[2] the tensions in Lukács' intellectual and personal pre-Marxist odyssey examined in the last chapter at least make it explicable. His efforts to manufacture a viable stance in conditions of increasing cultural fragmentation had produced neither a stable nor a consistent standpoint. Until the October Revolution of 1917 he saw no way beyond the impasse of bourgeois cultural disintegration and his ideal of a unified culture appeared practically groundless. During the war years he had repudiated both German *Kultur* and Western *Zivilisation*. The Russian Revolution resparked his hopes. According to his own testimony, his despair over the contemporary state of bourgeois culture subsided before a wave of messianic hope. Now the historical present was viewed as an explosive new ingredient pregnant with radically alternative possibilities. All at once, an authentic culture appeared as a definite historical possibility.

From a contemporary perspective it is perhaps difficult to imagine how Lukács could have so readily linked together his own utopian dreams and a concrete historical event in another country. The answer to this question lies in the immediate events which conditioned the writing of the essays that make up History and Class Consciousness. The work was a reflection on the practical and theoretical problems of Marxism written during the first eventful years of Lukács' communist career – from March 1919 to October 1922 – and partially revised for publication in 1923. Primarily, it was perceived by Lukács as an urgent response to the crisis of revolutionary politics in the early 1920s. He had actively participated in the short-lived Hungarian Soviet Republic where he served as Deputy Commissar of Public Education. Clearly this initial revolutionary victory and his participation in government substantiated his belief that the radical social struggles of the post-war period held the possibility of the realisation of his dreams of authentic cultural renewal. However, the difficulties encountered by the Hungarian Soviet Republic, its ignominious collapse, the subsequent failure of uprisings in Germany and the apparent lull in the 'revolutionary wave', all experienced at close quarters, compelled him to raise some fundamental theoretic-practical issues. He was especially determined to challenge the orthodox Marxist belief in 'inevitable' revolution as a consequence of the automatic workings of objective economic mechanisms. He firmly believed that this idea of an objective movement that would 'automatically' bring the proletariat to a consciousness of its 'historical mission' was a major obstacle to a truly Marxian understanding of the significance of praxis in a genuinely revolutionary theory.[3]

After the failure of the Hungarian Soviet Republic Lukács had eventually rejoined his exiled comrades in Vienna where he wrote for party journals. At the time of publication in 1923 the crucial issues were the failure of the March action, the idea of a communist offensive and the question of immediate revolutionary strategy.[4] It is clear from the temper of Lukács' essays that he saw himself as a witness to the final crisis of European capitalism; to the first of perhaps a protracted series of revolutionary struggles. With hindsight it is easy to say that he was mistaken about how history was moving, even dreadfully wrong, however, many shared his hopes. They believed that the bankruptcy of modern bourgeois society and culture had been confirmed by a futile imperialist war, its staggering human cost and the massive socio-economic problems engendered by it. The seemingly temporary setbacks to the communist movement did not alter this general prognosis. Lukács insisted that history was poised on the brink of a great epoch of revolutionary struggle but warned of the need to abandon complacency and discard the idea of inevitable revolution.

It was this climate of revolutionary euphoria that explains Lukács' revised attitude to history. Fettered by the dominant stream of the *Geisteswissenschaften*, his early thought had viewed history *as the embodiment of the processess of alienation and fragmentation which had destroyed the organic, integrated cultures of former times.* History signified the triumph of an increasingly mechanical world characterised by de-personalisation and pure objectivity. His new interpretation, while not discarding this characterisation of contemporary modernising processes, recast them in a more encompassing framework which both *allowed for and positively endorsed the possibility of a radically alternative future.* The historical emergence of a concrete radical socio-cultural alternative together with his own personal commitment to revolutionary praxis introduced into History and Class Consciousness a new dimension and new understanding of history. If Lukács' historical optimism was misplaced, his theoretical achievement remains almost undiminished in its insistence upon a dereified conception of history.

His new understanding of history compelled an immediate reassessment of his earlier dismissal of the Hegelian identification of the concept of totality with the entire historical process. Lukács now recognised this theoretical move as something more than a disguised lapse into 'reified' contemplation; it was the philosophical key to Marx's critique of political economy and the real emancipatory meaning of the Marxian concept of theory. On this basis, Lukács retrieved the Hegelian origins of Marx's Capital. By fusing its underlying concept of historical totalisation with the Weberian notion of 'rationalisation', he broadened the Marxian idea of fetishism into a general theory of the historical process. He was now able to show how economic categories were 'explicit forms of being, determinations of existence'.[5]

Lukács' Marxian idea of totality

Lukács' reconstruction of Marx's concept of totality demonstrated his deep familiarity with classical German Idealism. From Hegel he appropriated the fundamental conception of man's relation to nature as a historically constituted subject/object relation. Hegel, as previously mentioned, had quickly recognised that the subjective paradigm which underlay the Kantian idea of transcendental constitution was inadequate as an explanation of the manifold determinations of real concrete existence. While retaining the Kantian epistemological breakthrough (the idea of subjective constitution of experience, of the forms of objectivity), Hegel radicalised Kant's activism with *an additional ontological dimension*. The Hegelian subject *Geist* was the supra-individual producer of the historical world. Hegel replaced Kant's epistemological abstraction – the transcendental I – with a real finite-infinite agent engaged in incessant processual development. The result of this ontologisation of the principle of active subjectivity was the Hegelian claim that reality itself was a process; a historical process in which the social world was constantly recreated by generations of historical subjects who were themselves its products.

In History and Class Consciousness, Lukács adopted this Hegelian view of reality as processuality. The fundamental meaning of his concept of totality is encapsulated in the idea of the universal historical process. Yet, as a perceptive interpreter of Marx he had already assimilated important elements of critique that modified the Hegelian concept. He rejected the idea of *a philosophical decipherment of the total historical process* . Hegel had mystified the immanent motor of history and falsely ascribed the ultimate guiding role to a philosophical abstraction '*Weltgeist*'. He had therefore failed to consistently acknowledge the primary role of concrete social praxis and this was confirmed by his contemplative, backward looking view of philosophy which virtually neglected the problem of future history. Taking up Marx's solution to this failing with his identification of the proletariat as the contemporary, concrete agent of progressive historical forces, the first potentially conscious, collective subject and Marxist theory as an expression of its enlightened self-consciousness, Lukács maintained that 'totality' was a theoretically anticipated universal meaning of history, a meaning identical to the growing self-consciousness of the proletariat.[6]

This Marxian shift in Lukács' understanding of totality involved the appropriation of two decisive elements of the young Marx's critique of Hegel. The Hegelian principle of historical immanence was consistently adhered to by providing it with a concrete, real basis in a social class. At the same time, Lukács disposed of an ontologically pre-established meaning of history by reiterating the point that historical meaning *had to be created, was something to be realised by the free, conscious activity of a class of individuals acting collectively*. He reinforced these ideas when he opposed his concept of universal history to both the idea of an 'aggregate of individual historical events' and to a transcendental interpretation which opposed the actual events themselves:

> The totality of history is itself a real historical power – even though one
> that has not hitherto become conscious and therefore gone unrecognised –
> a power which is not separated from the reality (and hence the

knowledge) of individual facts without at the same time annuling their reality and their factual existence.[7]

Lukács was certainly emphatic about his own value commitment and its practical goal: 'the meaning of these tendencies' (the developmental tendencies of history) was 'the abolition of capitalism'[8] and, he could have added, the creation of a new socialist society and culture. Yet, he underlined that there could 'be no material guarantee for this certitude'.[9] In line with the practical orientation he ascribed to Marxian theory, he argued that the viewpoint of totality was an intellectual 'anticipation' only made possible by 'the accelerating power of thought'.

The perspective of totality was *a historically conditioned practical standpoint produced by the social conflicts and internal dynamics of bourgeois historical development*. It was an intellectual expression and clarification of real historical processes and social forces in the process of attaining self-consciousness. The historical emergence of this theoretical perspective was, according to Lukács who unquestioningly accepted Marx's own self interpretation, tied to the creation of a social class for whom the standpoint of totality was an authentic expression of its objective interests. Lukács endorsement of Marx's insight into the socio-historical conditionedness of theory confirms his claim that there could be no purely 'objective' proof of his theory.

Notwithstanding these important Marxian qualifications, Lukács acknowledged that the idea of historical totalisation at the conceptual basis of Capital was Hegelian. Marx had unfolded the mystery of the commodity by showing the structure of this form as a historically created form of objectivity which, in turn, conditioned corresponding forms of subjectvity and subjective attitude, i. e., wage labour. The real dynamism of this conception was shown by the fact that an initially appropriate form of subjectivity could in the process of historical evolution come into contradiction with the commodity. In reading Capital through the prism of Hegel's phenomenology of history, Lukács rediscovered Marx's early theory of alienation (prior to the full publication of the 1844 manuscripts in 1932) and *universalised it as a general theory of historical forms*. In the famous 'Reification' essay, the full implications of this interpretative reconstruction for a general theory of history can be gleaned from two important formulations:

> When Marx makes dialectics the essence of history, the movement of thought becomes just a part of the overall movement of history. History becomes the history of the objective forms from which man's environment and the inner world are constructed and which he strives to master in thought, action and art, etc.[10]

and:

> History is, on the one hand, the product (albeit the unconscious one) of

man's own activity, on the other hand, it is the succession of those processes in which the forms taken by this activity and the relations of man to himself (to nature, to other men) are overthrown.[11]

Perhaps surprisingly, and quite unconsciously on Lukács' part, his own notion of totality turned out to be even more encompassing than Marx's original. Still under the influence of Weber's theory of rationalisation and Simmel's sociology of forms, he conceived 'alienation' in terms of a general theory of human objectification. Thus he asserts 'history is the history of the unceasing overthrow of the objective forms that shape the life of man'.[12] The significance of this conceptual broadening is that now all 'forms of activity' including ideal and symbolic representation became interpretable in terms of the idea of alienation.

This general theory of historical objectification implied that both the social function of man-created objects and the corresponding subjective categories of their comprehension were historically specific and changed in the course of those actual practices in which these objects were created and the array of subjective attitudes (cognitive, aesthetical, etc.) realised. On this reading, human experience is always a socio-historical objectification. Always conditioned by previous historical development, humans reproduce and transform the socio-historical world through their own life activities. Historical creation therefore always presupposes an inherited level of social development. From a totalising perspective, history is a unified process constantly expanding the existing reservoir of techniques, meanings, rules and human possibilities through the reciprocal co-constitution of the social world by subjectivity and its conditioning world of objects. In the reproduction of the existing life forms new objective possibilities and subjective needs are revealed. This process of historical creation and augmentation involves not only increasing productive forces in the narrow technological sense but also changing schemata of social signification and perception. It amounts to a process of enrichment producing always new configurations both material and ideal, subjective and objective.

Lukács reaffirmed the Hegelian-Marxian theory of alienation. This process of historical enrichment, of constant cross-fertilisation between subjective and objective development, remained for the most part an unreflected product of the total life activity of the aggregated historical subjects.[13] The accomplished results of human actions rarely accorded with the original subjective intentions and the products entered a sphere of objectivity possessed of its own dynamic which often divorced these products from the subjective needs of their creators. Yet, Lukács insisted that the contemporary historical possibilities had engendered a practical standpoint that allowed the past and future to be drawn together and ascribed with a unified meaning as a total process. The concrete realisation of this totalised meaning ultimately depended upon the maturing class consciousness of the proletariat.

As the de facto heir to the accumulated wealth of the entire historical development, the proletariat was *objectively* in a position to crown history with a universal, truly human meaning. The realisation of this objective possibility depended upon the proletariat grasping its historically unique opportunity to be the first social class in history to *consciously make it*. The proletariat's privilege consisted in it being the first historically significant social class to be more than an object and unconscious instrument of immanent historical forces. Although Lukács stressed that the realisation of this historical 'truth' presupposed a revolutionary overthrow of the existing bourgeois order, he recognised proletarian self-consciousness, its knowledge of its own potentially autonomous subjectivity and historical creativity, as the pre-condition for the actualisation of this 'truth'. Fully conscious, the proletariat could practically take up its theoretically ascribed role as the bearer of the emancipatory meaning of history. In anticipation, Lukács nominated the proletariat *as the identical subject/object of history*. Like Marx before him, he argued that bourgeois society had created both the objective conditions and the subjective possibility of a transcendence of the alienation which characterised all previous historical soceities. However, this transcendence was to be a *fully conscious act of a collective social subject which had finally recognised itself as the real creator of the social world*.

The concept of totality also has other methodological functions in <u>History and Class Consciousness</u>. Aside from designating the universal historical process, it also signifies the methodological point that each concrete society was be viewed *as a whole*. The sum of all social and economic relations in any given society form a *contradictory unity conceivable as a 'negative totality'*. Economic categories and relations arose out of, and depended upon, specific social relations which they reciprocally transformed in the process of social reproduction; the two always inter-meshed and constituted *aspects of an ongoing unified process*.[14]

Here Lukács touches on one of Marx's central concerns which he otherwise neglects. Chapter Two indicated that the problem of socio-economic reproduction loomed large in the late economic manuscripts and became a decisive aspect of Marx's articulation of the concept of totality. Lukács' very different immediate interests caused him to refocus the emphasis on to the idea of universal history. He was primarily concerned with the practical and philosophico-methodological dimensions. The urgent needs of a contemporary historical crisis compelled him to underscore the very real, and tenuous, historicity of all socio-economic ensembles. It was imperative to view the isolated economic and social 'facts' of the bourgeois totality in the light of their immanent negative processuality. It was therefore essential not to fetishise the unity of these relations. This unity was not fixed but merely a 'moment' within a more encompasssing historical movement that manifested itself in present social contradictions. Lukács' immanent totalising perspective facilitated an ascription of a socialist meaning to history *projected from the standpoint of current contradictions*. But this meaning was an *anticipation;* the appearances of everyday life and their ideological reflection in bourgeois theory distorted and obscured this *becoming truth*. Lukács coined the term 'reification' (*die Verdinglichung*) in explanation of this *socially conditioned opacity* of the total historical process and its potential immanent meaning.

The theory of reification

A major implication of Lukács' claim regarding the opacity of everyday life was his theorisation of a *historically conditioned* 'false consciousness'. He argued that as the social function of objects and the corresponding subjective categories were determined by the historically specific character of social practices experience was subject to *'objective' distortions* which only rarely entered the consciousness of typical historical actors. Until the historical emergence of the proletariat, the opportunity to bring 'these objective forms that shape the life of man' fully to consciousness had never before existed.

However, even the proletariat was subject to these 'objective distortions'. To take hold of its singular opportunity it was required to overcome the contemporary form of social objectivity constraining both its self-knowledge and actions. Lukács termed the historically specific objective forms dominating modern capitalist society and constituting *a qualitatively new system of constraints, 'reification'*. His seminal essay 'Reification and the Consciousness of the Proletariat' (1923) asserted that the universalisation of the commodity form in bourgeois society ushered in a profound historical change in the dominant forms of objectivity and subjective comprehension which threatened to prolong the subjugation of man to historically determined 'false' appearances.[15] Here, Lukács' pre-Marxist critique of the qualitative change in the structure of alienation reappears in a Marxist framework.

In pre-capitalist times, Lukács maintained, insight into the historico-social deterimination of social being was veiled by the overriding predominance of apparently natural bonds stemming from a traditional organisation of production and social hierarchy. While the evolution of bourgeois society rapidly *socialised these formerly 'natural' relations* and promoted a consciousness of the social construction of all human institutions, its progressive displacement of natural bonds by commodification generated *a kind of 'second nature'* which soon rivalled the one that had dominated pre-capitialist social experience.[16]

Lukács described the new system of constraints accompanying the commodity in the following terms:

> Reification requires that the society should learn to satisfy all its needs in terms of commodity exchange. The separation of the producer from his means of production, the dissolution and destruction of all 'natural' production units, etc., and all the social and economic conditions necessary for the emergence of modern capitalism tend to replace 'natural' relations which exhibit human relations more plainly by rationally reified relations.[17]

Born of bourgeois society, modern reification entailed an ongoing process which gradually replaced traditionally regulated forms of production directed toward the satisfaction of socially fixed needs by indirect production for the market regulated only by profit and effective money demand. *'Natural', personal relations and bonds* were systematically overturned in favour of *impersonal, contractual ones, while customary, irrational, qualitative procedures gave way to rational, abstract and quantitative methods.* Parallel to these corrosive tendencies, the phenomenon of reification diversified and quickly permeated all other spheres of social life, all forms of consciousness including those not directly related to the revolution in productive methods.

Lukács also examined the consequences of this process. He considered the main objective consequence to be that the man made world took on the appearance of a *'second nature'* governed by its own *rational, quasi-natural laws.*[18] On the subjective side, the activity of production became something alien and superimposed on the producers.[19] Lukács' detailed elaboration of these consequences illustrated his great synthetic power.

Marx's critique of fetishism was the chief source of Lukács concept of reification. He took over from Capital the fundamental observation that the universalisation of the commodity form caused the abstract labour thus embodied to appear to the producers as an independent, phantom world of complex relations between things. Men were unable to recognise the social relations upon which this mysterious objective world with its own autonomous laws depended. Working from this insight, Lukács reconstructed the essentials of Marx's theory of alienation. The specialisation engendered by the bourgeois division of labour destroyed the original unity of traditional work processes. Exploding after the separation of peasantry from their traditional means of production, this specialisation fostered the abstraction of labour power which was the initial pre-condition for the universalisation of the commodity form.[20]

Rather than chart the actual historical course of this development, Lukács' analysis elaborates the modern manifestations of alienation. The bourgeois fragmentation of the unity of the productive activity tended to eliminate all purely individual, qualitative and irrational features from work. This reorganisation of work according to rational analysis and 'objective' requirements produced corresponding subjective effects. The fragmentation of work impacted disasterously on the producers. As the work process was reconstructed in accordance with the criteria of objective functionality quite independent of the workers' needs, his/her role was reduced to that of a cog in a largely mechanical operation. The rationalisation of the system eradicated the worker's individual idiosyncrasies and he/she consequently lost the sense of personal skill and mastery formerly attached to artisan work.[21] This total subordination to objective work rhythms and processes compounded the initial alienating consequences of the worker's separation from the means of production. The performance of repetitive and purely mechanical tasks demanded the almost complete disregard of the individual's total personality. It transformed activity into a form of contemplation which involved the quantitative expenditure of physical powers but no longer engaged the whole active person.[22] Finally, Lukács underscored the atomisation resulting from the enhanced power of objective organisation. Mechanisation and the physical dispersion of the work process broke up the traditional communal and social aspects of co-operative and organic work.[23]

Lukács' reconstruction of the Marxian theory of alienation smacked of Weber's influence. It fused together Marx's treatment of abstract labour with the Weberian theory of rationalisation. The emphasis placed on quantification and calculability as features of industrial rationalisation represented a step beyond Marx in exposing the multiple dimensions of alienation.[24] In fact, Lukács claimed that the complete self-realisation of capitalist production ultimately required a progressive rationalisation of all other spheres of life. Only this would bring them into conformity with the needs of the capitalist system. He supported this thesis with the aid of Weber's accounts of bureaucracy and law and cited modern journalism and marriage (as a contract of sexual exchange) as other examples which illustrated the deepening penetration of reified relations into every domain of modern social life.[25]

The question of reification was of immediate practical significance. Lukács explained that the processes of commodification had invaded the very psyche of the modern individual determining even his/her perception of the objective quality of objects. As a consequence, the social world acquired a 'new objectivity' seemingly independent of man and subject only to its own laws.[26] Lukács argued that this historically conditioned appearance largely explained the sense of impotence afflicting the working class in times of economic stability. Revolutionary politics required a concerted emphasis on ideological struggle to rend this insidious appearance. Marxism had to abandon a complacent trust in the 'historical inevitability' of socialist revolution and address to task of disrupting the reified hold of everyday consciousness.

Lukács' idea of reification also absorbed the negative meaning attributed to the totality of objective socio-economic processes by Simmel, Weber and his own pre-Marxist work. He stressed the *irrationality of the capitalist 'whole' despite the highly rationalised organisation of its partial spheres*. Each distinct sphere of bourgeois society possessed its own independent momentum and a certain autonomy from other spheres.[27] But *the totality of reified objectivities had escaped the control of man; the movement of society was dictated by the inner logics of its distinct spheres*. This was a contradictory, socially destructive dynamic ultimately beyond the controlling instruments of bourgeois rationality. However, within the terms of Lukács' new characterisation of history, these elements of *Kulturkritik* emphasising the increasing autonomy and oppressive weight of a dehumanised objective culture were incorporated into a more optimistic, anticipatory interpretation of universal history. They no longer foreshadowed an irreversible fate. This fate was *an appearance transparent to a totalising historical perspective*:

For the elimination of the objectivity attributed both to social institutions inimical to man and to their historical evolution means the restoration of this objectivity to their underlying basis, to relations between men; it does not involve the elimination of laws and objectivity independent of the will of man and in particular the wills and thought of individual men. It simply means that this objectivity is the self-objectification of human society at a particular stage in its development; its laws hold good only within the framework of the historical context which produces them and which is determined by them.

Viewed from the perspective of its immanent socio-political possibilities, the seeming autonomy and oppressive objectivity of the reigning bourgeois totality disappeared. It became *transformable once the inherited potential of this society's productive forces were realised.*

The cornerstone of Lukács' critique of bourgeois science was his assertion that the totalising perspective was inaccessible to its epistemological point of departure: the isolated individual. For this individual, society appeared not as a 'totality in process' but as a conglomeration of disconnected partial systems and spheres. The abstract methodology of bourgeois social science took these partial spheres as objects of specialised disciplines and presupposed the existence of distinct domains of fragmented 'facts'. Each specialised discipline monopolised its own segment of the societal whole proceeding to discover its underlying laws. Lukács argued that this positivist method merely took the 'facts' of bourgeois society as it found them and was unable to penetrate to their historically determined basis.[28] Seeing the reified character of the method, he compared its underlying contemplative attitude to that imposed on the modern industrial worker by means of the rationalised bourgeois division of labour. Like the worker chained to the tempo and rhythm of the machine, the bourgeois social scientist had to accept unquestioningly the reified appearance of a social objectivity moved by an inherent, lawlike necessity. To the contemplative gaze, the man-made, social world became an independent ensemble of autonomous, partial systems and the constitutive role of social praxis was lost from sight.

For Lukács, this unwitting concealment of the historical and therefore transient character of social objectivity, of the merely practical relations at its basis was the crux of the reified method.[30] Additionally, he insisted that the specialisation of bourgeois science and the resulting *compartmentalisation of knowledge destroyed 'every image of the whole'.*[31] In themselves, the 'facts' of bourgeois society were ambiguous and ultimately meaningless. To discover the real essential meaning of these social processes, the contemplative standpoint had to be discarded in favour of an alternative that allowed for the comprehension of the fragmented processes and objects of existing empirical reality as part of a becoming historical totality. Lukács conceded that class interest constantly inhibited members of the bourgeois from adopting this more comprehensive historical perspective. He argued, however, that practical considerations like economic crisis and the cognitive need to grasp the whole forced the bourgeois to periodically confront the question of totality.

Lukács reiterated that this question was closed to the epistemological standpoint of the isolated individual:

> No path leads from the individual to the totality; there is at best a road leading to aspects of particular areas, mere fragments for the most part, 'facts' bare of any context, or to abstract, special laws.[32]

The 'facts' of bourgeois society necessarily appeared to the isolated individual as immutable and untranscendable; one could *adapt to them but not change their underlying structure. Only the assumption of the standpoint of a collective subject allowed the question of society as whole to be really addressed.* The collective subjects referred to here were the social classes of modern society. Lukács maintained that the category of totality 'determined not only the object of knowledge but also the subject'.[33] The attainment of a totalising perspective which was the cognitive pre-condition for the defeat of reification depended upon the possibility of radical collective action. Limited to an attitude of calculated adaption and manipulating pursuit of individual gain, the bourgeoisie was not an acting, collective subject in the Lukácsian sense and therefore failed to rise above a reified perspective.

Lukács accorded this privileged historical role to the proletariat. His theory of class consciousness explained the link between class and a totalising perspective and indicated the practical necessities driving the proletariat towards the adoption of the latter.

Class consciousness

Lukács' understanding of a totalising perspective as a practically becoming, universal meaning of history presupposed the historical emergence of a concrete, collective social subject with the capacity to realise this meaning as a free, conscious creation. While he clearly designated the proletariat as the bearer of this privileged historical role, he did not pretend that the concrete social class was already capable of fully assuming this historical mantle. The process that would lead the proletariat to its maturity was fraught with obstacles and struggles. This was certainly not just a literary device Lukács adopted to enhance the significance of the final, inevitable victory. Following Luxemburg he seriously questioned the established Second International orthodoxy which claimed an uninterrupted development of class consciousness engendered by the economic contradictions of capitalism.

The issue of class consciousness received very little theoretical attention after Marx's own aborted efforts. The orthodox followed Engel's authoritative view that 'ever-increasing proletarianisation' and 'massive overproduction' signified a contemporary crisis of capitalism eventually requiring a change in the mode of production.[34] The role to be played by class consciousness in this scenario was far from clear.

The gradual improvement in the living conditions of the working class during this period and the mounting political strength of German social democracy combined to postpone any serious reckoning with the question of class consciousness. Although the stabilisation of bourgeois society engendered serious disputes over alternative strategies (orthodoxy versus reformism), the most popular interpretation of revolution was economistic. It was believed that swelling proletarian economic demands would automatically translate into revolutionary politics and class struggle.[35] During this halycon phase of growing prosperity, legislative gains and parliamentary success, it was easy to confuse party initiatives in education, entertainment and workers' culture with a developing class consciousness.

Lukács refused to entertain these ideas of socialism. Conceiving socialism as a radical transformation of the whole fabric of society and the replacement of the rule of inhuman, uncontrolled economic processes by the free, conscious activity and the forging of a collective cultural wholeness, he rejected social democracy's preoccupation with economic demands and incremental improvements in living conditions. These concerns neither provided the pre-conditions for socialism nor did they engender a consciousness of the need for it.[36] As far as Lukács was concerned, the moral credibility of social democracy had been destroyed by the capitulation to war sentiments in 1914 and its subsequent collusion in the suppression of revolutionary actions after the collapse of the Imperial Regime in 1918. At the same time, the economic hardship following the war at least temporarily discredited reformist's hopes for continued economic improvement and a slow evolution towards socialism.

Despite this apparently overwhelming historical judgment and his own fervently held theoretical opposition, Lukács did not completely dismiss the social democrats. He preferred to show that the previous successes of the movement were based on its representation of the immediate interests of the proletariat, i.e., the struggle for wages and conditions. His theory of reification explained the attraction of this outlook to the individual members of the proletariat. The seemingly unshakeable permanence of bourgeois institutions and the reified, fragmented character of everyday experience concealed the underlying structural connection between economic conditions and the political relations underpinning them. Immersed in the immediate interests of their own particular everyday struggles for improved wages and conditions, workers risked losing sight of the exploitative relations on which the bourgeois organisation of society was founded. The gains achieved within this organisation neither endangered its reproduction nor speeded the proletariat's recognition of its own long-term historical goal: the abolition of bourgeois society. The failure of the social democrats to see this and the workers entrappment in the reified immediacy of economic struggles constituted an 'ideological crisis' whose outcome would decide the fate of socialist revolution in western Europe.[37]

Against this background, Lukács' theory of class consciousness served a number of functions. It explained the unique historical position of the proletariat and illuminated the immanent historical forces linking its economic struggles and immediate interests to contemporary, epochal political conflicts. This linkage raised the objective possibility of the proletariat's attainment of a full class consciousness and the assumption of its genuine historical subjectivity. Lukács also hoped to alert the movement to the practical urgency of this ideological crisis. The linkage between immediate interests and ultimate historical goal by no means guaranteed an automatic transition from the former to the latter. In other words, Lukács insisted that the acquisition of class consciousness was a vital pre-condition of the process that would bring the proletariat to political maturity and a momentous advance toward the realisation of its 'historical mission'.[38]

The theory of class consciousness was inter-meshed with Lukács view of history as a self-totalising process. A consequence of this view was his refusal to 'naturalise' given social relations as objective circumstance. They had to be perceived as a moment within a dynamic historical process of interlinked social activities and practices. Consistent with this stance, he attributed only a qualified validity to empirical consciousness. Arguing for a conditioned understanding of consciousness, he asserted that spontaneous individual or mass consciousness engendered within a given form of social relations and practices could not be relied upon to provide an adequate view of that social reality.[39] He did not mean that empirical consciousness was absolutely false because he conceded that it did, in some sense, correspond to, and was determined by, a specific configuration of socio-historical objectivity. Instead, he spoke of the 'two-fold dialectical determination of consciousness'.[40] To understand what he meant it is necessary to elaborate his general account of historically conditioned 'false consciousness'.

Lukács totalising perspective represented a historically immanent standard against which empirical consciousness could be measured. He conceded the *subjective justification* of the immediate reformist consciousness of the isolated worker. This was a spontaneous response to the reified, seemingly 'natural' appearance of bourgeois social relations and practices. Yet, *assessed objectively from the higher perspective of immanent historical totalisation*, this *'necessary'* subjective consciousness completely missed the evolution of society and therefore failed to express the essence of the social situation facing it. In short, Lukács perceived *another point of historical determination of empirical consciousness requiring a 'two-fold' reflection for its integration*. This dialectical view enabled Lukács to provide an explanation of the practical failure of empirical consciousness to attain its subjectively intended goals. Without comprehending the real historical forces determining its actions and transforming the intended results, empirical consciousness was destined only to contribute to the realisation of *historically imposed objective tasks while believing it was prosecuting its own immediate aims and ends.*[41] Taking up a qualified reading of the Hegelian 'ruse of reason', Lukács argued that spontaneous empirical consciousness was *objectively inadequate even while possessing its own subjective necessity and 'truth'.*

This account of empirical consciousness implied its inability to capture the *true historical significance of its 'object'.* At this point Lukács introduced the idea of imputed class consciousness. Such an imputed consciousness was really a *construct of historical materialism that offered a historical standard of cognitive awareness against which to assess the empirical consciousness of particular historically effective classes.* Imputed class consciousness was derived by relating consciousness to the 'whole of society' understood as a processual totality, or, in other words, to the objective standpoint of totality. Encompassing all determinations of consciousness, this perspective gauged the maximum of cognitive potential belonging to the objective situation and interests of a particular social class. By relating empirical consciousness to a totalising perspective, consciousness was assessed against the objective interests arising from the class position from which it emerged. Lukács continued:

> By relating consciousness to the whole of society it becomes possible to infer the thoughts and feelings which men would have in a particular situation if they were able to assess both it and the interests arising from it in their impact on immediate action and the whole structure of society. That is to say, it would be possible to infer the thoughts and feelings appropriate to their objective situation.[42]

This constructivist concept of class consciousness was inferred not from empirical nor psychological contents but *from objectively ascribed real interests viewed in relation to the total historical process.* Lukács argued that only a limited number of objective situations determined by the productive organisation existed within any given society. Imputed class consciousness was derived by *imputing rational reactions appropriate* to these typical positions in the economic structure of society.[43]

This distinction between spontaneous empirical and imputed consciousness allowed Lukács to posit the idea of 'objective posssibility'. This category denoted *the unconscious historico-social limits which circumscribed the furthest possible cognitive horizon available to representative class actors in respect to the totality of history.*[44] The gist of this idea was that earlier historically significant classes neither could nor needed to attain the level of their own imputed class consciousness. Only the proletariat was in principle able and practically required to realise its class consciousness. Lukács concluded by insisting that this could only be achieved by the worker's practical immersion in the historical struggle for a revolutionary transformation.

The category of 'objective possibility' presupposed Lukács' theory of reification: all past history was characterised by historically determined 'false consciousness'. Past social actors were unable to grasp the real motor of their collective actions and the determining mechanisms behind social appearances. Referring to pre-capitalist society, he argued that the perfectly 'natural' appearance of existing social forms ensured the social actors' complete immersion in the traditional categories of their life situation. Amidst apparently timeless and natural insititutions and relations it was *objectively impossible* to pierce appearances and comprehend their essential historicity. This 'naturalness' obscured the economic basis of the estates and castes. In these societies, an economic sphere of life as such *did not exist*. Economic activities were embedded to a total, religious organisation and interpretation of everyday life and the cosmos. All other socio-economic categories were invisibly interwoven into this all-encompassing religious fabric and this lack of purely articulated social spheres, i.e. economic, legal, political, concealed from the participants the economic processes and factors operating beneath these forms.[45] These later forms remained *decisive for consciousness* even after subterranean economic developments gradually began to undermine the traditional order. For Lukács, Cervantes' Don Quixote typified this tragic dilemma of a privileged caste clinging to a disintegrating world long after its collapse. Lukács underlined that in this historical case self-interest and imputed class consciousness were mutually exclusive. Awareness of historical obsolescence was simply beyond the horizon of possible consciousness. It would have involved the recognition of the hopelessness of struggles to which these estates were objectively committed.[46]

The rise of capitalism engendered a new productive organisation and correspondingly new cognitive possibilities for class consciousness. The internal dissolution of organic, 'natural' social forms was acompanied by a increasingly more self-delineating economic sphere which came to exercise a pervasive influence over the entire social totality. Despite the general phenomenon of a seeming increasing autonomy of all partial spheres of society, the real impact of commodification was *towards the homogenisation of the structure of these spheres*. The capitalist economy both generated and demanded a more cohesive politico-socio-economic structure. The degree of autonomy previously existing between the state and economy in pre-capitalist societies was an immediate casualty of this development.[47] The dispossession of the feudal peasantry provided the initial conditions for a 'purely economic' determination of productive relations based on the sale of labour power. Losing their traditional, 'natural' appearance, these relations were finally perceived and articulated in purely economic categories: individuals were *socially posited* as wage labourers and capitalists. Only when these economic determinations became visible to the actors themselves for the first time was it possible, Lukács maintained, to speak of adequate class consciousness as a potential historical attainment.

Yet, even these new historical conditions did not ensure all social classes equal potential access to a real knowledge of historical forces. As the Cervantes example drives home, classes and strata owing their origins to pre-capitalist social relations *were bound to remain ignorant of the forces destroying their world*. Class consciousness was simply *incompatible* with their own objective interests.[48] Lukács observed that to speak of class consciousness in respect to the social residues of pre-capitalist society was rather problematical. Following Marx, he argued that the isolation imposed on the peasantry by the organic character of its life situation militated against both *the formation of a collective perspective and the identification of class interests*. The peasantry remained a class in itself without ever becoming a class for itself.[49] Such examples only reinforced Lukács main argument that these particular social classes and strata were precluded from real historical insight. An understanding of the historico-social determination of their spontaneous historical perspective disclosed that 'imputed' class consciousness was beyond their cognitive horizon.

The bulk of Lukács' subsequent analysis was devoted to the two classes historically attached to the modern organisation of production, bound in both their origin and destiny to the further development of this capitalist form of production: the bourgeoisie and the proletariat. Both these classes were contemporary contestants for hegemony and their class interests demanded they address all important questions pertaining to the structure and organisation of modern society.[50]

Since the French Revolution the bourgeoisie had attained the hegemony of modern society. Its class consciousness was expressed in the ideology of the 'Rights of Man'. This class consciousness enabled the bourgeoisie to act as a progressive historical force during the early phase of capitalist development but, Lukács maintained, its tragic contradiction was soon revealed by the historical emergence of the proletariat and the theoretical elaboration of the workers' standpoint. At the height of its ascendency the bourgeoisie's command of the productive process required that it attempt to understand the capitalist economic system and its immanent evolutionary processes *as a whole*. Yet, class interest imposed definite limits on its capacity to fulfil this task. The bourgeoisie was incapable of penetrating to the core of these processes and bringing them under practical control. Lukács perceived in this incapacity a 'dialectical' contradiction. Initially the bourgeoisie relied solely on its spontaneous class consciousness generated by immediate economic interests. It was able to act as the champion of emancipatory transformations. However, this initial strength became a fetter once its dominant position was consolidated and the objective socio-economic processes evolved further. Lukács maintained that the bourgeoisie's inability to transcend reification vitiated its understanding of these processes.

The bourgeoisie's attempt to theoretically comprehend the totality of capitalist society was grounded in the standpoint of the isolated individual. The perspective of private appropriation and distribution of commodities could not appreciate the immanent, potentially social, dimension of capital. As a result, the historical evolution of capitalist society always appeared to the bourgeoisie as an alien, uncontrollable, quasi-natural objective reality. This socio-historically determined limit to the perspective and potential enlightenment of the bourgeoisie both undermined its own efforts to theoretically appropriate the social whole and ensured its practical incapacity to deal with its contradictions.[51]

The tragedy of this socio-historical 'limit' was manifest in the historical transformation of the bourgeoisie from a progressive social force to an opponent of radical social change. This metamorphosis also highlighted the structural limits on the bourgeoisie's capacity for a truly conscious subjectivity. However, a deficient subjectivity and periodic economic crises were only a subordinate aspect of the threat to the bourgeoisie's ascendency. The main challenge came not from these fixed, purely objective limitations but from the increasing maturity of the proletariat as a new, organised, subjective force. The same process which produced the proletariat as a class struggling for the very means of its existence also generated *a new socio-historical perspective able to contest the adequacy of bourgeois consciousness and its ideological expressions.*[52]

Lukács dated the transformation of bourgeois theory into a 'mendacious consciousness' (*einer Falschheit des Bewusstsein*) from the time of the first proletarian attempts to wrest the hegemony of modern society. Subsequently, bourgeois theory degenerated from a genuinely great effort to comprehend problems which were insoluble from its own point of view to a vain apologetics aimed at masking the problems themselves. From this time, according to Lukács, every significant bourgeois thinker was confronted with a choice between their conscience and their class interest. Their insoluble theoretical problems, henceforth became moral ones. 'Mendacious consciousness' was a class-determined bourgeois response to the objective development of the proletariat and the intractability of its own practical dilemmas.[53]

Imputed class consciousness and the problem of mediations

Harking back to Simmel's idea of tragedy, Lukács' conception of the bourgeoisie emphasised its historical tragedy. Its own development of the modern capitalist organisation of production bore within the seeds of its own increasing degeneration, impotence and ultimate abolition. This tragedy, however, had an entirely different significance for the proletariat:

> Whereas for the proletariat the 'same' development has a different class meaning: it means the abolition of the isolated individual, it means that workers can become conscious of the social character of labour, it means that the abstract, universal form of the societal principle as it is manifested can be increasingly concretised and overcome.[54]

The possibility of this radically alternative historical meaning resided in the proletariat's potential capacity to transcend the distortions of a historically determined reification and realise its imputed class consciousness. Lukács recognised that there was nothing inevitable about this prospective process. Repeatedly he argued that class consciousness was an *objective possibility* opened up by the historical evolution of capitalist society. Its status was that of a practical imperative imposed on the proletariat as an indispensible condition of its conscious move towards a more rational and humane society. But it *was not an immediate possession of the members of this class.*

Like the bourgeoisie, the contemporary proletariat was a prisoner of reification which bound it to the 'facts' of capitalist society. In contrast to the bourgeoisie, the alleviation of its oppressed living conditions provided it with an immediate incentive to challenge existing arrangements but this in itself did not amount to an adequate class consciousness. As with all other immediate class perspectives, the spontaneous consciousness of the proletariat failed to disclose the essence of historical evolution. The antagonism between the immediate interests of the proletariat (which could be accommodated within the framework of existing bourgeois institutions) and its ultimate historical goal was disclosed only by a totalising perspective.[55] Immediate interests confined the proletariat to the economic struggle against the seemingly independent and lawful world of economic 'facts' which structures its lived oppression. On the other hand, class consciousness which related the proletariat's position to the totality of bourgeois society transfigured these 'facts', linking peripheral economic struggles as 'moments' of a process of historical movement which spilt over into political struggle positing socialism as its historical goal. This 'higher' standpoint required the proletariat to perceive the apparent disjointedness and autonomy of the separate spheres of bourgeois society and grasp their immanent historical tendency:

> Only when the immediate interests are integrated into a total view and related to the final goal of the process do they become revolutionary, pointing concretely and consciously beyond the confines of capitalist society.[56]

Despite the antagonism between the immediate interests and historical goal of the proletariat, Lukács saw a *developmental dynamic immanent* to its class consciousness. As with the bourgeoisie, he spoke of *the dialectical character of* the antagonisms inherent to these class perspectives. Like all previous hegemonic classes in history, the bourgeoisie was favoured by the compatibility between its *immediate interests and its ultimate leadership of society.* It needed only to assert its own interests to take charge. Its eventual decline was the outcome of an objective historical movement more than a consciously willed result. The great historical challenge for the proletariat *was the degree of conscious subjectivity* required for it to integrate its immediate interests and historical goal. The inherent dynamic posited here was not *a purely objective historical process but a real enhancement of conscious subjectivity.*[57]

Lukács clearly did not discount the significance of objective factors. In his essay 'Class Consciousness' he attributed an important role to objective factors in the disruption of normal bourgeois reified immediacy. The economic instability of the capitalist system which was manifest in periodic crisis impaired the normal, seemingly automatic, functioning of the market system. As a result of these fractures, which Lukács believed chronic, the appearance of capitalist self-regulation was exploded and the normally obscured connection between politics and economics exposed. Neverthelesss, the realisation of the radical possibilities latent in this unstable objective siutation depended upon *a subject factor: the historical maturity of the proletariat.*[58]

The Lukácsian analysis of empirical consciousness focused on an 'aspiration towards truth' expressed in the proletariat's suspicion of bourgeois 'immediacy'.[59] Material deprivation had led the proletariat to spontaneously question the justice of bourgeois relations. Such an 'aspiration towards the truth', however, only yielded the disposition towards a viewpoint transcending bourgeois society. The effective practical realisation of this possibility required the *translation of the disposition into knowledge and practical deeds.* Lukács repeatedly insisted that the required conscious subjectivity would not follow as an automatic product of immediate economic necessities and material interests. This essay, however, concluded with a call for the consideration of a *process of mediation* that would raise this 'aspiration towards the truth' to a realised class consciousness. This practical imperative implied an urgent task to avoid an imminent collapse into barbarism by transforming the opportunist reformism of the defeated worker's movement and therefore overcoming the objective crisis of capitalism.

Lukács' later 'Reification' essay returned to this latter problem apparently as an effort to clarify his own theoretical understanding of the concrete process. While this train of thought is again incomplete, it does amplify his ideas on the subjective dimension of the anticipated process that would raise the proletariat to a conscious, revolutionary subjectivity. The analysis is grounded in the Marxian theory of alienation. The capitalist system based on the sale of labour power reduced the individual worker to a mere object. Labour power was merely inserted where required into a rational, objective system of operations without the slightest concern for the personality to which it was bound. The system eliminated all sense of the worker's subjectivity reducing him/her to a 'cipher'.[60] Yet, Lukács maintained that the qualitative dimension of labour power could not be completely expunged. This was what distinguished labour power from the other materials consumed in production and allowed it to resist total reification. Commodity production actually introduced a radical split between the physical powers of the human being and its human subjectivity.[61] For Lukács, such a radical split was not confined to the experience of the proletariat but was a general feature of reified social experience in bourgeois society. Despite this, the bourgeoisie could sustain *the illusion of subjective agency* because the mechanisms of the market and commodity exhange engendered a belief in the effectivity of entrepreneurial decisions and free agency. By contrast, the 'brutal form' of the proletariat's alienation undercut all illusions regarding free agency. It required total subordination to objective requirements of the productive system and the minimalisation of consumption to the bare necessities of life.[62] The impact of this objective subordination was the creation of a split in the self-interpretation of the worker between residual elements of real subjective agency and degradation to the status of mere object.

Lukács argued that this minimal awareness of alienation was the foundation of a real resistance grounding the subsequent attainment of class consciousness:

> Corresponding to the objective concealment of the commodity form, there is a subjective element. This is the fact that while the process by which the worker is reified and becomes a commodity dehumanises him and cripples and atrophies his soul – as long as he does not consciously rebel against it – it remains true that precisely his humanity and his soul are not changed into commodities. He is able therefore to objectify himself against his existence while the man reified in the bureaucracy, for instance, is turned into a commodity, mechanised and reified in the only faculties that might enable him to rebel against reification.[63]

The proletariat's 'minimal subjectivity' acts as a rebellious core against a 'slavery without limits'. Yet, it is not quite clear as to what this 'minimal subjectivity' consists of? Commentators have sometimes interpreted Lukács' employment of the term 'humanity' as a recourse to the idea of 'anthropological limits' to total reification.[64]

While Lukács' own argument was not unambiguous on this point and his terminology aided confusions, there is fairly strong indirect textual evidence to counter such claims. His detailed summary of Marx's critique of Feuerbach indicates that he clearly rejected all forms of anthropological humanism.[65] He distinguishes Marx's humanism from all its predecessors by underlining its historical dimension: the idea of an *essentially historicised humanity evolving in the process of its own self-creation conditioned by concrete social totalities.*[66] This radically historicist conception of humanity greatly assists the construction of a consistent interpretation of Lukács' idea of the evolution of proletarian subjectivity.

In his critique of earlier humanism, Lukács argued that the unmediated opposition of abstract notions of the human to existing dehumanised bourgeois man only presented the problem 'in a confused form' and could 'not point the way to a solution'.[67] The real solution, he suggested:

> can only be discovered by seeing these two aspects [the human and the dehumanised] as they appear in the concrete and real process of capitalist development, namely inextricably bound up with a another: i.e. the categories of dialectics must be applied to man as the measure of all things in a manner that also includes simultaneously a complete description of the economic structure of bourgeois society and a correct knowledge of the present.[68]

Lukács' historicism supplies an interpretative key to his understanding of the proletariat's minimal subjectivity. Futhermore, the mentioned 'split' in proletarian experience between dehumanised object and posited subject becomes the basis of a truly historical dialectic of social transcendence towards enhanced forms of human subjectivity.

In depicting the specificity of commodity production, Lukács mentioned that the more organic forms of society posited labour as an immediate social category and fixed the producer as a subordinate, naturally given, social role. In striking contrast, capitalist society constructed the 'isolated individual' whose work had no immediate social significance.[69] This new individual was formally a free, universal subject of choice, responsibility and contract, while, at the same time, reduced by the division of labour to the position of an 'animate object'. *Posited as an abstract, general human subject, this subjectivity was denied by the actual conditions and requirements of the productive system.* Lukács viewed this historically determinate 'split' between *objectively posited abstract subjectivity and objective social function as the historical source of the 'self-consciousness of the commodity'*. It generated an ongoing, immanent process of self-recognition finally leading to the penetration of the reified structures of capitalist society.

Lukács' own analysis only followed the historical development of the proletariat as far as the formation of trade union consciousness. He clearly anticipated, however, that this would lead on to further stages of maturing political consciousness. But the question of the concrete mediations in this anticipated process remain unanswered. In the final analysis, he merely posited the proletariat as the potential bearer of the totalising perspective and underscored the *practical necessity of precipitating this decisive cognitive step*. In this regard, his theoretical recourse to the Leninist Party as a vanguard of the movement is especially disquieting. The Leninist Party fills a role that Lukács was troubled to fill. The explanation of this difficulty and the resulting important lacuna in his account of the dialectic of proletarian consciousness must be sought in the logic of Lukács' own analysis.

The reconstruction of the contradictory dynamic in the proletariat's objective situation provided an impressive immanent explanation of the motor of this development. It supplied a theory of motivation that did not rely solely on objective economic factors. The 'split' in the proletariat's lived experience fuelled the working-class struggle for political rights and a share of bourgeois material prosperity. Yet, the very plausibility of this account told against it as an explanation of the process of acquiring a revolutionary consciousness.

The crux of this dynamic was a struggle against deprivation and the worse excesses of alienation. In large measure, however, these prizes had already been won for a significant segment of the proletariat by trade unionism. In other words, *the very process which enlightened proletarian consciousness inevitably also diminished the causes that motivated the initial struggles.* Since Marx's death, trade union successes and the extension of their educational and cultural activities had provided an arena for the real expression of the proletariat's repressed subjectivity. In so far as Lukács envisaged the transformation of bourgeois society in terms of a revolutionary political cataclysm, the actual historical dialectic of proletarian consciousness appeared to have stopped short. In acquiring some of the trappings of bourgeois subjectivity, the edge had been taken off the motivation towards radical transcendence, towards class consciousness.

Lukács never really comprehended the degree of working-class accommodation to existing bourgeois society nor the limitations of his own theoretical argument. This is partially understandable. The perilous state of economic collapse and widespread working-class unrest after the First World War revitalised the belief that bourgeois society could not provide the conditions nor fulfil the demands required by the proletariat.

The absence of a theoretical solution to this problem of mediations precipitated the most notorious feature of <u>History and Class Consciousnes</u>. Having established the command of reification over proletarian consciousness and the short-term horizon of its immediate interests, Lukács clearly found it impossible to resist the temptation to posit the revolutionary Communist Party as a catalyst and practical instrument in faciliating the overcoming of these considerable obstacles to class consciousness. The Bolsheviks were a plausible candidate for this role. Convinced of the authenticity of the Russian Revolution, if initially critical of the Bolsheviks' activities within the Comintern,[70] Lukács nominated the party as the practical bearer of imputed class consciousness. The party apparatus was theoretically stipulated as the proletariat's guide to the assumption of its historical role.[71] The essay 'Towards a Methodology of the Problem of Organisation', which articulates this final standpoint, was written in late 1922 and undoubtedly reflects the unfavourable drift in the objective historical situation and to revolutionary prospects. Lukács' wholehearted adoption of the Leninist theory of the party reflected the failure of recent strategies premised on worker spontaneity and his growing awareness of the 'ideological crisis' facing the working class movement.

The details of Lukács' theory of the party and its internal inconsistencies cannot be dealt with here.[72] However, his depiction of the Communist Party bears a remarkable resemblance to his pre-Marxist ideal of totality only in a microcosmic form. He talks about the elimination of egoistic individualism, the total personality, self-discipline, positive freedom and the re-activation of individual praxis as exemplary features of the party organisation and ethic. This ideal of the party anticipates the overcoming of reification and marks the party as an authentic model of the future. While this ideal image has critical dimensions,[73] it functioned indirectly as an apology for the Bolshevisation of all the Communist parties attached to the Comintern. As the prospects of revolution dimmed, Lukács' view of the Russian Party took on mythological proportions.

Revolutionary faith in the party replaced a careful sociological analysis of the contemporary proletariat and its empirical existence.

The overcoming of reification

This lapse into a mythology of the Communist Party might be passed over as a failure of political judgment were it not for the fact that it is constitutive of the very theoretical core of History and Class Consciousness. It is an index of deep theoretical tensions running through Lukács' project.

This project centred around the problem of reification and its overcoming. This was at the heart of the contemporary 'ideological crisis' which Lukács hoped to avert with his theory of totality. There was, however, a real ambiguity in his theorisation of the problem of reification. He himself later drew attention to this difficulty in explaining the shortcomings of his early, most famous, work. In the 1967 Introduction to a new edition, he pointed to a Hegelian confusion in the work between the categories of objectification and alienation. Echoing Marx's early Hegel critique, he claimed that his depiction of the proletariat as the identical subject/object of history was a relapse into idealism.[74] While this self-criticism is exaggerated[75] it is not without substance. Sometimes the Lukácsian concept of reification appears to encompass all manner of functional relations between men. It becomes difficult to envisage what *unreified, socially emancipatory social activity could mean.* The only candidate seems to be free artistic creation. Márkus argues that this utopian idea of emancipated praxis had less to do with an idealist distaste for material activity than with Lukács' messianic vision of the socialist future.[76] Yet, his employment of the Hegelian framework to express his utopian vision – thus conflating the ideas of objectification and alienation – made it impossible for him to clearly articulate *the necessary limitations on human freedom.*

Clearly, Lukács' theory of historical totalisation presupposes reification as *an ineradicable moment of all human praxis.* Unfortunately, the conceptual framework of History and Class Consciousness denied him the means to designate a distinction between these inescapable aspects of historical objectification that could be 'pushed back' but never eliminated and those created by specific social arrangements that could be abolished. While he did consider 'rationalisation' one of the principal indices of de-humanisation in capitalist society, his retention of the idea of rational planning as a crucial element of the future socialist economy is proof that he never seriously entertained that idea of eliminating *all forms of reification.* His recourse to a modified version of the Hegelian identical subject/object simply denied him the possibility of addressing the question of non-reified interchange between man and nature. He was, therefore, unable to circumscribe the limits imposed on free, rational praxis by human finitude and objective being.

This conceptual ambiguity had a decisive impact on the final shape of his concept of totality. His depiction of history betrays a finalistic, Hegelian residue. Proletarian revolution is transformed into a metaphysical act upon which the meaningfulness of the whole of history depends. This is despite the very real contrary tendency which remained the main force behind his reconstruction of the concept of totality; this tendency posited 'totality' as a *present totalisation from the viewpoint of a particular limited future perspective perceived as the solution of a practically imposed 'historical task'*. The residual Hegelianism transformed this emancipatory concept of history into that of a *closed totality. No longer a practical resolution of present-day antinomies enlightened by a contemporary conspectus of the whole past leaving the future open to free, always revocable collective decisions, socialism now signified a millenial end of history.*

Such philosophical mythology was clearly a theoretical substitute for the anticipated process of mediations projected by Lukács. The designation of the proletariat as the metaphysical subject of history added philosophical support to the concrete historical dynamic of which he was convinced. The idea of imputed class consciousness was also clearly a product of philosophy mythology. It was nothing more than an intellectual projection reflecting Lukacs' revolutionary aspirations.[77] This theoretical abstraction was imposed on proletarian consciousness rather than expressing its real needs and concrete aspirations. Here again the *practical*, open-ended pole of Lukács' idea of totalisation concerned with promoting free, provisional praxis is swamped by the other *theoreticist* pole which construed totality as a closed theoretical truth to be bestowed on the oppressed class.

There is a real irony in this theoretical fiasco. Lukács had strong reasons for believing that he had freed his Hegelian ideas from mythology. The proletariat was not a *Geist*. It was an empirical, sociological reality possessed of at least the *potential* to become both the subject and object of its own praxis. He had also restricted his application of dialectics to the socio-historical realm. This clearly indicated his distrust of the metaphysical connotations of the framework. Yet, the mere positing of this theoretical identity with an exploited social class without analysis of its empirical existence and without being able to show concretely the mediations of its historical realisation was hardly adequate to avoid past errors.[78]

The historical conjuncture that sustained Lukács' historical optimism and his delicate theoretical equation dissipated as quickly as it arose. The next generation of leftist intellectuals faced a much more sobering historical situation. The fragmentation of the workers movement, the rise of Fascism and the economic collapse of the late 1920s. Although Lukács' work exercised a considerable influence on the members of the Frankfurt Institute of Social Research, a drastically changed historical situation compelled them to an increasingly more radical critique of his concept of totality.

The crisis of enlightenment: Horkheimer and Adorno against an administered totality

The Institute for Social Research was originally established in 1923 at Frankfurt. But the period and programme from which it derives its contemporary fame began when Max Horkheimer assumed its headship in 1931. From this time the Institute attracted a number of talented young theorists including Fredrich Pollock, Eric Fromm, Leo Lowenthal, Theodor Adorno, Walter Benjamin and Herbert Marcuse, who contributed to the Institute's journal and helped define the shape of what became known as critical theory. The following discussion is devoted to Horkheimer and Adorno who are justly recognised as the principal architects of this unique theoretical approach. Horkheimer laid down the novel inter-disciplinary research programme and wrote the essays which came to be regarded as the definitive formulation of this new critical social theory. From the time of his emigration to the United States in 1938, Adorno exercised a growing influence over the direction of the Institute's work. In collaboration with Horkheimer, he reshaped the Institute's philosophical perspective away from the more orthodox Marxian critique of political economy towards the radical position articulated in the jointly written Dialectic of Enlightenment and subsequently assumed the headship of the Institute after Horkheimer's retirement due to ill health.

While Lukács' History and Class Consciousness had no practical impact on the European Communist movement and was quite severely criticised by the Bolshevik leaders of the Comintern, it did influence the young intellectuals who became the core of the Institute. This chapter will consider both that influence and the subsequent direction of critical theory. Initially, it will focus on the Institute's reception of Lukács and especially Horkheimer's and Adorno's individual critiques of his concept of totality. Taking into account the dynamic character of critical theory as a response to the rapidly deteriorating historical situation, the exposition will distinguish two distinct phases. Although this strategy involves some simplification of the earlier period and some homogenisation of these thinkers' post-war thought,[1] it facilitates a manageable overview concentrating on the major question of the Institute's appropriation and critique of the concept of totality.

The new historical conjuncture

As surely as Lukács' thought was determined by the revolutionary prospects and messianic hopes of communists in the early 1920s, so too, critical theory was shaped by the evaporation of these conditions and the onset of the great crisis of European social and political life that emerged with the world depression and the rise of Fascism. Adorno alluded to this decisive extra-theoretical determinant of critical theory in the aphorism which opens Negative Dialectics: 'Philosophy which once seemed obsolete. lives on because the moment to realise it was missed'.[2] The failure of a socialist revolution in western Europe was perhaps the major ingredient in the development of critical theory.

This historical judgment was very much in the balance when Horkheimer began the reflections which were to lead him to the proposal for a new type of theory. Despite growing doubts and suspicions regarding the capacities of the fractured German working class and the authenticity of the Russian Revolution,[3] Horkheimer hoped that disunity could be overcome and give way to socialism. Yet, it was this deteriorating climate and the problems it raised for Marxist orthodoxies that were encapsulated in his early work. This drastically changed historical perspective is clearly one major difference separating his standpoint from Lukács'.

Horkheimer's first analysis of the contemporary worker's movement manifests this change. He rejected Lukács' hypostasisation of the proletariat as the identical subject/object of history to concentrate on its current empirical condition. He was particularly troubled by the increasingly obvious split which divided the workers into two distinct groups. Employed workers were relatively secure and reluctant to endanger their recently won stake in bourgeois society. They were educated and organised but lacked the essential motivation to challenge the existing order or embark on a revolutionary political course.[4] In stark contrast, the chronically unemployed clearly had an objective interest in radical social change but were unable to press their demands. They lacked education, organisation and a class consciousness that would provide theoretical understanding of the fundamental causes of their condition.[5] On the basis of this sociological characterisation Horkheimer maintained that within the contemporary proletariat radical motivation had become divorced from the capacities and resources required to actualise revolution. He argued further that this sociological split was reflected in the political fragmentation of the working class between reformist social democracy and a dogmatic Communist Party. The more moderate employed workers were generally aligned to reformism. The social democrats were integrated into bourgeois politics. They appreciated the complexity of the real world but had lost the radical will to change it. Furthermore, they subordinated theory to pragmatism. The Communists, who typically represented the interests of the chronically unemployed, sustained a revolutionary spirit only by discarding realistic political analysis and retreating to canonised theoretical authorities in the blind conviction that they somehow already possessed the truth.[6] Horkheimer castigated both political factions. The social democrats acquiesed to reified bourgeois social conditions while the Communists refused to face empirical realities.[7]

This scathing diagnosis of the contemporary divisions vitiating the workers' movement clearly shaped Horkheimer's understanding of the character and role of critical theory. His critique of the existing workers' parties suggested the need to disassociate critical theory from any direct links to either of the competing parties who had drained the political strength from the socialist movement. *As a corrective to the failings of both wings of the workers movement, theory had to remain independent.* While Horkheimer was profoundly influenced by Lukács' general reconstruction of Marxist theory, his position was distinguished from that of History and Class Consciousness by this basic questioning of Lukács' posited unity of theory and praxis. He had *designated Marxist theory as the self-consciousness of the proletariat* and, in turn, *identified the Communist Party as the concrete bearer of this theoretical perspective.* In view of the contemporary fracture of the proletariat and the failings of its main parties, Horkheimer was reluctant to sacrifice the independence of critical theory by aligning it directly to any political organisation. This was a largely implicit critique of Lukács restricted to the problematic political consequences of his theory. It did, however, indicate *a critical turn.* In the more thoroughgoing analyses of the programmatic essays, he critically explored other dimensions of the Lukácsian concept of totality.

A materialist attack on metaphysics

Horkheimer's early study 'Hegel and the Problem of Metaphysics' provides some insights into the broader philosophical stance which underpinned the first version of critical theory. The chief burden of this short essay was an attack on the Hegelian speculative identity between subject and object. While Hegel attempted to transcend metaphysics, this element of his thought involved a relapse into metaphysical thinking.[8] Horkheimer argued that the idealist identity of subject and object was 'a mere faith' resulting from the abstraction of thought from its concrete, total social situation.[9]

He rejected the idea of a 'total' systematic philosophical science capable of eliminating the discrepancy between rational concepts and real events. This naturally implied a repudiation of the Hegelian idea of the totality of history. In Horkheimer's view, 'total' systematicity and philosophy of history were metaphysical residues betraying a failed abstraction. A truly materialist theory as both practical and historical was simply incompatible with the idealist principle of identity. Critical materialism required the opposite principle of non-identity. Here he initiated a theme echoed by Adorno and increasingly central to their later collective efforts.

Alfred Schmidt credits Schopenhauer's pessimistic materialism with an important role in alerting the young Horkheimer to the shortcomings of classical metaphysics. This philosophical sympathy prompted Horkheimer's move to employ the category of nature *as a corrective and counter-balance* to the abstract idealist claim to identity and totality. This category provided a *limiting function defining the boundaries of human theoretical knowledge.* Horkheimer insisted that even with the growth of science and the extension of technical mastery over nature these boundaries would never completely disappear. Futhermore, the category of nature also evoked the material-corporeal foundation of the human species. Even the great advances of modern medical science and the future prospect of the elimination of socially unnecessary distress would not extinguish questions of human physical suffering and finitude. On both these counts, he defended a materialist emphasis on non-identity.

The emphases in this critique highlight Horkheimer's very discriminating appropriation of classsical idealism. Lukács' messianic hopes encouraged him to view the proletariat as the concrete instantiation of Hegel's identical subject/object. Even while he discarded the idealism permeating this theoretical framework, this distantiation *never amounted to a rigorous settling of accounts with the framework itself.* This failing explains his exaggeration of the idea of nature as 'social category' which created insuperable difficulties in articulating dimensions of the nature concept denoting something pre-existing and independent of man. Of course, Horkheimer followed Lukács in insisting that nature was always a social category, always conditioned by specific social significations and transformed by specific social practices. Yet, he qualified this idea by underlining the residual significance of the concept both as *potentiality* and *limit* on the social meanings historically ascribed to it. Like the young Marx, Horkheimer refused to ignored the biological restraints on human possibilities and the centrality of nature as the permanent arena and irreducible pre-condition of human activity. Recognition of these residual, albeit crucial, dimensions of the concept of nature precluded accepting the identity of subject and object, concept and being. Even the overcoming of reification and the establishment of a socialist realm of freedom would not change these residual significances.[10]

Non-identity was a crucial element of the early Horkheimer's espousal of materialism but not its principal meaning. He maintained that materialism could be defined neither solely in terms of general principles nor as an alternative metaphysical answer to the interpretation of ultimate being:

Materialism is not interested in a worldview or in the souls of men. It is concerned with changing the concrete conditions under which men suffer and, in which, of course, their souls must become stunted.[11]

The old type of metaphysical materialism affirmed the primacy of matter. Against this, Horkheimer conceived materialism as a *practical doctrine whose object and tenets changed over the course of history in response to the most urgent practical tasks.*

This practically orientated materialism repudiated the meaningfulness of ultimate metaphysical questions for practical action. According to Horkheimer, the quest for 'totality', for the 'enigma of being' relied on false assumptions.[12] It implied the possibility of discovering ultimate essences, supra-historical values and norms which could serve as an unchanging orientation for practical action. Moreover, it supposed that knowledge was eternally valid and autonomous from the ongoing processes of social evolution. Horkheimer emphatically rejected both these claims. These ideological views had to be undermined by exposing *the intimate relation between knowledge and social praxis.*[13] This was the contemporary task of materialism. To expose the social interests underlying all metaphysical systems and reveal both their transience and historically conditioned character.

Once theory was seen as conditioned by a whole range of socio-historical practices, the absolute knowledge sought by the metaphysicians was recognised as unattainable. This conditioning, including the interests of powerful social groups, meant that theory was always partial and relative.[14] It would be a mistake, however, to confuse Horkheimer's ideas with those of the sociology of knowledge. Deeply impressed by Lukács, Karl Mannheim at this time also argued for the historical relativisation of all worldviews and the appreciation of their ideological character.[15] While Horkheimer renounced any implicit standard of pure objectivity and acknowledged socio-historical distortions in the evolution of knowledge, he also insisted on the discovery of the objective basis of all knowledges and the recognition of their partial truth. Here he conceded Hegel's positive contribution to the tradition of practical materialism:

> Recognition of the conditional character of every isolated view and the rejection of its absolute claim to truth does not destroy this conditional knowledge; rather, it is incorporated into the system of truth at any given time as a conditioned, one-sided and isolated view. Through nothing but this continuous delimitation and correction of partial truths, the process itself evolves its proper content as knowledge of limited insights in their limit and connection.[16]

Hegel thought that this process of corrective transcendence culminated in Absolute knowledge: a totalised system. Critical theory exposed the illusory character of this supposition. Horkheimer underlined the need to recognise the traces of subjectivity in its own concept formation. But this did not mean that knowledge and object were one nor that the object would one day be distinguished with perfect clarity.[17]

The idea of non-identity signified for Horkheimer an *irreducible and indispensible tension* between concepts and their objects . As an untranscendable condition of human knowledge, this tension implied both a *progressive impetus* and an *'infinite task'* in efforts to theoretically approximate historically evolving objectivity. The practical character of critical theory is most clearly illuminated in this provisional, historical view of knowledge. In the changing circumstances and evolving perspectives of history, the acquisition of knowledge was never exhausted and remained open-ended. The ideal of a 'final truth' had to be dispensed with. Knowledge required a practical orientation concerned to achieve concrete improvements and grasp the essence of the real forces tending in this direction.

Having abandoned the aspiration to the Absolute, the contemporary task of philosophy was more modest. Recognition of the tension between concept and object strengthened Horkheimer's conviction that the full spectrum of empirical studies were needed in the research programme of critical theory. Philosophy would have a *critical role*, informing empirical research of its concealed socio-historical assumptions. It would reinforce the point that the process of knowledge acquisition remained provisional, constituting 'truth' only within the limits of a consciousness aware of its own historical conditionedness. This role meshed neatly with the overall aim of an inter-disciplinary critical theory those goal was *the mutual enrichment of critical philosophy and empirical research both to the end of radical social change.*

A materialist concept of totality

Horkheimer's thorough critique of its metaphysical residues never amounted to a repudiation of the concept of totality. A *modified concept of totality was crucial to his idea of materialist critique.* However, it needed to conform with a theoretical conception that underlined *the historicity of all knowledge,* that entertained the possibility of *radically changing future perspectives* and even contemplated *its own historical limits.* These requirements are captured in one of Horkheimer's early aphorisms:

> To all those who are primarily concerned with the unhampered
> development of human potential and of justice, these classes [here
> Horkheimer refers to social classes and Marxist theory as class theory]
> must appear as the decisive structural principle of our time, for the
> realisation of such goals depends on their elimination. There are other
> differences, other structural principles which, given the same interest in
> the free development of men and justice, may appear as fundamental as
> social classes. The difference between the sick and the healthy would be
> an example.[18]

Horkheimer argues that the principle of social classes is *practically decisive in the contemporary epoch* owing to the centrality of social contradictions and their impact on other existing antitheses.[19] However, this priority was practical, not trans-historical.

This awareness of the historical limits of Marxist theory compelled Horkheimer to significantly modify inherited formulations of the concept of totality. Critical theory 'constructs a developing picture of society as a whole, an existential judgement with a historical dimension'.[20] Such a conception required sufficient flexibility to accommodate new historical developments within the capitalist world without requiring a shift to a wholly new perspective. It was derived from the pattern of recurrent events and relations which constituted a self-reproducing totality.[21] While the underlying structure persisted without radical transformation its *theorised concept retained an epochal significance*:

> The stability of the theory is due to the fact that amid all change in society the basic economic structure, the class relationship in its simplest form, and therefore the idea of the supersession of these two remain identical. The decisive substantive elements in the theory are conditioned by these unchanging factors and they themselves therefore cannot change until there has been a historical transformation of society. On the other hand, however, history does not stand still until such a point of transformation has been reached. The historical development of the conflicts in which the critical theory is involved leads to a reassignment of degrees of relative importance to individual elements of the theory, forces further concretisations, and determines which results of specialised science are to be significant for critical theory and practice at any given time.[22]

This formulation reveals the key features of Horkheimer's new understanding of the concept of totality. The materialist emphasis is exemplified in the practical demand to respond to changed circumstance and to incorporate the special sciences as an auxiliary aid in the programme of conceptual re-adjustment. As well, he stresses the non-ontological status of theory. Class theory may have an epochal significance but its horizon has now receded from 'universal history'. Practical orientation means that the concept frames *only the present possibilities of the existing society understood as an epochal self-reproducing system of social relations*.

Linked to this conscious retreat from the Lukácsian idea of universal history, Horkheimer undertook a revision of his concept of progress. Lukács had perservered with an *objectivist, albeit anticipatory, idea of progress*. Like Marx, he viewed capitalism with all its flaws and oppression as an objective advance over all previous societies: it had greatly enhanced human productive forces and created the material conditions for the possible realisation of a socialist society. The actualisation of the Hegelian identical subject/object provided a dynamic historical perspective which served both as the culmination of universal history and as a standpoint which allowed the objective measurement of historical development. Horkheimer viewed this clear-cut objectivism as an apology for the invariant historical spectacle of human suffering.

In an aphorism entitled simply 'Progress' he outlined the only meaning the notion could have for socialists in the present historical situation. Dismissing reactionary efforts to deny progress, he continued:

As if it weren't perfectly obvious what progress the socialist mean, what progress the reactionaries resist, both theoretically and in practice. It is the improvement of material existence through a more purposeful restructuring of human conditions. It can be said emphatically that this improvement means more for most people than the implementation of a relatively accidental value, whether they know it or not. To them, it is the most important thing on earth.[23]

This is clearly a qualified defence betraying Horkheimer's disquiet with all blasé affirmations of contemporary progress. He stands firmly by the *practical meaning of the concept* – the improvement in the material conditions of the working masses as a result of developing productive forces in the present, and especially, the socialist future – despite his opposition to any thought that such progress was *historically necesssary or that it be used to justify past and present human suffering.*

The latter theme was reformulated in another striking passage:

That history has realised a better society out of one less good, that it can realise a still better one in its course is a fact. However, it is another fact that the path of history leads over the suffering and poverty of individuals. Between both these facts there is a series of explanatory connections but no justifying meaning.[24]

The critical tone struck here becomes more strident as Horkheimer's hopes for radical social change disappeared. He reiterated Burckhardtian pessimism deflating the idea of rational progress as some sort of 'mystical necessity'. Progress was *possible but not historically determined. Nor could progress compensate for the suffering of past generations.*[25] Social progress was to be perceived *as a historical task.* The idea was abused when dogmatically asserted to justify present suffering as a 'necessary cost' of actions intended to promote better conditions in the future. The crux of Horkheimer's critique of progress was his rejection of an *objective calculus of suffering and improvement.* Historical progress could be asserted *only on the basis of a particular hierarchy of values*; this was never *absolute progress nor could it provide amends for incaluable pain and loss.*

Horkheimer's critique of progress fused his materialist pessimism with a Kantian ethics. Kantian elements were already apparent in his view of nature as a 'limiting category' serving to restrict the metaphysical excesses of idealism. Another Kantian idea enters here with the view that human intentions ought not be submitted to a utilitarian calculus. Individuals are ends in themselves and not to be reduced to expendable means in pursuit of external, 'higher' purposes. Even Lukács' efforts to stress the *contradictory character of historical progress* had not, as far as Horkheimer was concerned, rescued the apologetic objectivist concept which legitimated past and present human suffering as the '*unavoidable cost*' of future harmony.

Critique of imputed class consciousness

Horkheimer's critique of objectivism extended to the notion of imputed class consciousness. This was already foreshadowed in his analysis of the contemporary fragmentation of the proletariat and his distantiation of critical theory from direct party allegiance. In theoretical terms, Horkheimer simply disassociated critical theory from Lukács' *ontologisation of class consciousness*. Although Lukács viewed imputed class consciousness as a *theoretical construct*, he had described theory as the *self consciousness of the proletariat*. Consistent with his desire to eliminate quasi-metaphysical philosophical hypostatisation from critical theory, Horkheimer refused to transform a *methodological ideal into a historical entity*.

Horkheimer was here concerned particularly with a more mediated understanding of the unity of theory and praxis. He continued to uphold this maxim and Lukács' practical orientation of theory towards a revolutionary goal but wanted to *rescue critical intellectuals' theoretical autonomy from the sociological forces Lukács had deemed them to be representing.* He retained the idea that the proletariat was the *posited addressee* of critical theory, however, dismissed its Lukácsian identification as also *the subject of the theory*. He no longer conceived theory as the adequate class consciousness of the proletariat. Rather, it was a *cultural product determined by the contradiction between material conditions and the cultural complex of ideals and norms to which society had given rise but not yet fulfilled.* Historicising this cultural complex, Horkheimer argued that this contradiction was articulated according to the *historically specific standards of knowledge pertaining to the sphere of theory as a cultural formation*.

This mediated understanding of the unity of theory and praxis explicitly opposed the idea that the proletariat's sociological situation guaranteed correct knowledge.[26] It also repudiated Lukács' identification between the stance of the Communist Party and correct theory.[27] While theory was a cultural product conditioned *by a practical concern and extra-theoretical interests, it could not be reduced to class consciousness.* Horkheimer insisted that class consciousness remain a real empirical life praxis and political activity. Critical theory, he claimed, was neither 'detached' like the liberal intelligentsia nor 'deeply rooted' like totalitarian propaganda. It was located in a process of *interaction and dynamic tension* with advanced sectors of the workers and the rest of the class.[28] Combining cultural autonomy and *engagément*, critical theory was a *totalising theoretical construct*, open and responsive to historical change but forged from the standpoint of a possible future of contemporary society. As a consequence of this *engagéd* autonomy, the theorist was the spokesperson of a *self-reflexive truth* unafraid to criticise utopian tendencies amongst the workers or the ideologists of the status quo.[29]

Close analysis of Horkheimer's revision of the theory/praxis relation reveals that he had not really disposed of the problem underlying Lukács' theory. He had drawn attention to a serious difficulty in attempting to eliminate the unacknowledged hypostatisation of class consciousness. However, the distinction between empirical consciousness and a totalising perspective was still crucial to Horkheimer's own view. While rejecting Lukács' extreme identification of theory with a not yet constituted historical subjectivity, he also wanted to avoid the reduction of theory to the level of empirical consciousness. Critical theory never pretended to listen to the real needs of the workers as expressed in the Institute's own early empirical studies but, in line with its own revolutionary aspirations, bemoaned the pervasiveness of the authoritarian character structure.[30] This was a strategic response to current political exigencies and the inadequacies of Lukács' position but one not without difficulties of its own. It blunted critical theory's initial empirical orientation and encouraged a mood of cultural pessimism. Finally, it also opened up a potentially decisive theoretical lacuna: namely, how to ground critical theory?

The importance of this question can be gauged from the theoretical role played by imputed class consciousness in Lukács. In <u>History and Class Consciousness</u> it served as an *immanent measure of history*. The party as its actual custodian and its potential bearer, the proletariat, were both accorded an epistemological privilege. The perspective of totality facilitated the penetration of reified appearances hastening the acquisition of conscious subjectivity. Horkheimer desired to detach the practical efficacy of the totalising standpoint from identification with the view of the Communist Party. Yet, he still endorsed the validity of the perspective:

> Critical theory has a dialectical function of measuring every historical
> stage in the light not only of isolated data and concepts but of its primary
> and total content, and of being concerned that this content is virtually
> operative.[31]

How did Horkheimer propose to validate this epistemological privilege remembering that he had renounced the idea of total knowledge and underlined the historically conditioned character of critical theory?

It should be recalled that Lukács tied questions of 'truth' and historical objectivity to praxis. Inseparable from question of historical realisation, his concept of truth possessed a *real open-ended dimension* in tension with the Hegelian theoretical framework. This framework ultimately imposed an ontological-historical imprimatur on his version of truth despite his own intentions. History signified the rational unfolding of truth and this was theoretically confirmed by the designation of the proletatriat as the identical subject/object of history.

Although discarding the metaphysical assumptions behind the Lukácsian framework, Horkheimer remained convinced that the critique of political economy comprehended the essential core relations and structures of capitalist society. This insight bestowed upon the theory its epochal significance and validity. Nevertheless, Horkheimer's qualifications betrayed this conscious weakening of these claims:

> There are no general criteria for judging the critical theory as a whole, for it is always based on the recurrence of events and thus on a self-repro-ducing totality. Nor is there a social class by whose acceptance of the theory one could be guided. It is possible for the consciousness of every social stratum today to be limited and corrupted by ideology, however much, for its circumstances, it may be bent on truth. For all its insights into the individual steps in social change and for all the agreement of its elements with the most advanced traditional theories, the critical theory has no specific influence on its side, except concern for the abolition of social injustice. This negative formulation, if we wish to express it abstractly, is the materialist content of the idealist concept of reason.[32]

In this conception, truth does not mean correspondence with an unjust world nor is it a property of propositions but a practical attitude concerned with a radical transformation of this society. The emphasis on a 'concern for the abolition of social injustice' registers Horkheimer's ethical interpretation of this perspective. Marxism is primarily an 'existential judgment' on the contemporary capitalist world.[33]

By the late 1930s, however, the further deterioration of the historical situation, the complete defeat of the European workers' movement and the emigration of a whole generation of leftist intellectuals from Germany decreed a more pessimistic assessment of the historical forces working in favour of this radical transformation. No longer able to rely on objective historical forces, critical theorists decided to redouble their critical disposition. Horkheimer declined the retreat to transcendental foundations for his own critical stance despite a general sympathy for Kant and his theoretical modesty. While he occasionally spoke in anthropological terms such as an 'idea of a reasonable organisation of society' 'immanent in work',[34] he more generally sought a concrete source of critical values. This preference is explicable in terms of his antagonism to contemporary philosophical anthropology in Scheler's existentialist variant, and more positively, in his allegiance to the *programme of immanent historical self-critique*. This programme dictated that critical values were to be sought only in the *concrete contradictions and suffering emanating from existing capitalist society*.

The idea of immanent critique was a central principle of Horkheimer's critical theory. It was articulated most clearly in his notion of ideology critique. The claims of bourgeois ideology were contradicted by their material negation or non-fulfilment. These contradictions were a ready source of concrete values orientated to the critique of the present:

> To show the contradiction between the principle on which bourgeois
> society was founded and the actual reality of that society involves
> bringing out how justice was onesidedly defined in terms of freedom and
> freedom in terms of negation, and substituting a positive conception of
> justice by offering a groundplan for a reasonable society.[35]

Horkheimer proposed to derive the critical values which were to serve as the
foundation of critical theory from the immanent historical conflicts and
contradictions of contemporary capitalist society. The mere existence of *mass
misery and deprivation indicated deficiencies in capitalist society and served
as the basis for formulating negative values providing a critical, orientating
function.*

This attempt to sustain an immanent critique deprived of Hegelian
presuppositions guaranteeing an absolute historico-ontological objectivity was
not without difficulties.[36] The need to modify critical theory in response to
worsening historical conditions, however, soon clearly dwarfed these
unresolved theoretical questions. In fact, the re-interpretation of critical theory
represented by <u>Dialectic of Enlightenment</u>, co-written with Adorno, involved
many revisions and a fundamental reversal of Horkheimer's early cautious
endorsement of the concept of totality.

Adorno's early philosophical programme

The radical modification of Horkheimer's initial understanding of critical theory
was not simply the result of tragic historical experience. Certainly the drastic
change of perspective was influenced by the historical convergence of events
including the failure of socialist revolution in the west, the triumph of
authoritarian Fascist regimes in Germany and Italy, the ossification of the
Russian Revolution and the first-hand experience of capitalist stabilisation with
the New Deal. However, it was only an intense period of collaboration after
Adorno's arrival in the United States in 1938 that crystallised the new
uncompromising reappraisal of historical development and existing
authoritarianisms including 'state capitalism'. The significance of Adorno's
contribution to <u>Dialectic of Enlightenment</u> can be gauged by a brief analysis of
his early ideas.

Prior to his emigration Adorno had already contributed to the Institute's
work. Already in the early 1930s his essays on popular culture and musicology
were published in the Institute's *Zeitschrift für Sozialforschung*. At this time he
was also developing an original philosophical perspective and programme in
unpublished lectures and papers. Many of these ideas reappeared in the
collaborative work with Horkheimer.

In the very beginning of his lecture 'The Actuality of Philosophy' (1931)
Adorno rejected the traditional view of philosophy as an attempt to 'grasp the

totality of the real'.[37] He maintained that all attempts since Descartes to generate this totality as a product of autonomous reason had failed. The first part of his analysis surveyed the contemporary philosophical spectrum indicating the aporias which had engulfed all efforts to surmount the difficulties encountered by the traditional search for essential truth and unified meaning. Adorno's starting-point was the diagnosis put forward in Lukács' Theory of the Novel. When experience itself no longer provided an immediately meaningful totality, philosophy could not simply reassert an obsolete meaning. The attempt to discover a rational meaning in a fragmented and contradictory reality would lapse into ideological apologetics. Adorno charged that the present social order was contradictory and suppressed 'every claim to reason'.[38]

He also agreed with Horkheimer in rejecting Lukács' equation of truth with the universal historical process. Lukács perpetrated the idealist error of imposing rational categories on irrational concrete history. This alleged failing of 'identity thinking' was to increasingly become the object of Adorno's philosophical critique. 'Identity thinking' was a product of reification. It was a mode of thought which operated on the principle of making unlike things alike. To commit the mistake of equating the real with rational concepts, with abstract universals, involved the same error as that of bourgeois political economy. It assumed the reality of universal exchange which abstracted from the differential concrete labours and uses lying at its base. Similarly, to perceive history in Hegelian, rationalistic terms was to gloss over lived material suffering as a mere contingency.

Despite similar themes and objects, there is a noticeable difference of philosophical emphasis between Horkheimer and Adorno at this pre-collaboration stage. Inspired by materialist and Kantian influences, Horkheimer's scepticism was a response to the idealist suppression of the category of nature, the extravagant claim to total knowledge and the transcendence of concrete, contemporary issues. While Adorno shared all these concerns, his own critique focused on the *ideological character of the implied totality concept and his aim was to expose the reified perspective behind it.*

Clearly, this was the reason why Adorno relied so much on Theory of the Novel. His critique of reified history in 'The Idea of Natural History' (1932) reveals this debt to Lukács. There he explored the Lukácsian concept of 'second nature'. It will be remembered that Lukács viewed the world of everyday bourgeois convention as an oppressive sphere of alienation. It was familiar but rigid and stifled immediate aspirations. In other words, it appeared as a 'second nature'. While Adorno credited Lukács with the discovery of the phenomenon of reification – the apparent necessity of this *socially constructed nature* – he had provided no way of deciphering it.[39] According to Adorno, it was the work of his friend Walter Benjamin which offered this key to the problem of reification. Benjamin had drawn the resurrection of second nature 'out of the infinite distance into the infinite closeness and made it an object of philosophical interpretation'.[40]

Benjamin's ideas mediated Adorno's reception of Lukács. The Origin of German Tragic Drama (1928) provided Adorno with an alternative *anti-Hegelian conception of history*. In Benjamin's analysis of seventeenth century *Trauerspiel* he found a key to historical interpretation employable as a corrective to Hegel's idealist assertion of historical progress.[41] Benjamin deciphered the masks and emblems of death prevalent in this almost forgotten *Trauerspiel* in terms of the allegorical theme of the fall and decay of nature.[42] Lacking the modern progressivist understanding of history, the authors of these tragic dramas viewed historical phenomena in *purely naturalistic terms* as caught in the inevitable natural process of decline and decay. Thereby, the human institutions and conventions described by Lukács as 'second nature' were submitted to an equally de-mystifying thrust. To the allegorists, nature was intrinsically historical, but in the alternative sense of 'changing', 'passing' and 'withering'. Characteristically, Adorno's appropriation of these ideas was very selective and dispensed with much of Benjamin's underlying philosophical structure. However, inspired by this unfamiliar understanding of history as nature, he set out a programme of unveiling all such mythic interpretations as 'historically produced illusion'.[43]

Adorno's 'The idea of Natural History' employs the double connotations of the concepts 'nature' and 'history' in this attempt at contemporary de-mystification. Both concepts are employed as *cognitive concepts which demythify reality by means of reciprocal critique*. In other words, the concept 'nature' exposes the non-identity between the *concept of historical progress* and *actual historical reality* by drawing attention to the material nature violated in the name of historical 'progress'.[44] Similarly, the concept 'history' unmasks the ideology which views existing social arrangements as 'natural', essential or true *by evoking their historical production.*[45] Against past philosophical programmes to assert either concept as ontological first principle, Adorno argued that these proposals resulted in an apologetic, fatalistic reconciliation with present social conditions. Lukács' historicist critique of apparently 'natural' social relations succeeded in exposing reification *only to succumb to the danger of condoning irrational material suffering by celebrating a dubious 'historical progress'*.

Adorno's was an accentuated, double critical perspective. This unified approach was premised on a dialectical understanding of these concepts:

> to comprehend historical being in its most extreme historical determinacy, where it is most historical, as natural being or. . . to comprehend nature as historical being where it seems to rest most deeply in itself as nature.[46]

This technique of dialectical conceptual juxtaposition was also deeply indebted to Benjamin. Unlike the Hegelian Lukács who conceived truth primarily in terms of historical becoming, Benjamin viewed history as a capricious interplay of contingencies set on a course of eternal decline without redemption. Richard Wolin has explained that this particular view of history rested on Benjamin's genuine fascination with Jewish mysticism. He interpreted the Kabbalist myths as expressions of an eternal human longing for redemption. His interpretation of two of these myths reveal the pristine world as an unfragmented, divine totality. Its original condition allowed perfect communication between all living things and their divine source. Sin, however, shattered this perfection and knowledge became necessary as a means of distinguishing good from evil. For Benjamin, the course of history corresponded to the milleniums since the Fall in which the search for knowledge expressed the sense of permanent human exile and the need to re-establish the disrupted harmony.[47] In this eschatological interpretation of history, the origin became the goal of diremption and the philosophical task was the interpretative penetration of the darkness and uncertainty obscuring the original truth of language overlaid in the course of historical 'progress'. The quest for truth did not necessarily imply the restoration of the original condition. A dynamic reading of the notion of origin rendered it as a dormant potential still residing in the original condition.[48]

Perceiving history as a realm of contingencies and a process of decline, Benjamin disassociated his concept of truth from it. In accord with his mimetic theory of language,[49] he maintained that truth was revealed not by the subjective contents of language but through its revelation of our original mimetic capacities to create correspondences between ouselves and the world. Linguistic physiognomy expressed the, as yet, undisturbed connection between man and the surrounding environment. The truth, therefore, could not be formulated by the interpreter. The interpreter's role was to recreate/reconstruct the original connection between a past text and the form of life which had engendered it so that the hidden structure and meaning of the former was redeemed *just as it was immediately and unintentionally transparent to the original addressees*. For Benjamin, the revelation of the unintentional truth of any surviving artifact was achieved by fragmenting the constitutive elements and reconstituting them into appropriate constellations.[50]

Adorno adopted this technique of reconstituting constellations in his theory of 'historical images'. As with Benjamin, the truth emerged not as a result of conceptual mediation but was produced by the sheer power of the constellation's representational image. Wolin describes this release of redemptive truth in regard to Benjamin's decipherment of the allegories of seventeenth century drama:

> The 'dialectic of allegory' causes all manifest content to be transformed
> into its opposite: the death's head becomes an angel's countenance.
> Basing itself on the theological conception of the diametrically opposite
> relation in which profane life stands to the life of salvation, it goes all out
> in its attempt to dramatise the wretched nature of all earthly life in order
> thereby to set in contrast all the more emphatically the blissfulness of the
> life beyond. . . . By proceeding through this antithetical system of
> references the allegories of the *Trauerspiel* sought to pile ruin upon ruin,
> thereby illustrating not only the sheer hopelessness and futility of earthly

existence, but more importantly, the sovereign hope of mankind that rests with the Almighty redeemer.[51]

Benjamin intended his constellations to reveal essential contradictions that illuminated the hidden truth concealed in everyday historical remnants.

Again, Adorno's appropriation of Benjamin was selective. Just as with Lukács, from whom he adopted the idea of 'second nature' while repudiating his concept of totality, he set about applying a materialist turn to some of Benjamin's theologically-inspired concepts. He dismissed Benjamin's recourse to original ontology and his view of second nature as the return of archaic myth.[52] All myths were embedded in specific historical conditions and had to be explained as such.

In his lecture 'The Actuality of Philosophy' Adorno signalled the task of contemporary critical philosophy as interpretation.[53] While clearly distinct and autonomous from scientific research, philosophy was still bound to this form of conceptual questioning. Scientific questioning fulfilled an indispensible propaedeutic role dissolving phenomena and preparing them for philosophical re-appropriation in constellations. These constellations he called 'historical images'.[54] These images were phenomenal mimetic representations which evoked a unity amidst fragmentation and contradiction without relinquishing this dissolution and abstracting from contradiction. In this way they de-mystified and de-reified without ideological totalisation.

The critical interpretative role Adorno attributed to philosophy was predicated on his affirmation of Lukács' view of the inherently contradictory character of bourgeois reality. In contrast to Lukács, however, this role did not imply the transcendence of contradiction. Rather, it should render contradiction perceptible while preserving and concretising the antagonistic tension. According to Adorno, this was accomplished by revealing the *contradictory truth of a specific social totality as it appeared in the form of an object or phenomenon within a particular configuration.* In a fragmented reality bereft of coherent meaning and incapable of furnishing a unified truth, there was no alternative but to salvage 'fleeting traces of truth' by rearranging the fractured elements.[55]

Adorno's theory of fragmentary truth highlighted his critique of the traditional philosophical quest for meaningful totality. He attacked recent philosophical developments like phenomenology because its attempt to transcend the dominant neo-Kantian subjectivisim faltered on the notion of intentionality. While Adorno found much of interest in Husserl, he criticised his objectivist critique of psychologism for falling short. For Adorno, the continued recourse to the transcendental ego repeated the habitual assertion of the primacy of subject over object in the attempt to secure a rational, non-contradictory account of experience.[56] Adorno followed Benjamin in maintaining truth as something not comprehended by the intentionality of the knowing subject. He reiterated the materialist idea of non-identity maintaining both subject and object *as co-determinants*. Against Husserl's idealist stress on intentionality, he argued that materialist critique must cling to the concrete objects and phenomena themselves. Their philosophical reformation into constellations revealed the concealed truth of their unintentional being. Adorno echoed Benjamin's dictum 'Truth is the death of intention'.[57]

This brief overview of Adorno's early philosophical programme clarifies those tendencies and influences which provoked his particularly hostile reception of Lukács' concept of totality. It is true that Adorno's 'historical images' still implied a modified idea of totality. They crystallised a *unity* within contradictory reality. However, this concept was very far from the humanist emancipatory understanding of the historical totality bequeathed by Lukács. The radicalism of Adorno's stance is manifest in his critique of progress. While Horkheimer had been concerned to excoriate all traces of apologetic objectivism from the concept, this was a moderate critique preserving the belief in historical progress. Progress, for him, was an indispensible 'regulative idea'. Adorno, on the other hand, had imbibed Benjamin's profound suspicion of this idea. Not only did the discontinuous character of history undermine the possibility of conceiving it as the bearer of rationality, it also challenged the idea of 'uneven development'. The later Benjamin's view of history as a 'series of calamities and disasters' captures perfectly Adorno's sceptical claim that the idea of progress smacked of reconciliation with an unjust and false reality.

The objective movement of contemporary history only confirmed Adorno's deeply rooted suspicions. The present historical disaster necessitated a redoubled assault on the ideology of progress. The object of his philosophical attack undergoes transformation from the 1930s to the 1940s. The theme of reification gives way to the critique of the idea of progress in Dialectic of Enlightenment. But this noticeable shift is explicable in terms of the early thematics. It required only the deteriorated historical circumstances to occasion Adorno's heavy reckoning with all previous philosophical myths and illusions. Susan Buck-Morss is correct in seeing the decisive impress of Adorno's perspective and methodology on the first collaborative effort of the two leading thinkers of the Frankfurt School.[58]

The myth of Enlightenment

Completed only in the last years of the Second World War, Dialectic of Enlightenment was a despairing response to the failure of revolutionary politics, an exposé of the totalitarian tendencies in the fully administered epoch of state capitalism, a provocative re-assessment of the meaning of bourgeois progress and a message to the future. In theoretical terms, the critique of reification was displaced by the more encompassing critique of instrumental reason which identified the progress of civilisation with humanity's conquest of internal and external nature.

The new configuration of critical theory was in many respects an elaboration of Adorno's early pragrammatic essays in the light of the contemporary historical tragedy. Benjamin's continuing influence is also evident. Despite his own tragic death in 1940, his last thoughts on history probably helped to shape the perspective of Dialectic of Enlightenment. During the war Adorno held his surviving manuscripts for safekeeping. The methodology and virtually all the key ideas of the joint work were, however, already present in Adorno's early essays. The recourse to antithetical conceptual pairs like enlightenment/myth, reason/barbarism, progress/regress, and science/magic, facilitated the formation of constellations illuminating the critical truth of the contemporary situation. The 'myth' of Enlightenment as rational progress was set against the reality of its own concrete history.[59]

Adorno and Horkheimer were well placed to record the refutation of some of Lukács' central theoretical claims. Witnessing the almost complete victory of Fascism and the stabilisation of state capitalism under the New Deal, they could confidently dismiss the view that reification had its own internal limits in the formalism of its own rationality. The reorganisation of capitalism, the overcoming of chronic economic stagnation/crisis and the domination of total administration using political control and market research all pointed to a new pinnacle of manipulation. Not even subjective need was protected from the incursions of instrumental reason. Mass consumer culture appeared to stifle worker discontent and material prosperity ensured accommodation to the existing social arrangement.

In view of this diagnosis, Benjamin's critique of the idea of progress seemed more telling and culturally relevent than Lukács' revolutionary optimism. The apparent disappearance of critical theory's posited addressee and onset of a fully administered society refuted Lukács' idea of socialism constructed by collective, conscious praxis. Horkheimer and Adorno responded to this situation by radically breaking with the orthodox Marxian framework of the earlier critical theory. This involved a complete change in the meaning of the concept of totality. It no longer denotes the aim of theoretically capturing the historical dynamic of society in its immanent unity and open processuality from the standpoint of proletarian interests but designates the quality of contemporary history under the reign of administered domination. The authors achieved this major theoretical turn through a synthesis of the Benjaminian critique of 'progress' with a re-interpreted Weberian concept of rationalisation. The substantive crux of the synthesis was their despairing warning against the increasing instrumentalisation of reason and the emergence of a comprehensively regulated society as the impending fate of modernity. In this scenario, the defeat of fascism would not rehabilitate human freedom because the ominous signs of rationalised domination were already well advanced in the state capitalist regimes like the United States.

This revision of critical theory represented a radicalisation of the Lukácsian concept of reification. The association of reification with the processes of bourgeois commodification still played a role in the idea of instrumental reason but only a subordinate one. Commodification was a decisive step in the process which universalised domination. It was a mode of identity thinking which came to permeate the whole social totality:

> Since, with the end of free exchange, commodities lost all their economic qualities except for fetishism, the latter has extended its arthritic influence over all aspects of social life.[60]

However, Adorno and Horkheimer were unwilling to *confine reification solely to the epoch of the commodity*. In their new conception commodity reification was *but one moment in the more encompassing process of increasing domination which began with the quest for self-preservation through the conquest of nature and the original division of labour*.[61]

Clearly in these terms it is problematic even to speak of reification. The authors link the development of civilisatory rationality with the barbaric domination – of the self, of others and nature. In this perspective, humanity's separation from nature and the evolution of its relation to nature as to a mere object is seen to involve both *the repression of the natural in man* and *the distortion of human cognitive interests in the service of a 'logic of domination'*.[62] This dialectic possesses its own paradox:

> As soon as man discards his awareness that he himself is nature, all the aims for which he keeps himself alive – social progress, the intensification of all his material and spiritual powers, even consciousness itself – are nullified and the enthronement of the means as an end, which under late capitalism is tantamount to open insanity, is already perceptible in the pre-history of subjectivity. Man's domination over himself, which grounds his selfhood, is almost always the destruction of the subject in whose service it is undertaken; for the substance which is dominated, suppressed, and dissolved by virtue of self-preservation is none other than that very life as functions of which the achievements of self-preservation find their sole definition and determination: it is, in fact, what is to be preserved.[63]

The identification of the subject with a distorted rational faculty and the dissolution and reduction of all phenomena to the terms of this distorted rationality marked the genesis of identity thinking and human self-renunciation.[64] Civilisation is the history of the progress of domination which proceeded from the attempt to eliminate the non-identical, the 'other' in the cause of self-preservation.

Latent in the view of self-preservation as the reproduction of the self is the idea of the selfhood of the subject as unified *ratio*. Adorno and Horkheimer maintained that this understanding of selfhood instigated the process whereby knowledge was invested with increasing autonomy. The process received its first social expression in the original division of labour. Borrowing from Durkheimian sociology of knowledge, they argued that the fundamental categories of logic reflected these initial social relations of domination.[65] These ideal categories were instruments of man's attempt to report, order and explain the surrounding environment in the interests of his own self-preservation. While they were only means to this end, they preserved and exemplified the formal irrational structure of domination. In the course of enlightenment, rational knowledge usurped the position as goal of the process and, demonstrating a primitive lineage of domination, it imposed itself on the world without regard to existing distinctions and human suffering.[66]

The radicalism of the authors' interpretation was revealed in this application of the concept of enlightenment to the whole civilisatory process. Enlightenment signified *not the antithesis of myth but the continuance of its innermost logic*. Myth was the first form of enlightenment; a intellectual product of man's need to subordinate the world to his own categories of order, regularity and explanation.[67] The further development of rationality, however, required that myth be submitted to critique. The self-understanding of enlightenment involved the critical exposure and overcoming of all vestiges of myth. The rational pretensions of all former worldviews were demolished at the altar of reason itself. This process of critical self-reflection culminated in the critical rejection of the fundamental categories of classical philosophy. Here the last refuge of myth was exposed. Not even these categories could escape the critique of superstition. The outcome of this critical dialectic was paradoxical to say the least.

The dialectic of enlightenment was ultimately self-destructive. The torch of criticism eventually consumed even its own inspirational categories and touchstones. 'Truth', 'freedom', and 'enlightenment' itself were all sacrificed to the inquisition of positivist analysis and demoted to the level of anamistic magic.[68] Yet, ironically, not even positivism could extricate itself from the fate of all previous standard bearers of enlightenment. Its desire to exempt itself from the tribunal of critique revealed, Adorno and Horkheimer asserted, *its own metaphysical bias*.[69] *Instrumental reason ignored its own historical pre-conditions and invested both formal rationality and existing power with an absolute status like that claimed by the old metaphysical truths.*

This resistence to self-consciousness betrayed the *persistence of myth*. The absolutising of reason in the notion of formal rationality, the idea of reason as a natural automaton of calculation *signified its transformation into myth*. The overwhelming adoption of quantitative, mathematical procedures represented an inversion of ends and means identical to that noted in the Weberian analysis of rationalisation. Thinking was reduced to a thing and its reified function was that of mere instrument.[70] At the same time, however, this mere instrument usurped the position of the absolute.

The practical and theoretical programme of instrumental reason was the conquest of nature. To assimilate nature into the categories of subjective reason and eliminate otherness by suppressing the non-identical by means of identity categories. The later Adorno orientated his whole critical thrust to the ultimate fallacy of this programme: its formalist abstraction. As the instrument of rational universality, abstraction denied the particular. It rendered the qualitative uniqueness of every situation imperceptible. Abstraction treated every historical situation as a mere repetition of what had already gone before. Its ideal of 'universal law' exemplified the myth of eternal recurrence which denied the possibility of new beginnings. In addition, abstraction divorced reason from its own corporeal, material basis in the concrete, particular individual.

For both Adorno and Horkheimer, Kantian philosophy provided a clear expression of the domination entailed in the project of enlightenment. Since Kant, thinking had been conceived as the unceasing activity of subjective synthesis. This completely empty and formal notion of self-consciousness reduced it to self-preservation and the affirmation of identity. This philosophical interpretation of the essence of thinking was a definite cultural expression of the reified *naturalisation of a specific mode of thought linked to commodification and its permanent quest for equivalence*. All aspects of the external world and nature within were reduced to the constitutive activity of the subject. In realising its pretensions to universality, reason itself became *particular and constricted* . The sensuous substrata of all conceptualisation was ignored as a mark of its own inherent self-renunciation. As Adorno argued in Negative Dialectics: 'the principle of absolute identity is self-contradictory'.[71]

Adorno and Horkheimer maintained that this domination of the non-identical in the environment and the repression of nature within provoked periodic instinctual rebellions. In modern societies, however, these outbursts were manipulated by Fascist ideology and total-administrations to serve the interests of over-rationalised, increasingly irrational, systems of domination.

This radical and complex critique has to be analysed on several distinct levels. As ideology critique, it claimed the substantially illusory character of the self-emancipatory triumph of civilisatory reason. Beneath the regulated surface of modern social life accumulated repression signified an imminent threat of violence; a violence orchestrated by unrestrained irrational powers. The historical experience of Fascism and the post-war realisation of the atomic age with its awesome potential for human self-annihilation showed that such fears were hardly groundless. At every point Adorno and Horkheimer drew attention to the nexus between the features of modern rationality and its parallels in irrational social actuality.[72]

The crux of this link was the assertion that enlightenment had collapsed into almost total reification. The critical dimension of reason had lapsed into resignation before an increasingly irrational, 'given' system of institutions and powers. The ideals of enlightenment and progress were exposed as ideologies and unmasked as a return of the ever-same myth that had escaped destruction and overcoming.

At this point the revised concept of totality was elaborated. Modern society was a new system of total domination characterised by new manifestations of alienation, de-personalisation and administrative repression. It was this aspect of total administration that facilitated the paradoxical inversion of ends and means which threatened to negate the dearest achievements of the civilisatory process:

> Through the mediation of the total society which embraces all relations and emotions, men are once again made to be that against which the evolutionary law of society, the principle of self, had turned: mere species beings, exactly like one another through isolation in the forcibly united collectivity.[73]

The total technical and economic apparatus of modern society achieved the goal of virtually expunging every trace of subjectivity not required by the self-calculating movement of material production. Everything that could not be subordinated to the demands of technical logic was expunged as entirely superfluous.[74] In this process, uniformity necessarily replaced individuality.

The implications of this radical revision of the former emancipatory significance of the concept of totality were not lost on Adorno and Horkheimer. With the total control and manipulation of all domains of society, the hitherto major forces of social resistance to totalitarian tendencies were defused and seduced into acquiescence. The advent of the totally administered society stripped the emancipatory potential from the totality concept. 'Rational totality' was not an alternative social organisation posited in the immanent future but the false reality constraining present human existence. In modern society, *totality needed neither be deciphered nor postulated: it was directly present.* The historical crisis of liberal capitalism had been averted by the emergence of a new total form of domination and control. In this perspective, Fascism was no historical aberration but the inexorable continuation of trends already evident in late capitalism. Politics, economics and culture were all now characterised by careful administration, iron control and subtle manipulation. This negative critique was extreme and unrelenting:

> Instead the conscious decision of the managing directors execute as results. . . the old law of value and hence the destiny of capitalism. The rulers themselves do not believe in any objective necessity, even though they sometimes describe their concoctions thus. They declare themselves to be the engineers of world history. Only the ruled accept as unquestion-able necessity the course of development that with every decreed rise in the standard of living makes them so much more powerless. . . The masses are fed and quartered as an army of unemployed. In their eyes, their reduction to mere objects of the administered life, which preforms every sector of modern existence including language and perception, represents objective necessity, against which they believe there is nothing they can do. Misery as the antithesis of power and powerlessness grow immeasurably, together with the capacity to remove all misery permanently.[75]

This stark picture of a society totally controlled and manipulated, in which the traditional working class was pacified by incremental improvements in living standards and a stupefying mass culture, where almost all critical opposition was quashed, has often earned Adorno and Horkheimer the charge of historical pessimism and cultural aristocratism. The influence of Weber's ubiquitous notion of rationalisation on their interpretation of modernity lends credibility to the view that they promoted the resurgence of the historical pessimism which had permeated the culture theory of the *Geisteswissenschaften*. Yet, despite the validity of some of these claims, Dialectic of Enlightenment cannot easily be assimilated to the theories of cultural tragedy. Against such interpretations it should be underlined that the author's analysis departs from the perspective of missed historical opportunities and existing materio-technical potentialities for emancipation. The perspective remains that of liberation even if the addressee has been reduced to a handful of lonely authentic individuals and praxis renounced as an agent of instrumental activity.[76]

Dialectic of Enlightenment almost invites misinterpretation. While the authors roundly condemn philosophy of history[77] and explicitly censure the view of totality embraced by Lukács, they appear to manufacture their own *even grander history of decline which coincides with the evolution of instrumental reason and the concominant refinement of domination.* The only way to make partial sense of this blatant inconsistency is a recollection of the methodology underpinning the critique. Adorno's 'historical images' and 'constellations' *consciously relied on extreme formulations and contradictory fragments for the very purpose of igniting the concealed truth behind the ideologies of progress, social rationality and material prosperity.*

This approach certainly clarifies the aims of the authors' critique. Their historical images are, in Adorno's terms, 'negative constructs'. Later he argued in similarly provocative manner 'Universal history must not be construed but denied'.[78] This strategy is also apparent in the historical construct presented in Dialectic of Enlightenment. Adorno and Horkheimer despaired for the immediate future and were determined to destroy the ideology of progress. Adorno later, in opposition to Hegel, defined world spirit as 'permanent catastrophe'. This extreme image, like many in Dialectic of Enlightenment, repudiates the return of complacent quasi-theological optimism which implicitly consecrates past suffering and legitimates the existing repressive domination of a fully administered 'false' totality.

The extreme pessimism of Adorno and Horkheimer's diagnosis of modernity was predicated on the belief that Fascism represented the paradigmatic form of contemporaneity. The 'continuity thesis' which interpreted Fascism as the political form corresponding to monopoly capitalism seemed vindicated by many developments in the United States. The evolution of Soviet Russia also appeared to corroborate a general movement towards totalitarian domination. The historical construct of Dialectic of Enlightenment crystallised this horrendous contemporary outlook. It conceded no positive image of historical development. Adorno sustained this pessimism virtually to the end. The only image of history he was prepared to contemplate was a negative one: from the 'slingshot to the megaton bomb'. This image clearly represents not an alternative philosophy of history but a sensuous evocation which challenges the present by recalling its links with the barbaric past.

For Adorno, such images were 'shock tactics' employed in the hope of realising their opposite. They were never offered as an account of historical fate. Unlike Weber, who viewed the processes of rationalisation as the irreversible 'fate' of modernity, he and Horkheimer understood the predicament of modernity as a product of reification: something man-made and changeable. Their account of history mourned lost oppportunities, registered unrealised social potentials and bemoaned the lack of a contemporary social force capable of relieving the increasingly desperate situation. The ultimate fate of humanity stood in the balance.

The reinterpretation of the Homeric Odysseus myth in <u>Dialectic of Enlightenment</u> was an especially forceful utilisation of these shock tactics.The same Homeric world had served Lukács as a normative standard of integrated culture. Even the Marxist Lukács employed this idea of cultural community as an ideal for the socialist future. Ironically, and perhaps not accidentically, this epic story was now turned to the opposite purpose: to demonstrate the deep historical roots of the instrumental attitude and repressive rationality. In a clever inversion of Lukács' interpretation, the Odysseus tale was viewed not as an evocation of a sensuously existing totality of meaning – the expression of a closed unified culture utlimately destroyed by the social processes which instigated diremption – but as *the anticipation of the modern literary hero*. Odysseus' quest to find himself after losing himself *foreshadowed the paradigmatic idea of the modern novel*.[79] Unlike Lukács' epic hero, who performed as a surrogate for the community and whose ultimate fate was never in doubt, Adorno and Horkheimer viewed Odysseus as the proto-bourgeois individual who owed his success to the clever exploitation of the discrepancy between word and object.

It is tempting to view this interpretation of Homer as a conscious critique of Lukács' vision of an integrated culture. Such a view is corroborated by Adorno's acknowledged anathema to the idea. He always maintained that 'a liberated mankind would by no means be a totality'.[80] He believed the ideal of a rational, perfectly integrated community to be the product of the myth of 'total reason'; another instance of reified thinking which suppressed all manifestations of the non-identical.[81] However, more important than any implicit critique of Lukács was the fact that this interpretation of Odysseus represented an exemplary execution of the methodology of 'historical images'. The classical myths were approached through the prism of bourgeois rationality. In this way they served to *de-mythologise the origins of Western culture, exposing in it the sources of barbarism and instrumentalism*. The method's object was to jolt the present and undermine its subjugation to an idealised past.[82]

While motivated by despair, the intent behind <u>Dialectic of Enlightenment</u>

was clearly one of critical intervention in the present. When judged in the light of subsequent events, its underlying presuppositions seem extreme and excessive. Particularly the assimilation of all forms of modernity to the model of Fascism. Dubiel also stresses that the thesis of proletarian integration was not a product of new research, new experiences or new information 'but a radical intensification of a pessimistic view of socialism's chances in Germany'.[83] However, this provocative text was intended to preserve and articulate an emancipatory, critical perspective in admittedly dark times. The authors saw themselves as the true defenders of the spirit of the enlightenment:

> As the organ of this kind of adaption [to the status quo], as a mere
> construction of means, the Enlightenment is as destructive as its romantic
> enemies accuse it of being. It comes into its own only when it surrenders
> the last remaining concordance with the latter and dares to transcend the
> false absolute, the principle of domination.[84]

Despite the passages which bemoan the lack of resistance to administered monopoly capitalism, although they refused to posit a concrete political goal, failed to address a definite sociological subject and even went so far as to question the contemporary fetish for practically utilisable theory, it would be a mistake to characterise Dialectic of Enlightenment as a retreat into philosophical despair.[85] The authors presuppose resistance to contemporary society as the rationale of their intervention. They hoped both to preserve and evoke the emancipatory forces of an epoch which had created the 'capacity to remove all misery permanently'.[86] Indeed, this was a fragile hope, one stripped of illusions to the point of judging bourgeois reality too harshly, but one which sustained emancipatory aspirations and had not capitulated to the prevailing reverence for existing social reality.

The antinomies of critical theory

If, on close inspection some alleged inconsistencies in Dialectic of Enlightenment disappear, substantial theoretical difficulties remain outstanding. A sympathetic appreciation of Adorno and Horkheimer's critical intentions and unique methodology cannot disguise the heavy price they paid for adopting this extreme critique of instrumental reason.

The most troublesome consequence of their chosen strategy was the accusation turned against *the very reason they relied upon to execute their critical project*. Adorno and Horkheimer claimed that discursive logic was raised on the basis of actual domination[87] and that the deductive forms of science reflected hierarchy and coercion.[88] In insisting that human reason was contaminated by the instrumentalising process of enlightenment, they, at the same time, rendered the claims of their own critical reason problematic. If the whole structure of reason only reflected domination *then even the project of rational self-criticism was undermined*. Although they maintained an undisguised hostility to philosophical irrationalism, their own reluctance or inability to clarify the limits of their critique of enlightenment, to distinguish what was historically retrievable from this evolution, risked the collapse of their critique into irrationalist nominalism.

Another consequence of the author's genuine desire to evade the compass of a logic of domination was a conscious withdrawal from the goal of positive theoretical knowledge and a distantiation from the aims of the positive social sciences. It implied the abandonment of early critical theory's commitment to a inter-disciplinary research programme involving the synthesis of philosophy and empirical social research. It has already been noted that the diagnosis of modernity presented in Dialectic of Enlightenment was based more on past experience than new contemporary research. After the war, Adorno did contribute to the empirical studies on The Authoritarian Personality (1950). However, his philosophical thought was already crystallised around the idea of a purely negative dialectic which sustained its critical posture only by the repudiation of a scientific knowledge wrought from the suppression of the non-identical. Habermas has perceived this tendency as a retreat into philosophical speculation.[89] He substantiates this claim by analysing the author's temporal extension of the concept of reification. While the concept of instrumental reason did not completely dispense with specific historical analysis, most attention was directed at the traditional epistemological problematic of subject and object. Compared to the Marxian programme to explain exploitation and domination with a historico-structural analysis of capitalist society as totality, this radicalised strategy to relocate domination in the cognitive-instrumental dimension of human activity seems abstract and minimises, if only by omission, the intersubjective conditions of this development.[90] Furthermore, it problematises even more the perspective of emancipation which now demands an unspecified revision of man's relation to nature.

Habermas has argued that Adorno and Horkheimer consciously chose to work within such unresolved theoretical *aporias*. Viewing human reason with suspicion, they could not, nevertheless, completely abandon it. Having questioned reason and impuned theoretical logic, they reverted to an aphoristic mode of discourse. This aesthetical, only indirectly rational, mode of argumentation was the only one compatible with the new negative philosophical task. It gave expression to the human capacity for mimesis through which instrumentalised nature could evade homogenised rationality and make its 'speechless accusation'.[91] With only the brutalised instrument of reason at their disposal, Adorno and Horkheimer were unable to provide a theoretical account of the reconcilation with nature prefigured in the primordal human mimetic capacity. The image of mimesis offered an inarticulable potential for an alternative, non-instrumental, reconciliatory and emancipatory human appropriation of nature.[92]

Needless to say, the form of emancipation foreshadowed by this image was shadowy and inexact. Nor was it linked to the sphere of social praxis. It did, however, testify to the authors' determination to maintain the critical autonomy of philosophy and their aspiration, despite great disappointments, to transcend the 'given'. To view this strenuous critique of the concept of totality as its dissolution would be a superficial judgment. Adorno and Horkheimer always asserted their continuity with the tradition under examination. Their aspiration to transcendence clearly vindicates this claim. In submitting their theoretical inheritance to a telling critique, they not only exposed some of its most questionable theoretical difficulties and excesses, they also joined its project of critical enlightenment and emancipatory self-transcendence. If this will to transcendence signifies their perpetuation of the tradition of totality thinking, the fragility of their final stance raised even more fundamental questions regarding the tradition itself. Despite their radicalism, did not Adorno and Horkheimer remain too much captives of the tradition and its specific understanding of emancipatory totalisation? This is a question to be engaged in the conclusion. For the moment it is enough to recall that their stern warnings against the speculative metaphysics of the totality concept did not prevent them from committing similar exaggerations. Their idea of the totally administered society was more a myth of totality (in a negative sense) than anything ever perpetrated by Hegel. While Adorno and Horkheimer positively typified the radical historicist tradition's search for an immanent, radical transcendence, they also exemplified its proneness to overstatement and utopian ardour in resistance to existing society.

The anti-humanist challenge to radical historicism

Chapter Seven

Michel Foucault: anti-totalising scepticism or totalising prophecy?

With <u>Dialectic of Enlightenment</u>, the radical historicist tradition of totality thinking totters on the brink of internal self dissolution. Several commentators have read the critique of instrumental reason and the totally administered society as the final collapse of the emancipatory hopes first articulated variously by Hegel, Marx and Lukács. The last chapter attempted to qualify this view arguing that despite the bleakness of Adorno and Horkheimer's mature vision and the theoretically damaging aporias in which they *chose to work,* their continuity with the emancipatory, historicist tradition was secured by a historiosophic critique of bourgeois modernity and an aspiration to radical transcendence. Nevertheless, their work did represent an exceedingly pessimistic account of modernity and a searching *internal* interrogation of the tradition of totalising historicism. Not surprisingly, it has taken a thinker from *outside* the historicist tradition to surpass the radicalism of their self-criticism. The work of Michel Foucault (1926-1984) crystallises, within the rough domain of social theory and historiography, a number of anti-totalising currents in French intellectual culture and mounts the most trenchant questioning of the emancipatory credentials of historicist critique and Marxian totality thinking. The very radicalism of Foucault's anti-totalising rhetoric would alone warrant his inclusion in any study of radical historicist totality thinking. However, it is also clear from the immanent development of his own thought as reflected in his last writings[1] that Foucault himself was drawn to the tradition of historicist critical theory (which he chose to call 'critical ontology'). His late essay on Enlightenment evidences a desire to refashion and actualise a vital contemporary idea of critique and culminates with the reconstruction of a unified tradition of critique stemming from Kant and Hegel to his own work.

This alleged convergence therefore makes it quite fitting that this chapter explores Foucault's critique of totality. Such an analysis cannot amount to an assessment of his work as a whole though it does require the contextualisation of this critique within his project. Investigation of the basis of Foucault's radical step beyond the position articulated by the Adorno and Horkheimer in <u>Dialectic of Enlightenment</u> brings into relief another episode in the totality story. It will clarify much of the post-structuralist animus against the concept and permits a critical assessment of one influential version of this anti-totalising tendency. It will also point to some striking parallels between Foucault's stance and that of the late Frankfurt School without glossing over the fundamental differences. The similarities between his globalising critique of modernity and their own raises the spectre of a repressed totalising aspiration in Foucault's own work while some of the differences prompt serious questions regarding both the adequacy of his own professed alignment with the historicist tradition and his reconstruction of the contemporary meaning of critique.

Foucault's critique of totality is embedded in a series of historical works which explore the history of the modern human sciences; psychiatry, medicine, psychoanalysis, political economy, criminology and sociology. What distinguishes Foucault's account from that of conventional historians of science is his fascination with the underside of this triumph of human reason. His primary concern is to provide a critique of the way in which the human sciences have functioned as instruments of power, social control, discipline and exclusion. He reveals this hitherto unsuspected story to expose the complicity of the human sciences in the institution of the radically new modern configuration of power/knowledge, to arm us against the humanist illusions sanctioned by these discourses, to dramatise the frightening completeness of contemporary social control and register this as crisis. Hayden White succinctly captures Foucault's perspective when he suggests that his discourse aims to disclose 'the madness lying at the very heart of reason'.[2] From his first investigation of the scientific constitution of the category of insanity to that of sexuality in his last, Foucault stubbornly returned to the *culpability* of the human sciences in the process whereby modern society has strengthened its hold over the population and extended the sway of power into all social interactions.

Foucault's interest in these issues was initially whetted by his early training in psychology and philosophy. His intensive studies in psychology and psychopathology in the early 1950s was followed by experience of psychiatric practice in mental hospitals. His utter distaste for these practices aroused his scepticism against the scientific pretensions of the human sciences and their studied indifference to their own violence.[3] Foucault later claimed that his interest in the question of power and its relation to the production of 'truths' was instigated by such contemporary events as the Lysenko scandal aganst the historical background of the great historical shadows of Fascism and Stalinism. But the historical watershed in the crystallisation of this concern was really the events of May 1968. These events seemed to confirm the bankruptcy of the French Communist Party, to question the orthodox Marxist scenario of revolution and to feed rising suspicions that the concept of totality served both *totalitarian and exclusory purposes*. The subsequent dispersion of politico-social struggles around schools, prisons, reformatories and psychiatric clinics reinvigorated this underlying theme in all Foucault's previous work providing it with a new intensity and sharpness of vocabulary.[4]

The critique of the human sciences

The methodological basis for Foucault's critique of totality was laid down in The Order of Things (1966). There he retrieved and explored the allegedly flawed anthropologism at the heart of the modern human sciences. Foucault locates the emergence of anthropocentric form of knowledge at the the end of the eighteenth century and sees its paradigmatic formulation in the philosophy of Kant. This Copernican revolution also initiates the process of self-reflection that made possible the birth of the sciences of man. Kant's critique of metaphysics marked the demise of the Classical age which had been dominated by a *representationalist mode* of knowledge presupposing a seamless correspondence between language and the world of objects. Kant's critical exploration of the classical mode of representation problematised the process of representation exposing both its unsuspected reification and ultimate dependence on subjective synthesis. The crux of the anthropocentic turn was Kant's refusal to acknowledge this demise of an objectively co-ordinated metaphysical order as a defeat of knowledge, as a collapse into finitude and contingency. Instead, he transformed the constraints of this meagre, finite subjective basis into the *transcendental condition of all knowledge* reconciling subject and object and thereby rescuing the quest for an intersubjectively secured objective knowledge from the debris of human contingency.[5] This dubious manoeuvre was, however, flawed from the outset. The anthropocentric form of knowledge and the human sciences for which it immediately provided scope were stricken by a deep *aporia*. Like the hero of Lukács' modern novel, Foucault's modern finite and conditioned epistemological subject is set before an infinite quest for knowledge but without the powers to ever realise it. The modern mode of knowledge caves in under the weight of its own self-contradiction. Foucault sees the impossibility of the task and its antinomies registered in the 'doubling' that plagues modern anthropocentric thought. He delineates three sets of oppositions: the empirical and transcendental, the cogito and the unthought, the perfect a priori and the return to origin. These doublets record the various contradictory paths and approaches traversed by modern anthropologism in its ultimately unsatisfactory attempts at self-transcendence. The heart of this critique of anthropologism is a rejection of the modern concept of totality in the modifed critical form crafted by Kant which preserved totality only as a *regulative idea*. Foucault contends that the *aporia* constructed into the principle of Kantian epistemology and the pressures of its unstable doublets are manifest in the voracious dynamism which characterises the modern scientific will to knowledge.

Later in his intellectual development Foucault will argue that the aspiration to totality which underpinned the sciences of man also involved a terrible human cost. The human sciences unquenchable thirst for knowledge facilitated their enlistment in the formation process of the modern disciplinary regime of increasing social control. These burgeoning 'sciences' furthered the astounding metamorphosis of power in the modern bourgeois epoch which advanced its expansion, enhanced its fecundity and saturation into every crevice of society.

Assault on totality

In The Order of Things and Archaeology of Knowledge, however, Foucault was still primarily concerned to resist the manifold consequences of the reign of anthropologism in the historical human sciences. This required a relentless assault on the ideological humanism constitutive of modern historical consciousness and philosophy of history. Martin Jay has noted that this ensured his hostility to all theoretical varieties of the concept of totality.[8] The Archaeology of Knowledge (1969) commenced with a ringing endorsement of a radical shift in the preoccupations of contemporary historians who had broken with anthropologism. The Introduction offers a celebration of this inchoate revolution in the self-image of history and its break with a totalising anthropological justification of history as progress and 'old-age collective consciousness'. Foucault's direct assault on totalising history is perhaps the best place from which to unfold his very comprehensive critique of the concept of totality. He begins by arguing that the still incomplete epistemological mutation in history:

> has broken up the long series formed by the progress of consciousness, or
> the teleology of reason, or the evolution of human thought; it has
> questioned the themes of convergence and culmination; it has doubted the
> possibility of creating totalities.[9]

One commentator has characterised the intellectual milieu in which Foucault came to maturity as one dominated by the attempt to escape Hegel.[10] In his own work this influence comes to fruition in a repudiation of the very idea of a global, totalised or totalising history. Such totalisation only betrays the narcissism of the present which demands that the past be related to it in terms of continuity and growth. This continuity/progress is an ideological fiction foisted on the past to legitimate present interests and perspectives.[11] Foucault recoils from this distortive privileging of the present as an attempt to impose an illusory identity on recalcitrant, dispersed events. The search after origins effects a false homogenisation of profuse events in order to validate the superiority or the progressiveness of the present, to demonstrate its necessity. Foucault does not deny the inescapable impact of the current regime of knowledge/power, the impossibility of ideology-free interpretation but he does aspire to discard the illusions of presentism and relativise the claims of the contemporary age, to reveal its real historical contingency.[12] The study of history reveals no constant or unified process; it has no aim or end, no *telos*, no direction nor cumulative meaning. To view history as a singular process, the historian is compelled to ignore discontinuities, ruptures, changes, the vast plurality of contesting narratives and transient, irregular discourses. The so-called continuity of history is a sleight of hand resulting from the *manufacture* of a fictitous supra-individual subject: a Hegelian 'spirit' or Marxian 'proletariat'. Nothing is changed when the totalising historian resorts to abstract principles like 'freedom' or 'progress' to articulate these themes of continuity and growth. Foucault had already demonstrated in <u>Madness and Civilisation</u> that the gradual triumph of rationality was equally a tale of increasing violence and insanity. On the one hand, the result of quite dispersed processes of rationalisation, temporally dislocated and violently unified and, on the other, something specific to western capitalism. His counter-discourse views the realm of the historical as one of contingency, inconstancy, disorder and chaos. This is not to deny the historians' interest in the discovery of unitary processes, principles of correlations and coherence but to acknowledge the necessity to establish them on another basis than that of a single unitary totalising process and a fictive macro-subject. Adopting a Nietzscheian motif, Foucault chose to view history is a site of permanent struggle and fluctuating power. Comforting illusions of reconcilation and ultimate harmony only serve to veil this radical historical openness, to disarm and lull into complacency.

It is easy to catalogue Foucault's ledger of the failings of total history. Totalising historical consciousness ascribes to history continuity, direction, purpose, meaning and closure. The critical historian, on the other hand, must redress this ideological distortion by underscoring discontinuity, unevenness and dispersion, decentredness, contingency and a structure of series. (Foucault takes over this structuralist notion from the Annales School to denote the methodology which seeks to eschew storytelling articulated through the synthesis of contemporary consciousness in favour of a problem solving, explanatory conception of history focused on the plurality of uneven, complex levels within historical configurations.) Against 'total history' Foucault opts for a 'general history' which overturns the above presuppositions of totalisation and seriously raises the questions of real historical dispersion:

> The problem that now presents itself – and which defines the task of a general history – is to determine what form of relation may be legitimately described between these different series; what vertical system they are capable of forming; what interplay of correlations and dominance exists between them; what may be the effect of shifts, different temporalities, and various rehandlings; in what distinct totalities certain elements may figure simultaneously; in short, not only what series, but also what 'series of series' – or, in other words, what 'tables' it is possible to draw up.[13]

Foucault's discontent with the idea of totality is not confined to a suspicion of philosophies of history *à la* Hegel which ventured to ascribe progress, reconciliation and ultimate meaning to history as a whole. He not only rejects the construction of, using Martin Jay's terminology, 'longitudinal' totalities, he also wants to dispense with the stock anti-positivist methodological device in social theory of conceiving society 'as a whole', of forming 'latitudinal' totalities. Here again structuralist interests play an important role. He wants to dispense with the search for the 'principle – material or spiritual – of a society, the significance common to all the phenomena of a period, the law that accounts for their cohesion. . .'.[14] However, it soon becomes apparent that his motives in this anti-totalising crusade are as much political as theoretical or methodological:

> I believe. . . that this particular idea of the 'whole of society' derives from a utopian context. This idea arose in the western world within this highly individualised historical development that culminates in capitalism. To speak of the 'whole of society' apart from the only form it has ever taken is to transform our past into a dream. We readily believe that the least we can expect of experiences, actions, and strategies is that they take into account the 'whole of society'.... But I believe that this is asking a great deal, that it means imposing impossible conditions on our actions because this notion functions in a manner that prohibits the actualisation, success, and perpetuation of these projects. 'The whole of society' is precisely that which should not be considered except as something to be destroyed. And then, we can only hope that it will never exist again.[15]

In the post-1968 Parisian conversion to localised political struggle and anti-Marxism, Foucault shared with the *Nouvelle Philosophie* a critique of globalising political strategies and movements.[16] Globalism reproduces the logic of domination against which these movements putatively struggle. It imposes an *impossible* global scenario upon all which involves the hierarchisation of demands according to a long-term and universal strategy. The freedom, interests and strategic flexibility of particular struggling groups is inhibited as they are required to accept the logic of modern society. Foucault maintains that the idea of society 'as a whole' is a utopian ideal that paralyses local initiative. The perspective of the whole must generate a truncated and partial politics because, of necessity, it is required to abstract from so much that has concrete political effects. The totalising political perspective of Marxism has tended to either subordinate or ignore that vast domain of 'unpolitical' politics, of oppression and conflict not reducible to class and economics – sanity, insanity, illness, crime and sexuality – which Foucault now problematises and liberates from silence. This non-totalising emphasis approaches politics 'from behind and cut(s) across societies on the diagonal'.[17] Foucault clearly perceives the incipient traces of *totalitarianism* in a totalising view of society. It hinders theoretical research, constrains political actions and limits the political imagination to the ossified and monolithic global movements which had perpetrated the great political disasters of the twentieth century.

Foucault's claim that the viewpoint of 'society as a whole' was 'utopian' was interlinked with a strong anti-theory rhetoric most clearly expressed in interviews. In the same way that a view of the whole is said to *totalise* in the perjorative sense that it abstracts, limits, imposes and closes, generalising theory which makes a strict inter-subjective claim must also be repulsed because its universalising logic is part of the system of western civilisation responsible for so much oppression and so many exclusions. Even attempts to transcend the present by positing alternative utopian futures do not escape Foucault's sceptical eye. Theoretical utopias also perpetuate the logic of domination materialised in the present system. Utopian visions never transcend the past but reproduce selective aspects of it through reliance on historical models. They typically also make a claim as the solution of general problems and therefore capitulate to a totalising logic The 'universal' intellectual *imposes* these visions and commitments on the forces of local social struggle by *ascribing* interests to them from some 'higher' standpoint. The oppressive present is to be opposed not by alternative utopian systems but by actual, excluded experiences. Rather naïvely Foucault once suggested that the 'actual experiences' of the counter-culture – drugs, sex, communes and other forms of consciousness – supplied a rough outline of a future society.[18] Generally his assault on totalising views of society was a protest against the pretensions of the traditional intellectual and the *reification* of theories and associated political movements which *abstract from real experiential needs and stifle the concrete aspirations of local struggles.*

The denial of subjectivity

Much of Foucault's critique of the recourse to the concept of totality in the conceptualisation of history and society echoes objections already familiar within the radical historicist tradition of totality thinking. Despite the different sources of his own theoretical inspiration, different emphases and methods of argumentation, there remain certain affinities between Foucault and the leading figures of the Frankfurt School. One need only point to the early Horkheimer's critique of the metaphysical excesses of Lukács' Hegelianism, his reluctance to view the Communist Party as the concrete historical bearer of a totalising perspective,[19] Adorno's later misgivings regarding the 'truth' of the whole[20] and their shared suspicion that the idea of progress provided an ideological legitimisation of suffering by its exclusion from emancipatory calculus. Yet, beyond these elements of a shared critique of totality, Foucault's assault on anthropologism reaches a qualitatively new intensity. In his sights was a critical annihilation of the idea of subjectivity.

Chapter Three presented a reconstruction of various critiques of the totality concept within the *Geisteswissenschaften*. There it was argued that the prevailing cultural pessimism induced a disillusionment with notions of historical progress and scepticism toward totalising history after the fashion of Hegel. A typical philosophical expression of this sceptical pessimism was the *fragmentation* of the previously *unified* totality concept into *multiple* concepts of totality, each accorded a differing *value connotation*. Weber, for instance, repudiated the idea that history signified a process of emancipation. He provided a rather pessimistic anticipation of the imminent future in the form of a negative utopia, viewing the dynamic tendencies of modern society as a threat which promised only more alienation, de-personalisation and further encroachment on human freedom. In this scenario, at least partially shared by Simmel, all positive evaluation was directed to subjective totalisation, the individual subject being conceived variously as the sole creator and final arbiter of values, the true subject of culture and the only unit accessible to hermeneutical understanding. This pessimistic retreat into subjectivity recurs in the darkest days of Frankfurt School's cultural reflections when Adorno and Horkheimer viewed those few remaining authentic individuals as the only surviving addressees of critical theory.

While Foucault shared with Weber, Simmel, Horkheimer and Adorno a rather stark and harrowing view of modern society, the strength of his antagonism to the totality concept is confirmed in efforts to track it down to the enclave of the subject: to even eject it from this sanctuary where it had invariably found support within the radical historicist tradition. Foucault's critique of totality, including even the idea of subjective totalisation, is grounded in a virulent anti-humanism and anti-subjectivism.

Foucault utterly rejects the essentialist idea of the subject common to both empiricist and rationalist streams of modern philosophy. He dismisses the idea of a *unified* and invariant subject as the origin and site of the creation and legitimisation of all values, both of the 'laws of reason' and of free moral/social actions – therefore also as the *ultimate guarantee* of the possibility of reconciliation of reason and freedom. Here, Foucault's stance is the junction and radicalisation of two trends of thought. Firstly, the historicist criticism of the atomised rational individual of the Enlightenment. This tradition including Hegel and Marx emphasised the *historico-social constitution of subjectivity*. It retains, however, the idea of a historically shaped form of subjectivity as a *critical standard* against which to judge social conditions that oppress its self-affirmation and unfolding. In other words, it retains the idea of emancipation. Secondly, the Nietzschean idea of the subject as a mere 'fiction', 'popular prejudice' or 'ideological' construct which both unknowingly serves the unconscious, anonymous 'will to power' and – in its modern exuberation – fundamentally distorts it. Such Nietzschean ideas (also deeply influencing Heidegger) are found, transformed and concretised in the psychoanalytical conception of the ego. They form the basis of the idea of the de-centred subject central to Freudian metapsychology. Here, the rational ego is merely a layer/component in the complex structure of the personality. It is the buffer and compromise between the conflictual demands of instinctual drives (id) and social regulations (superego) the identity and unity of which is always based on repression and sublimation. The Freudian concept of *therapy*, however, retains the practical emancipatory idea of enriching and maintaining this ego identity.

In Foucault, the simultaneous radicalisation of both these trends results in a wholesale repudiation of the idea of subjectivity. Not only a specific historical product both the universality and the unity of which is *illusory* (already implied in the critique of anthropologism), but also as a product of social repression and subjugation. There is no coherent or constant human being or condition that would sustain such a notion. Foucault sees the individual subject as a *product of historically changing practices and discourses*. His work represents a constant attack *on the very idea of subjectivity itself*. For him, *subjectification* has always been a historical mode of *subjugation*. The modern subject is a 'fictive atom of an ideological representation of society', product of overlapping discourses and disciplinary practices.[21]

> The individual is not to be conceived as a sort of elementary nucleus, a primitive atom, a multiple and inert material on which power comes to fasten. . . . In fact, it is already one of the prime effects of power that certain bodies, certain gestures, certain discourses, certain desires, come to be identified and constituted as individuals. The individual, that is, is not the *vis-á-vis* of power; it is, I believe, one of its prime effects. The individual is an effect of power.[22]

Like Ibsen, who peels away the layers of Peer Gynt's life only to reveal its radical insubstantiality, Foucault's aim is to peel away the historically imposed, fictive, forms of individualisation stripping subjectivity of everything but its minimal power to resist and struggle, eliminating all limitations.

This critique of the concept of the subject is successively radicalised by Foucault. Initially it is the methodological/historical aspects that dominate. The tools of methodological anthropologism lead inevitably to the *aporias* outlined in The Order of Things. However, Foucault's anti-subjectivism is not merely based on a negative critique. As with his account of modern historiography, he is convinced that recent intellectual trends offer a way through the impasse of anthropologism. He relies principally on the structuralist turn in modern linguistics and anthropology to provide a radically anti-humanist methodological alternative. The first fruit of this alternative model was Foucault's archaeology.

According to this method, it was necessary to break with the search for meanings which presupposed simple, fictive entities like philosophical systems, *oeuvres,* authors and subjects. The hermeneutical approach involves a flagrant and impermissible reduction of complexity. The interpreter sets out to tailor a plethora of historical events to a single meaning, to tailor them afterwards into some neat causal, intelligible chain in intellectual history.[23] To escape the subjectivist trap that promises a fully retrieved meaning – the utopian totality –

the archaeologist disdains meanings and excavates the hidden forms of regularity or rules inaccessible to consciousness which make it possible for subjects to say what they do. Thus Foucault was concerned less about ideas of madness than about the discursive conditions that made 'madness' a possible object of knowledge This 'positive unconscious of knowledge' was the discursive rules which provide the necessary preconditions of statements and allocate the places and functions of authors and audiences. To these epochal *epistemes* Foucault accorded a radical autonomy residing in the structuralist requirement that they be understood strictly in terms of their own discursive rules and unity. Of course, as a unified complex of unconscious rules and presuppositions, the *episteme* was a totalising concept akin to the Hegelian *Zeitgeist*. Foucault clearly qualifies this with the assumption of a plurality at any given point of time but this only renders the concept in some respects even more abstract.

In any case, the advantages accruing from this methodological procedure which delved below the level of the text, consciousness and subjectivity, avoiding the simplifications of hermeneutics and opening up a great uncharted system of unarticulated limits were soon offset by other inherent disadvantages. As Foucault's interests turned back to the investigation of the contextual social practices in which the scientific discourses of the human sciences were embedded, his affirmation of the total autonomy of these systemic conditions of possibility of meaningful discourse for a posited audience prevented him from explaining anything about the actual functioning of the discourse in question. To overcome this difficulty he was forced to discard the radical autonomy of the discursive rules.

The reappraisal occasioned by this difficulty allowed Foucault amongst other things, to widen and intensify his critique of the concept of subjectivity. The resulting genealogical approach enabled him to refocus attention on the network of concrete institutions and practices that actually imposed specific forms of subjectivity on modern humanity. From the time of Discipline and Punish (1975), the enterprise of archaeology is subsumed in a Nietzscheian style genealogical unmasking which links discursive knowledges with the institutional regime of contingent socio-historical practices from which they emerged. Genealogy assumes that knowledge and truth are always interpretations generated by a correlate matrix of practices. This interwoven network of practices, procedures, institutions, disciplines, knowledges and truths constitutes historically contingent regimes of truth/power. Genealogy at the same time preserves Foucault's trenchant methodological anti-subjectivism. The constitution of these knowledges, and their complementary disciplinary practices are accounted for without reference to any form of subjectivity:

> I don't believe the problem [of the constitution of objects] can be solved by historicising the subject. . . . One has to dispense with the constitutent subject, to get rid of the subject itself, that is to arrive at an analysis which

can account for the constitutent subject within a historical framework. And this is what I would call genealogy, that is, a form of history which can account for the constitution of knowledges, discourses, domains of objects etc., without having to make reference to a subject which is either transcendental in relation to the field of events or runs in its empty sameness throughout the course of history.[24]

Genealogy reveals the 'politics' of these discursive regimes as the labyrinthine play of complex mosaics for which questions of intention, decision or aim, miss the point that power is already invested in real and effective practices.[25]

However much this methodological ingenuity receives its impetus from perceived shortcomings in the traditional anthropologism of the human sciences, Foucault's anti-subjectivism, like his critique of the idea of 'society as a whole', is not the product of solely scientific considerations. In fact, the *anti-science* emphasis of the genealogy resides in Foucault's desire to emancipate historical knowledge from the hegemony of unitary, scientific discourse and unite its erudition with local struggles. So paradoxically, the source of his relentless anti-humanist rhetoric is an alleged emancipatory project. The emancipatory potential of this anti-humanist, anti-subjectivist exercise consists in the elimination of all limitations on human possibility. When all is demonstrated to be contingent historical construction, *even our received forms of subjectivity*, then it is evident that *almost nothing* has to be the way it is. Liberated from the chains of all historical necessities, individuals are radically free to create themselves from the infinite possibilities. Alerted to the historical contingency of the received straightjacket of identity which constrains the individual by imposing *selected* characteristics, desires, gestures, etc., contemporary social struggles can more uninhibitedly assert the excluded claims of *difference*.

Doubtless, the radicality of Foucault's suspicions against the idea of subjectivity must be sought in his continued sympathy and empathy for the insane and marginalised. First-hand experience of the violence and coercion inherent in conventional categorisation, in its impact on the insane, provoked a profound scepticism of even the most taken for granted social constructs. While Foucault shared this suspicions with other anti-psychiatrists like R. D. Laing, his own train of thought led him to historically explore the whole power/knowledge ensemble that sustained it.

The carceral society

The real basis of Foucault's political aversion to the idea of the subject lies in the thoroughgoing character of his critique of modernity. Unlike Weber, Adorno and Horkheimer who view the ideal autonomous modern subject as a potential or actual ally in the struggle against the increasingly rationalised, administered, totalitarian society, Foucault goes so far as to doubt the bona fides of modern subjectivity. He spies here just another shape of oppression. However, the possibility of this depth of oppression is inseparable from the pervasive character of modernity and its disciplinary regime of normalisation. Ironically, Foucault's radical scepticism regarding all ideological forms of totality – even that of the subject – is curiously connected to, and nutured by a negative image of totality: that of the carceral society. Like Horkheimer and Adorno, Foucault's critique of metaphysics and philosophy of history does not prevent him from allowing the concept of totality to slip back into his own image of modernity. Modern western society is a singular historical phenomena demonstrating in its very accidentality the ominous 'success' of totalisation in the sense of an interlocking of all the various requirements and practices of power into one system.[26] Miraculously, and in a way which seriously detracts from the force of his totality-critique, totality now becomes a legitimate concept for the analysis concerning the most important object: the present.

The spirit of totalisation which Foucault so remorsely attacked in his early works as the instrument of an overblown and deformed rationality in the shape of the modern human sciences takes it revenge in his account of modernity. The critique of civilisatory reason which persisted as an undertone in the histories of madness and the clinic now asserts itself as a *global* critique of modern society. He insists in the first chapter of Discipline and Punish that this work is no academic history of the past but 'the history of the present'. His portrayal of the evolution of disciplinary techniques, judicial punishment, criminology and penal institutions from the end of the classical age through the nineteenth century expands ineluctably into a savage condemnation of the modern 'disciplinary society' which, despite Foucault's purportly purely descriptive brief, easily manages to evoke the suggestion of increasing total domination. The key to this shift is Foucault's staunch belief that the rapidly expanding disciplinary institutions of the nineteenth century initiated a confrontation with the problems of organisation, administration, surveillance and control of large populations that rapidly became constitutive problems of modern politics.[27] The 'carceral network' was a microcosm which prefigured the new techniques, instruments, attitudes and powers which now dominate modern societies. The experts, technocrats, administrators and managers preside over a closed system of supervision and control that evidences no essential difference from the institutions of correction:

> Prison continues, on those who are entrusted to it, a work begun
> elsewhere, which the whole society pursues on each individual through
> innumerable mechanisms of discipline. By means of a carceral
> continuum, the authority that sentences infiltrates all those other
> authorities that supervise, transform, correct, improve. It might be said
> that nothing really distinguishes them any more except the singularly
> 'dangerous' character of the delinquents, the gravity of their departures
> from normal behaviour and the necessary solemnity of the ritutal. But, in

its function, the power to punish is not essentially different from that of curing or educating.[28]

The birth of the prison ushered in a new age where the economy and society required a new form of individual subordination. The systemic demands of this new social ensemble engendered a whole range of disciplinary mechanisms and professionals whose principal task it was to ensure the *normality* of the population. The imperatives of the new political economy required the productive service from individuals in their concrete lives. The regime has to gain access to the bodies of individuals and to exercise control over their acts and attitudes. Thus the network of penal institutions were joined by the teacher, the social worker and the factory manager as agents of an overarching system of normalising power that judged the individual from the cradle to the grave, shaping body, gestures, aptitudes and behaviour according to the 'universal rule of the normative'. The nascent human sciences prove indispensible in this regime engendering and legitimating a whole arsenal of therapies and techniques appropriate to the required new shape of subjectivity. Inter-meshed with disciplinary practices, they were organs of a new social power whose domination is infinitely detailed, productive, ineluctable and de-centred.

In this new regime, the position of the professional and the adminstrator may be enhanced but they do not control the workings of the whole. Modern society is a complex matrix of many mechanisms that somehow fit neatly together without designer or controller.[29] The 'judges of normality' are *omnipresent* but as *arms of a subjectless, normalising power* all the more effective because of its radical dispersion.

The parallels between Foucault's account of the 'carceral society' and Horkheimer and Adornos' view of the totally administered society are striking. In each case modernity is presented as a virtually seamless, closed system articulated by organisations and institutions of domination that have a life of their own tied to a logic of functioning that shapes, controls and directs every aspect of life, even of those who apparently direct, control and benefit from the system. They share the idea of society as a negative totality already anticipated in Weber's frightening negative utopia: the 'iron cage'. However, despite the similiarity of these assessments, they all arrive at this shared diagnosis by clearly distinguishable routes.

Horkheimer and Adorno understand the totally administered society as a product of the last phase of bourgeois development. The crises of liberal capitalism were followed by a period of structural transformation which produced the new forms of 'state capitalism'. The society emerging from this metamorphosis was characterised by concentrated economic power in vast corporations, the strengthening of the state power with its intervention into the economy and the resulting fusion of economic and political power, the extension of administrative control over the population through centralisation of organisation and the manipulation of advertising and the culture industry.

Horkheimer and Adorno view this tightened control as a result of *psychic* manipulation made possible by the new technology of propaganda and the weakening of the individual ego as a consequence of the post-liberal decline of the bourgeois family and the increasing socialising role of mass society.[30]

Foucault focuses his own analysis of incipient totalitarianism on the early institutions of confinement and the discovery of the corporal disciplines. The new nineteenth century regime of power/knowledge mastered the techniques of *bodily discipline* which rendered the individual a compliant material for social moulding. Foucault underscores the importance of these new instruments of corporeal mastery because, in line with his critique of subjectivity, he views individuals as formless, conditionable beings whose subjectivity is nothing more than a precipitate of habitual drilling exerted on the body.[31]

There is a certain complementarity in these two constructions of the disciplinary, adminstered society. Horkheimer and Adorno never bothered to fill in the detail of their account of totalitarian modernity. Rarely do they speak of precise mechanisms and techniques of control. Although they occasionally mention the role of the institutions of mass society like the school, the trade union and the club, they preferred to draw attention to the most striking recent manifestations of creeping reification and concentration of power: to increasing economic monopoly, extension of the state power and the burgeoning consumerism which exposed the population to a subtle incorporation and subordination to the system. Foucault's analysis of the techniques of micropower certainly enriches this account. With scrupluous empirical detail, he is able to show how relations of power are interwoven into the social experience of sexuality, the family, schools, medicine, social work and social science. He demonstrates that every capillary of modern life is saturated with the effects of power; he details the mechanisms and techniques whereby power circulates, whereby control is exerted and exercised within a *subjectless, multiform and fluid* grid of inter-relations. This image of an anonymous, pervasive domination clearly converges with Horkheimer and Adorno's thesis of total administration and control.

Despite the similarities of these diagnoses and the complementarity of the analyses in some important respects, the two critiques part ways on several vital issues that can best be put down to a difference of critical standpoint and its theoretical consequences. This difference is most easily approached by a consideration of the question of *resistance* which is articulated in both theories but most fully by Foucault in his analytics of power.

Foucault on resistance

While Horkheimer, Adorno and Foucault paint uncomprisingly harrowing portraits of modern *global* domination, neither party relinquishes the possibility of resistance. Seemingly, the former come closest because they perceive no sociologically significant addressee for their revamped critical theory. The working class has been co-opted by the allurements of material prosperity and the culture industry, the critical intelligentsia was either annihilated by Fascism or scattered on the wind of emigration. Only the isolated survivors remain, marooned and surrounded by a compliant and incorporated, mass society. Horkheimer and Adorno's critical theory is a helpless message of the isolated survivors set adrift in the hope of a future reception. The message *implies the possibility of resistance* and the authors provide two, admittedly fragile, reasons for hope. Firstly, they present a *historico-philosophical unmasking* of the instrumental form of social organisation that has led to the triumph of domination. History has presented opportunities to reverse the march of instrumental reason and even if these have not yet been taken the possibility of a reversal remains open: domination is *a contingent fact* of contemporary history, not its *necessary meaning*. At the same time, the theories of non-identity and mimesis hint at a residue of nature not assimilable to the requirements of domination. Here at least resistance finds a minimal platform.

Foucault is much more theoretically explicit on the question of resistance. Despite the gloom of his *totalised* vision of modernity and its comprehensive systemic domination, resistance is a vital element of his genealogical theory of power. At the centre the genealogical approach lies Foucault's Nietzscheian assertion that all discourse both carried a hidden power and derived from the practices of power.[32] This renewed interest in the nexus of power and knowledge required a rethinking of the available understandings of power. The conventional views which see power as a 'property', a 'privilege', something pertaining to and exercised over subjects, something to be appropriated, something exercising a prohibition, concentrated in a class or the state all seemed inadequate:

> The analysis, made in terms of power, must not assume the sovereignty of the state, the form of law, or the over-all unity of a domination are given at the outset; rather these are only the terminal forms power takes. It seems to me that power must be understood in the first instance as a multiplicity of force relations immanent in the sphere in which they operate and which constitute their own organisation; as a process which, through ceaseless struggles and confrontations, transforms, strengthens, or reverses them; as the support which these force relations find in one another, thus forming a chain or a system, or on the contrary, the disjunctions and contradictions which isolate them from one another; and lastly, as strategies in which they take effect, whose general design of institutional crystallisation is embodied in the state apparatus, in the formulation of law, in the various social hegemonies.[33]

Foucault maintains that the static, transactional, oppositional and repressive metaphors of power simply fail to capture the *dynamic productivity, the omnipresence, fluidity and inherent relationalism* of modern power. Modern power is *expansive, always utilising rather than negating oppositions in the service of its own increased saturation and circulation.* To capture this fluidity and relational character of modern power, Foucault often has recourse to the image of the endless battle where victory is only a momentary respite, constantly eclipsed by recharged resistance and a changing alignment of forces and strategies. And where power is ever present, so is resistance:

> Where there is power, there is resistance, and yet, or rather consequently, this resistance is never in a position of exteriority in relation to power. . . .
> These points of resistance are present everywhere in the power network. Hence there is no single locus of great Refusal, no soul of revolt. . . .
> Instead there is a plurality of resistances, each of them a special case. . .
> by definition, they can only exist in the strategic field of power relations. But this does not mean that they are only a reaction or rebound, forming with respect to the basic domination an underside that is in the end always passive, doomed to perpetual defeat. Resistances do not derive from a few hetergeneous principles; but neither are they a lure or a promise that is of necessity betrayed. They are the odd term in relations of power; they are inscribed in the latter as an irreducible opposite.[34]

De-centred power always finds a similarly dispersed resistance. It inhabits the same place as power, not as its 'counter-stoke' or passive underside but as its own inverse energy.

One does not have to look too far to find the historical underpinning of these reflections on power. Foucault perceives his work as a response to the collapse of a *global, revolutionary politics.* In an interview he contemplates the 'end of politics' which had gained its meaning from the existence of revolution.[35] May '68 and its aftermath registered a decisive rupture marked by the strategic impotence of the putative revolutionary party, an explosion of *local, dispersed resistances* to dominant socio-political hegemonies and the the total incapacity of the existing political vocabularies (especially the Marxist) to do them justice.[36] Foucault's reflections on power fill this theoretical vacuum by articulating a new configuration of resistance and theorising its possibility.

Yet, in Foucault's hands the post-1968 struggles assume trans-historical significance when appropriated in terms of a Nietzscheian influenced analytics of power. In this framework where the totalising will to knowledge is *abstracted from* its specifically modern anchorage in the expanding complex of the new disciplinary practices and human sciences and *historically generalised as an omnipresent, anonymous power in general,*[37] resistance is no longer 'a real sociological entity' but something *equally ubiquitous and amorphous* 'in the social body, in classes, groups and individuals themselves which in some sense escapes relations of power'.[38]

Although affirming the inevitability of resistance, Foucault's account of it is hardly reassuring. The 'something' which escapes relations of power is a shadowy figure. Indeed it is a limit but its status is unclear. Undoubtedly this difficulty, as others raised against the 'analytics of power', arises from

Foucault's grim adherence to a genealogical scepticism. Yet, what he summons up here is clearly the completely empty remnant of the 'subject' as the mere *possibility* of ending/overcoming any concrete determination. His determined anti-humanism and critique of totality in all its emancipatory versions necessarily excoriates all historically recognisable causes and candidates for resistance leaving only 'the other' of power as a minimal placeholder.

Genealogical *aporias*

Foucault's genealogical critique is critique without illusions. His is a timely reminder that humanism and its values, concepts of totality and totalising theory have served to further and legitimate domination, sustain illusions. Nevertheless, the question remains whether this critique is not too one-dimensional and *totalising* in its condemnation of all emancipatory values, theories and projects?

The concluding assessment of Horkheimer and Adorno at the end of Chapter Six highlights the dilemmas of their critique of enlightenment. A *critique of civilisatory reason* forged with *rational* means inevitably collapses into *aporias*. Horkheimer and Adorno accepted this but at considerable cost. Foucault, too, chooses the *aporetic* path of a rational unmasking of the human sciences and its associated institutional practices and he takes an even more uncompromising step with his critical destruction of the putative motor, albeit itself conditioned, and beneficary of enlightenment: the human subject – Man. The question immediately arises: does Foucault fare any better or worse than his predecessors on this road?

Disillusionment with revolutionary hopes plays a decisive role in deflecting both the Frankfurt School and Foucault along the paradoxical route of a wholesale critique of reason using rational means. While never a Marxist, Foucault maintains that his thought was decisively shaped by the political question of the desirability of revolution. However, the problematising of emancipatory discourse tied to revolutionary projects also blended with elements of a sustained methodological critique of the human sciences to produce an especially potent mixture. Foucault's methodological divorce from anthropologism raises awkward questions regarding his own critical standpoint. Given his genealogical indictment of all discourse as incriminated products of *particular* regimes of truth which govern their discursive possibilities, a cloud of uncertainty surrounds the status of his own work.

Foucault has repeatedly stressed the 'political' character of his own work. He has gone so far as to speak of his historical writings as 'only a function' of the local struggles in which he involved himself.[39] This is certainly in keeping with his idea of the *specific intellectual* who foregoes the *universalising task of speaking the 'truth' on behalf of mankind* in order to use his/her expertise to develop *strategies*[40] which further local struggles in his/her own specific orbit.[41] He views the contemporary philosophical task as:

the question as to what we ourselves are. That is why contemporary philosophy is entirely political and entirely historical. It is the politics immanent to history and the history indispensible to politics.[42]

Yet, Foucault's genealogical perspective allegedly precludes identification with these struggles. Identification would signify a capitulation to humanism, a lapse in the *anti-totalising scepticism* which guards against *ideological co-option*. Only such extreme caution allows the engaged philosopher to avoid *legitimating* aspiring contestants in the struggle over truth and thus sanctioning another in the long series of *regimes of truth* responsible for so much *violence and oppression*. Furthermore, the *spectre of substitutionalism* is always a threat to the universalising intellectual: identification allows the intellectual *to speak for the oppressed and define their interests*. Foucault would assert that he does not reject emancipation but he *refuses to identify or name it for fear of collusion in new totalitarian regimes of power/knowledge*.

This curious *engaged detachment* is inscribed in the genealogist's positivist inclinations. Rather than attempt to render historical actions comprehensible in terms of intentions, consciousness and context, the geneaologist offers an *explanation* of action and meaning in terms of horizons and underlying practices. Methodological detachment allows Foucault to detour the quagmire of meanings and self-understanding and externally grasp the configuration of practices/discourses in their complex structure. This positivist leaning manifests itself also in Foucault's bracketing of validity claims. He addresses the question of truth only to demonstrate its power effects and the functional role it plays in maintaining a given discursive regime. Foucault's historiography maintains a *descriptive* poise that comes from a deliberate avoidance of normative and validity considerations.[43] He prefers to remain the spectator unmoved by a history reduced to a raging kaleidoscope of contingencies rather than posit fictive continuities and thus become immured in the *totalising* logic of domination and ideological co-option. The result, as Charles Taylor has noted, is the unearthly relativism of the complete *outsider*:

> Foucault's monolithic relativism only seems plausible if one takes the outsider's perspective, the view from Sirius; or perhaps imagines oneself a soul in Plato's myth of Er. Do I want to be born a Sung Dynasty Chinese, or a subject of Hummurabi of Babylon, or a twentieth-century American? Without a prior identity, I couldn't begin to choose. They incarnate incommensurable goods. . . . But this is not my/our situation. We have already *become* something. Questions of truth and freedom can arise for us in the transformations we undergo or project. In short, we have a *history*. We live in time not just self-enclosed in the present, but essentially related to a past which has helped define out identity, and a future which puts it again in question.[44]

The strains imposed by Foucault's strategic methodological detachment reveal themselves in the difficulties that numerous commentators have pointed out.[45] Chief amongst these is the problem of critical values or perspective arising from Foucault's retreat into genealogical relativism.

This problem has been sharply formulated by Nancy Fraser. On what basis, she asks, does Foucault advocate resistance to domination? Why prefer struggle over submission? How does he distinguish the forces of domination from those of the dominated unless having recourse to an unacknowledged normative terminology?[46] Clearly Foucault foregoes the normative foundation that might have been provided by humanist values. He rejects these values and refuses to posit alternatives so as to escape the totalising logic of the form of life and theoretical discourse he opposes. But such a refusal hardly resolves the difficulty. Foucault commits a methodological self-ostracism which transforms him from *engaged social critic* to *indifferent alien who sees only the ceaseless, meaningless rotation of domination and resistance*. As Taylor insists, however, western civilisation does possess an identity constituted by the historical accumulation of *past struggles and their ideological expressions*. No matter how incompatible and contestable are the values which have solidified in this process of historical accumulation or identity formation, they cannot be dispensed with *simply because it is through them that present suffering is articulated as suffering, it is the struggle around them that defines who we are*. And this is precisely the question Foucault rightly views as the burning issue of contemporary philosophy when he asks 'what we ourselves are'.

Foucault's uncompromising critique of totality appears to strip him of the tools required to formulate any sort of positive answer to this question. He appears content with a radically sceptical strategy – a purely *negative* critique – leaving no stone unturned in pursuit of *accommodatory illusions*.[47] He sustains a vigil against the immanent domination of the contemporary regime of truth and his work stands as humanism's counter-discourse. The attitude determining this stance is encapsulated in Foucault's conviction that the contemporary moment is neither 'privileged' in a way which would justify rewriting history in its terms nor 'bad' but simply 'dangerous'.[48] The historical moment confronting the contemporary individual demands constant vigilance. Yet, the product of this viligance is an exceedingly *one-sided, one-dimensional, portrait of the present*. Foucault offers a *totalitarian* interpretation of contemporary institutions, practices and the human sciences as a unified matrix of domination. Out of a radical anti-totalising vigilance that views '*everything*' as dangerous, emerges a seamless, totalised view of the present.

Many commentators have noted the one-dimensionality of Foucault's view of modernity. Sometimes it is explained as a *rhetorical device* born of Foucault rejection of conventional theoretical discourse in favour of a more *aesthetical mode of presentation*.[49] Foucault has spoken of his works as 'fictions', as 'fireworks'. This move is again very similiar to the stance adopted by Horkheimer and Adorno in <u>Dialectic of Enlightenment</u>. They too chose an aesthetical mode of discourse as one less contaminated by the totalising logic of reason. Their aphorisms were intentional exaggerations constructed to *provoke, to warn, to register the crisis of a social totality that had seemingly co-opted resistance and overcome crisis.* Despite these striking similiarities, however, there is something more *theoretically* substantial and *problematic* in Foucault's one-dimensionality: and this is his new 'theory' of power.

Power revisited

It has already been noted that Foucault's histories of madness, the clinic and the prison coalesce into a *global, one-dimensional* view of modernity as the *carceral society.* Indispensible to this thesis is Foucault's new conceptualisation of power which was envisaged as accounting for the *new forms, modalities and reach* of power that emerged in the early nineteenth century with the unique fusion that took place between innovative new institutional structures, disciplinary practices and scientific knowledge. The modern disciplinary form of power is characterised by its *ubiquitousness.* It is all-pervasive, constant, local and *productive* in so far as it perpetually moulds and creates the practices required to sustain its specific form of life, the role of the prison is not to *repress* delinquency but to *create* it as a threat to society which provides the rationale for further expansion of the apparatii of social control and domination.[50] In this ineliminable, omnipresent form, *micro-power or bio-power* simply takes possession of the body and shapes individuals to its own requirements through training, discipline and routine. Under Foucault's gaze, the secret enclaves in which power has concealed itself are revealed. Theoretical criteria of well-formedness, coherency and validity, as well as institutional licensing which empowers some individuals and excludes others, lose their innocence and are assimilated into the modern matrix of imposed order and domination. Included in this notion of power are naturally also the older forms of power like state authority, economic and social coercion and prescription, those *global strategies which traverse the social whole shifting according to the ebb and flow of struggle and resistance.*

Foucault's new concept of power is clearly as *amorphous as it is subjectless.* Not only is this vast modern mosaic anonymous and bereft of intention but it is also rather ill-defined. The lack of definition in Foucault's concept of power stems undoubtedly from its *globality.* One commentator has remarked that, in Foucault, power:

> tends to occupy the 'anonymous' place which classical treatises in
> metaphysics reserved for substance; without location, identity, or
> boundaries, it is everywhere and nowhere at the same time.[51]

The theoretical origins of this amorphorous globalism lies in the Nietzscheian roots of Foucault's version of power. For Nietzsche, there is no order in the world other than that *imposed* on chaos by the human will-to power. Stripped of this original subjectivism, Foucault's idea of power, at its most fundamental level,[52] retains this *constitutive, transcendental function,* power being the source of all form. This understanding facilitates the putative dispersion of power intimated by Foucault as nothing is untouched by this anonymous, amorphous *constitutive power.*

Whatever the gains Foucault derives from this *decentring* and *dispersal* of power in terms of explaining some significant features of modernity,[53] the resulting subordination of cultural values and norms (including truth) to the service of power and their *radical reduction to* networks of power/knowledge forces him to embrace relativism. The *problem of values* which manifests itself in Foucault's *anti-humanist, anti-totalising, detached methodology resurfaces as a lack of discriminatory criteria within his ideas on power.* In other words, Foucault dispossesses himself of the means to articulate the idea of power as *coercion or domination. The ubiquity of power* in this conception transmogrifies it into an *inescapable and normatively neutral phenomena.*[54] Yet Foucault's own historical studies point to many instances of institutional arrangement, disciplinary practices, constraint on bodies and persons that clearly involve a power that is both *coercive, dominating and at least potentially eliminable.* Foucault's general characterisation of modern power as *inescapable, all-pervasive and productive* can succeed only by *levelling and blurring all discriminatory categories and nuances* concerning modern power and therefore simply avoiding the vital political questions of distinguishing instances of *eradicable and coercive* power. Despite Foucault's claim that his *global scepticism* leads to *'pessimistic activism',* it might more plausibly be argued that the inescapability of power relations engenders a *fatalism.*[55] Since ubiquitous power and domination always engenders resistance, the pessimism of Foucault's account of the modern social totality is matched by an equally unsupportable optimism for which any issue or field of action is equally worthy and promising. Foucault's lack of discrimination – just because of the pervasiveness and interlocking of all forms of power – seems to condemn resistance to futility. It is true that all social life is immersed in power relations but this does not mean the necessity to capitulate to the *inevitability of coercion and domination.*

The lack of discriminatory criteria stemming from the *globalism* of Foucault's critique of modernity grounded in this *ubiquitous* understanding of power leads to *critical myopia.* To view the modern social worker as another agent of *normalisation,* of an *all pervasive societal surveillance* may find some justification in view of the increasing incursion of welfare instrumentalities into the lives of relatively powerless beneficiaries. However, to lump together all processes of *socialisation* and *individuation as forces of normalisation* and *subjection* is to lapse into hyper-critical vacuity. Foucault commits this unfortunate conflation because the theory of power on which he depends is unable to articulate the distinction between forms of *constraint* essential in any process of individual socialisation and the forms of power which mark coercive restraint on already developed needs and abilities which could be satisfied in view of some project for change.

The difficulties with Foucault's *global* critique, with his iconoclastic new ideas on power evidence the inherent problems of his *totalising* critique of modern reason. In this critique the *dialectical, contradictory* aspects of historical modernity fall out: all that remains is the one-dimensional portrait. It is true that occasionally Foucault mentions demonstrably positive elements of these processes like the 'democratic revolutions' – the creation of parliamentary representative regimes and formally egalitarian juridicial frameworks – but this is usually only to emphasize its 'darker side' with the complementary growth of the carceral, disciplinary matrix of micro-mechanisms which are asymmetrical and non-egalitarian.[56] As Habermas has argued, Foucault's global critique filters out those aspects of reform to law and political institutions which represent unmistakeable gains in civil rights and legal security.[57] However, even if he was to pay more detailed attention to these historical gains, there is nothing in his theoretico-conceptual armoury which would allow him to articulate them. For him, such eighteenth century discoveries as 'progress' and 'individuality' are nothing more than carefully crafted ideological instruments of power. Ultimately, Foucault's totalised image of the carceral society suffers from its own *imbalance* and fails to do justice to the complexity of modernity.

Conclusion

In his last thoughts on the question of the Enlightenment and its historical contemporaneity, Foucault concludes with his own formulation of the contemporary meaning of critique:

> The critical ontology of ourselves has to be considered not, certainly as a theory, a doctrine, nor even as a permanent body of knowledge that is accumulating; it has to be conceived as an attitude, an ethos, a philosophical life in which the critique of what we are is at one and the same time the historical analysis of the limits that are imposed on us and an experiment with the possibilities of going beyond them.

For Foucault this critical task is primarily a work on 'our limits, that is, a patient labour giving form to our impatience for liberty'.[59] This understanding neatly encapsulates the tension in his project. His critique is a practically orientated enterprise guided by an *anti-totalising scepticism* which perceives historical *accumulations as oppressive limitations* and refuses to legitimate them. Everything is open to question and no limits are to be accepted as 'necessary'. Foucault's contribution to this task was his various *genealogical* studies which revealed the historical 'limits', the *political* underpinnning of many contemporary social phenomena, institutions, practices and knowledges. At the same time, Foucault presupposes a *'we'* that according to his own radical historicism can be nothing other than a result of *historical accumulation*. This *'we'* is the object of critique: critique must analyse the limits imposed on *'us'*.

However, this *'we'* already possesses an identity and aspirations stemming from its historical past. Even if aspects of our identity and aspirations are matters of debate and struggle, considered by all or only some of us to be *limitations* to be overcome, it still remains the case that our own self-understanding and vision of possible futures is largely conditioned by this historically sedimented and always evolving identity, this *'we'*. The liberty Foucault views as *the object of our impatience is quite meaningless without it.*

Yet, as Foucault's critique of totality reinforces, he is unwilling to acknowledge any *core of identity or value aspirations* in modern subjectivity as the basis of a critical perspective. The liberty he would have us impatiently seeking is entirely without *positive content*. He contrives to *methodologically suppress his own orientating critical values* – obviously the product of contemporary progressive political sympathies – in order to avoid their *co-option by* the existing power/knowledge regime of the carceral society. This *engaged detachment* is a product of his one-dimensional, global critique of modernity. As Richard Wolin has observed, the 'portrait of ubiquitous domination he draws is so totalising and convincing that there is no prospect of escape'.[60] Foucault is sufficiently hostile and suspicious of present society to prefer a *theoretical leap into anti-totalising sceptical relativism* which transforms history into a *contingent process of relentless change marked only by the ceaseless rotation of power and resistance.*

This theoretical *leap* is one which loses touch with the tradition of critical historicism reconstructed in the previous chapters. While Foucault eventually came to recognise the affinities between this tradition and his own programme, his critique of totalising *anthropologism* obstructs the path to a fuller convergence. As the similarities between his course and that of Horkheimer and Adorno reveal, the affinities are real, but Foucault's unfortunate and premature celebration of the death of man commits him to a more radical course which even threatens the rationale of his critical enterprise. As the conclusion shall argue, Horkheimer and Adorno are open to the charge that their searching reassessment of the tradition of totality thinking remains immured within the concept criticised. Their *totalising* critique of the administered society collapses in *theoretical aporias* and a political cul de sac. This difficulty returns with Foucault, only in his case the humanist *faith* which sustained Horkheimer and Adorno is *disclaimed*. His even more emphatic critique of totality points to the same theoretical and practical *cul de sac* but with the added consequence that its thorough annihilation of 'man', paradoxically, dislocates critique from the orientating source of its meaning. The elimination of historical identity in the name of the critique of totality leaves Foucault's 'politics immanent to history' without even a tentative direction, without the prospect of emancipation, a restless *will to change*.

Conclusion

The preceding chapters present a rather complex tale, a series of episodes, theoretical gains, losses and metamorphoses in a story which has not reached its conclusion. The founder of the tradition of radical historicism never abandoned the *religious* dimension which had always underpinned traditional philosophical ideas of totality. In this story Hegel was a transitional figure who proposed a compelling synthesis of old and new elements. Under the impact of the bourgeois revolution he presented a humanist reading of the totality concept and largely developed the conceptual framework for a purely *immanent* understanding of history and human meaning. For Hegel, the totality of history constituted a processual development whereby humanity attained both a consciousness, and actualisation of, its freedom as a lifeworld. While this process clearly had for Hegel an essential theologico-metaphysical meaning, his emancipatory, humanist optimism can hardly be denied.

Marx quite consciously dispensed with metaphysical residues and relocated the concept of totality on the *practical* terrain of revolutionary praxis. Responding to the failure of liberal reform and philosophical critique he reasserted Hegel's emancipatory optimism without philosophical dress. He renounced the philosophical *idea of history* to give expression and assistance to the concrete struggles of real individuals (acting as social classes). The concept of totality now reverberates with the significance of practical *anticipation*. It is the *theoretically clarified* perspective of a class of potential agents in a process of radical social transformation. Yet, it could not be said that Marx completely escapes Hegel's philosophy of history. His late works reveal unmastered traces of Hegel. The unconscious historical finalism of <u>Capital</u> points to unresolved tensions in Marx's concept of totality.

The historical and cultural conditions which had sustained the emancipatory optimism of Hegel and Marx receded towards the end of the nineteenth century. In a climate of rapid industrialisation, national self-assertion and political stabilisation, radical philosophy of history with its future orientated commitment to the complete reorganisation of society lost credibility. The leading thinkers of the *Geisteswissenschaften* shared a distaste for full-blown philosophy of history. Although theoretically guarded and anti-speculative, their work, nevertheless, discloses a disturbing new image of history. Increasingly they perceive the de-personalising, alien, objectivist trend of social processes. In Weber, this amounts to a negative utopia, the 'iron cage', which crystallises these forebodings of cultural and bureaucratic ossification into a vision of negative totality. This potentially tragic vision, shared by the pre-Marxist Lukács, highlighted the increasing autonomy of the spheres of objective culture. Both Weber and Simmel almost despair of bringing the independent 'logics' of modernity under rational control in the interests of human subjectivity. As a result, the meaning of history undergoes a rather profound inversion. Its formerly emancipatory meaning dissipates before a new look of oppression, de-personalisation, alienation and imprisonment.

History and Class Consciousness marks a new turn and a re-awakening of radical historicism. Lukács offered a unifying synthesis of the two preceding interpretations of totality. While sustaining his mentors' stress on the qualitative increase in alienation/reification in bourgeois society, he subordinated this insight to a revived Marxian affirmation of the emancipatory meaning of history. In perceiving the increasing oppression of objective cultural processes through the prism of the Hegelian-Marxian paradigm of alienation, he restored a critical, humanist concept of totality. He reopened the practical, cultural meaning of the concept by viewing history (the socialist future) as the possibility of meaningful social experience as free, collective, conscious, always revocable, activity. Yet, Lukács also resuscitated the idealist scaffolding of totality. This perspective for him was synonomous with the elimination of reification and the culmination of history.

Lukács' vision of emancipatory historical totalisation as revolutionary praxis quickly crumbled before the castastrophes of Fascism, depression, the political defeat of the Communist movement and the eventual stabilisation of capitalism. Reeling from this series of historical disasters in the 1930s and 1940s, Horkheimer and Adorno pursued a radical, if paradoxical, course. Simultaneously, they mounted a withering critique of the concept of totality as part of an instrumentalising logic of enlightenment while restoring a negative image of totality with their view of totally administered modern society.

The most important aspects of this paradoxical course are reproduced in the work of Foucault. He set out quite consciously to destroy the concept of totality and thus represents a radical challenge to the tradition of radical historicism. His political experience and theoretical training inclined him to view the totality concept as an agent of oppression and normalisation. For Foucault, emancipatory commitment implied eternal, anti-totalising scepticism. Yet, as with Horkheimer and Adorno, this anti-totalising intent is accompanied by an unexpected re-evocation of totality in the form of an ultra-pessimistic vision of modernity as the carcereal society. Despite Foucault's scathing methodological and political repudiation of the totality concept, he does not hesitate to salvage it for polemic and probably for other purposes.[1] His view of the normalising society and ubiquitous power effect a vision of relentless modernity caught between all-encompassing institutionalisation and meaningless resistance. However, the similarities and correspondences between the leading Frankfurt School thinkers and Foucault could not disguise the even more fundamental discrepancies which ally the former to the tradition of radical historicism and make the latter its unrelenting opponent. In the last chapter, it was argued that Horkheimer and Adorno preserved their emancipatory intent with a defence of modern autonomous bourgeois subjectivity. Without disguising their concern for instrumentalising distortions, they still clearly affirm the idea of autonomous subjectivity as a historical legacy and a positive human value. Foucault, on the other hand, true to Nietzsche, holds consistently to an anti-totalising view of history that refuses to see in modern subjectivity anything more than an oppressive social mould, an ideology imposed on modern individuals by normalising power. He preserves the idea of emancipation but denies it content for fear of substitutionalism or co-option. He therefore parts ways with radical historicism which still clings to an emancipatory project concerned to build *on the present*, to liberate a historical potential and human value immanent to, yet currently constrained by, existing society as a historical legacy of social forms and values.

This project – history as a practical, emancipatory totalisation – is one confined to the historical experience of modern western civilisation. The preceding study has attempted to incorporate this sense of dynamic historical experience as a vital determinant of the changing fortunes of the radical historicist concept of totality, its changing theoretical articulation and reception over a period of more than 180 years. The idea of universal history was a meaningful project only for a social existence constituted in its very being by an awareness of its historicity.[2] This experience of modernity was forged by the new dynamism of the economy and society which finally overturned traditional late feudal socio-political forms. These dynamic processes saturated all spheres of modern industrial life generating their own new ensemble of life forms, subjective experiences and social possibilities beyond the comprehension of earlier times.

In his address 'The Subject of History' Habermas encapsulates the multiple historical components contributing to the experience he terms 'modernisation'.[3] This analysis captures the essential features of the dynamic epoch which gave birth to this constantly shifting understanding of the concept of totality. Bourgeois society institutionalised an objective economic mechanism for the self-expansion of production and this transformation to economic dynamism built on constant technological change instigated its own parallels in other spheres of modern life. In modern culture, the old respect for tradition gave way before permanent innovation and novelty. The increasing complexity of the interlocking socio-economic system generated a need for greater regulation and closer control. The economic imperatives of a purportedly self-adjusting productive system conflicted with, and increasingly gave way before, socio-political demands for increased administrative manipulation. The liberation of bourgeois commerce from the constraints of tradition was accompanied by the emergence of a universal morality which transcended all parochialisms and questioned all relations based on domination and force. The disintegration of the power of tradition also signalled the failing capacity of the old culture to provide worldviews and sustain convincing interpretations of the whole. This constant erosion ultimately involved the relinquishment of the *cognitive* demand to *reproduce the totality* and the simultaneous subjectivisation of attitudes and beliefs.[4]

According to Habermas, this originally diverse but increasingly unified historical process engendered the modern consciousness of progress, crisis and self-emancipation so conspicuous in all configurations of the radical historicist concept of totality. The experience of progress, crisis and emancipatory aspirations was constitutive of the cultural meaning of the radical historicist totality concept. These elements of modern social experience permeate the conceptual structure of the concept of totality from Hegel to Foucault, albeit with very different accents, evaluations and emphases. But the differences should not obscure the underlying commonalities. In each case, the elements coalesce into *historical constructs* which unify and diagnose modern experience. Despite the shifting configurations always re-articulated in accordance with the tempo and perspectives of contemporary history, these basic elements are constant and permeate this whole tradition of cultural self-reflection in modernity. Agnes Heller anchors the continuity underlying totality thinking in the embeddedness of its conceptual elements in the experience of dynamic modernity:

> Human existence over the last two hundred years is experienced as
> historical existence. Philosophies of history answer the questions about
> the sense of historical existence and so they satisfy the needs of our time.[5]

In other words, the categories of totalisation 'express, formulate and satisfy our needs'.[6] According to Heller, we are all born philosophers of history.

A sympathetic recognition of the embeddedness of the categories of totality in our everyday historical experience is clearly pertinent to any tentative assessment of the tradition of radical historicism. In its light, many of the attacks on the concept as a metaphysical residue appear rather superficial. While these criticisms do not completely miss the mark when aimed at all remnants of classical philosophy of history, they typically fail to acknowledge both the radical historicist tradition's own reckoning with its relapses – evidenced in its ongoing self-critique – and to appreciate the continuing existential basis of these categories in the everyday experience of modernity. The paradoxical return of the concept of totality in such a vehement anti-totalising thinker as Foucault illustrates its indispensibility and affinity with modern self-reflection.

With this in mind, it may be instructive to briefly recall the Frankfurt School critique of totality. With some justice their late work has been interpreted as a disintegration of the emancipatory understanding of totality expounded by Hegel, Marx and Lukács. Adorno and Horkheimer gave this emancipatory tradition a searching examination and found it wanting on several crucial points. They questioned the emancipatory credentials of the concept and exposed its affinity with other modes of instrumental rationality they accused of suppressing the non-identical, ironing out the antinomies of contemporary existence, justifying past and present misery and lapsing into the myth of its own absoluteness.

The ferocity of this critique almost obscures the fact that Adorno and Horkheimer inevitably remained on the ground of the same category they challenged. The absence of a positive articulation of emancipatory hopes does not conceal the real continuity. The vehemence of critical theory's denunciation of the idea of progress, its re-interpretation of contemporary crisis and re-affirmation of the emancipatory autonomy of a critical perspective itself indicate continuity with the conceptual basis of radical historicism. The most striking and theoretically debilitating example of this continuity is the idea of a totalised modernity they share with Foucault. Theirs is the 'false' totality of the administered society while his is the normalising carcereal society. Here Horkheimer and Adorno perpetrated another myth which severely hampered their programme of de-mythologisation and displaced their critical efforts away from the practical problems of contemporary social and political action.

Negative dialectics arrived at a theoretical and political cul-de-sac. Unable to provide a positive account of emancipatory possibilities, it ceased to seriously grapple with the practical problems of the immanent contradictory dynamics of modernity. While Adorno begrudgingly retreated from the 'identity thesis' and proposed a distinction between totality 'as a category of mediation' and of 'domination', he never really overcame the limitations of the perspective shaped by working class political defeat, Fascism and war. Without a plausible political perspective, his emancipatory perpective lapsed into an act of faith.

The one-dimensionality of late critical theory induced a crisis for the idea of totality which was compounded by the evolution of anti-humanist critiques of totality in France like that of Foucault. This crisis, however, did not spell the end of radical historicism. Rather, the traditions' successors have been compelled to assimilate these shortcomings and critiques, to modify its concept of totality and reconstitute a viable emancipatory perspective. In the light of Agnes Heller's claim that the conceptual elements of the totality concept are embedded in modern experience, these efforts at critical resurrection are not really surprising. They are, however, disparate and impossible to reduce to a single paradigm. Habermas' project has already taken on a firm shape while others are still in outline and gestation. But already their reflections on the concept of totality provide a thoughtful contemporary balance-sheet.

Habermas has devoted much of his work to a critical reassessment of the tradition from which he emerged. He is primarily concerned to put the positive legacy of this tradition to contemporary use in critical social theory. His continuity with the radical historicist tradition is confirmed by his endorsement of its essential idea:

> The self-constituting subject of history was and is a fiction; in no way meaningless, however, is the intention, both expressed and hidden in it, to link the development of socio-cultural systems to the steering mechanisms of self-reflection in the sense of a politically effective institutionalisation of discourses (self-produced higher level of inter-subjective communities).[7]

Habermas repudiates Lukács' idealist conceptual mythology which remained trapped in the philosophy of the subject. His own programme calls for a paradigm shift to what he calls the paradigm of intersubjective communication. Despite the originality of this idea, his critique of the concept of totality owes a great deal to Horkheimer and Adorno. Like them he repudiates the idea that the totality of history could be a possible object of knowledge. He extended this critique with the denial that any predictive content could be derived from hypothetical anticipations of history based on the idea of an immanent historical direction.[8] The concept of universal history is only applicable to the reconstruction of the past, not to the future immanent in the present contradictory totality. Heller has implicitly seconded this point by transforming the idea of socialism into a philosophical utopia which may express needs, future aspirations and measure their radicalism but cannot be ascribed to history as an immanent goal.[9] Both Habermas and the Budapest School take very seriously the view that critical theory acknowledge its own historical perspective. It is a grave mistake to confuse one's own totalising standpoint with that of history in general. All histories are narratives of specific historical subjects. The empirical diversity of real historical subjects is incompatible with the idea of a history of histories. In concert with this limitation on the idea of universal history, Habermas has especially emphasised intersubjectivity. His dismissal of the conceptual mythology of a total social subject (in the dress of *Geist* or the proletariat) amounts to an effort to rehabilitate and problematise the obvious diversity of social subjects in advanced pluralistic societies. Modern mass democracies grapple with conflict between heterogeneous social interests. Like the early Horkheimer who tempered his political engagement with an insistence on the critical autonomy of critical theory and maintained its irreducibility to the self-consciousness of any single social subject, Habermas has detached his theory from any direct political partisanship. For him, critical theory is a cultural reflection which responds to a *human* emancipatory interest by fostering rational debate amongst a pluralist public. Here Habermas definitely signals his scepticism regarding the possibility or even desirability of a unified historical subject in modern society. He addresses himself to a general public which shares a common interest in emancipation and a potential for rational discussion. Yet it is not clear that Habermas has freed himself from all the residues associated with the ideas of a collective historical subject and class consciousness. A brief look at an alternative conception brings out a remaining problem.

The Budapest School reconstruction of critical theory has also criticised their former mentor Lukács' notion of a single historical subject. Márkus maintains that the project of contemporary emancipation involves not only the possibility but also the desirability of a *plurality of radical subjects*. The unity of mankind is not to be construed under the category of one class subject but as a practical commitment to solidarity and creative tolerance between a number of radical subjects, forms of life and a plurality of values.[10] This formulation goes beyond Habermas whose idea of dialogical *consensus* (abstractly prefigured by critical theory) continues to assert the *privilege* of theory to know the interests of others. Implicitly, Habermas preserves the elitist substitutionalism which he saw so clearly when rejecting Lukács' idea of imputed class consciousness.[11] This shift from the single agent and collective subject of history (Lukács' proletariat as identical subject/object) to a diversity of potentially radical subjects and plurality of competing values and theories has profound consequences for the radical historicist concept of totalisation. Totality thinking from Hegel to the Frankfurt School generally acknowledged the historical conditionedness of its critical perspective only to simultaneously discover a new ground for a universal claim. The contemporary recognition of the *conditionedness* and *particularity* of its own standpoint and values finally allows the *conditioned, practical, democratic and open-ended* emphasis of the tradition (previously always in tension with universalistic, theoreticist, substitutionalist and closed elements) to fully assert itself.

The final assault on conceptual mythology also extended to the idea of reification. Habermas dismisses the thought that reification could ever be completely eliminated. His <u>Legitimation Crisis</u> tackles the problem of the historical accumulation of an ossified 'second nature' in the form of oppressive social institutions and structures. Working with the distinction between 'lifeworld' and 'systems',[12] he focuses on the problem of developing politically effective control mechanisms for democratic imput and making contemporary planning authorities more responsive to a self-reflexive public will. He denies the idea of a total re-absorption of these institutional systems into the social integration of the lifeworld.[13]

This more cautious assessment of the prospects and possibilities of real emancipation in modern industrial societies is echoed in Habermas' defence of the idea of historical progress. He reiterates the early Frankfurt School's view that the idea of objective progress implies a unilinear, necessary development of humanity towards its self-realisation. But the rejection of this indefensible dogma does not lead him to embrace the position outlined in <u>Dialectic of Enlightenment</u>. Polemical anti-evolutionism is inimical to his attempt to reactivate the positive side of critical theory as a theory of modernity. Progress has to be a differential concept recognising variable tempos and levels of historical change; the unity of history resulting from the capitalist development of the modern epoch should not disguise the plurality of histories.[14] It is not possible here to consider Habermas' sophisticated proposal for a theory of historical evolution linked to this revised concept of progress. However, the intention behind this proposal involves a determination to salvage important elements from earlier radical historicist formulations of totality plagued by previous overstatement. The idea of progress must be resurrected to overcome the radical negativism of Horkheimer and Adorno. On this point, Habermas is again joined by Budapest School thinkers. Heller proposes to limit the notion of progress to the status of a necessary regulative idea.[15] A similar view is elaborated by Márkus who maintains that progress can never be inferred from the empirical continuity of history. 'Progress' is a theoretical *construct* which imposes a 'higher unity' on this continuity from the perspective of a definite *willed future*. It is therefore an *evaluative idea* resulting from the deliberate choice of certain already existing values and practical ends and the claim for their universal validity. 'Progress' is to be realised when these selected values and aspirations are consummated in the future by complementary social praxis.[16] Márkus emphasises that the choice involved here should not be an irrational decision but one grounded in a systematic analysis of the present causes of social misery. Nevertheless, it remains a choice in a double sense. Both as *one posited solution* to contemporary ills amongst others and one which also *claims* universal validity.[17] These various reformulations of the concept of progress represent a concerted effort to reconstruct a defensible concept of progress from the debris of its previous objectivist interpretation.

Many of the above critical observations and reflections on the radical historicist tradition owe a great deal to the earlier scepticism of Adorno and Horkheimer. Yet, the great error of these later critical theorists was the abandonment of ideology critique for the radical turn to the critique of instrumental reason. This totalising strategy led not only to the theoretical *aporias* mentioned at the conclusion of Chapter Six but also to their profoundly negative vision of modernity. In Habermas' view this vision completely discounted and underestimated the survivals of reason in cultural modernity which were a direct legacy of the bourgeois tradition. Not just responsible for the massive expansion of the productive forces celebrated by Marx, the bourgeois order also provided fertile ground for the evolution of individualist patterns of identity formation, autonomous aesthetic experience, universalistic notions of morality and law and the institutional structures of democratic decision-making.[18] Habermas greatly modifies the judgement encapsulated in the idea of the administered society and the 'myth' of the 'false' totality associated with it. His claim is that late critical theory completely overlooked the intersubjective potential residing in the bourgeois public sphere.

Habermas does not dismiss the real obstacles to the effective realisation of democratic ideals in contemporary political life. He is, however, convinced that bourgeois public institutions were, and are, a positive force for progressive social change. Discarding the view that they are merely part of the apparatus of domination in monopoly capitalist society creating the appearance of individual freedom, he sees them as the site and vehicle, albeit fragile and flawed, of decisive contemporary social struggles and resistance to the logic of 'self-regulating' bureaucratic systems and processes.

This re-evaluation of the bourgeois public sphere and its emancipatory contribution to present potentials and possibilities advances the argument implied by his modification of the concept of reification. Habermas consciously retreats from the idea of a totalising instrumental reason. In his view, the trend to increasing reification:

> derives less from an absolutised purposive rationality in the service of self-preservation, an instrumental rationality gone wild, than from an unleashed functionalist rationality of system preservation, which treated lightly the rationality claim of communicative socialization and empties the rationality of the life-world.[19]

Not denying the pernicious effects of expanding functionalist rationality, Habermas underlines its *contradictory character* and *limits*. His focus is the crisis of functionality and his theoretical aim remains to explore the avenues whereby the closures of reification could be re-opened and those inescapable pockets of systemic functionality be rendered more publicly responsible and accessible to democratic forms of control. This emphasis on democratisation again parallels the evolution of Budapest School thinkers. They reject the simple Cold War view of modernity as a capitalism versus socialism dichotomy. For example, Heller and Fehér suggest a tentative framework for modernity which includes three historical dynamics – capitalism, industrialisation and democracy – which have evolved in various configurations of combination, complementation, inhibition and conflict over the last two hundred years.[20] The Soviet 'dictatorship over needs' represents one configuration in which industrialisation has had the upper hand while the societies of the west represent another, dominated by capitalism. In this historical framework, Fehér and Heller argue that the emphasis must fall on *democracy and democratisation* as a means of advancing individual's control over their own life and providing them with mechanisms to employ their utopian energies in the pursuit of radical alternatives to the present. Socialism means not the elimination of all historical contradictions nor the creation of an integrated cultural totality but the radicalisation of democracy in an effort to increase the scope of principled self-determination in every sphere of life.[21]

In this very short survey of contemporary reflection on the historicist tradition, there exists a clear tendency to dismiss all philosophical mythology of the revolutionary historical subject and the extremely negativist idea of a 'false totality'. The emancipatory intention and the emphasis on a open-ended, practical vision and conceptualisation of collectively determined, creative historical praxis is affirmed while dispensing with the radical historicist's overstated claims inscribed in concepts like reification, total historical subject and universal history. Habermas and the others refocus attention on contemporary social contradictions and struggles as the basis for future emancipatory change. This does not mean that contemporary radical historicism affirms a mindless optimism. On the contrary, the dominant mood is rather pessimistic but it is one that still sees reason for hope. This mood is nicely captured in Habermas' view of modernity as an 'uncompleted project'.[22]

A continuing dynamic historical conjuncture of crisis, 'progress' and emancipatory aspirations keeps alive the theoretical inspiration of radical historicism. The historicist concept of totality originally signified a great attempt to meet the practical and philosophical demand for an immanent understanding of a future-directed society from the perspective of emancipation. Even the utopian, mythological elements (both positive and negative) which survived as residues in these immanentist interpretations of history represent a conscious attempt to harnass the dynamic possibilities of modernity to the social imagination of the present as future-directed transcending images of liberation or threat. In their excesses, however, they reproduced the errors of philosophical abstraction which the radical historicist tradition never ceased to criticise in traditional philosophy. More dire, they opened up the possibility of theoretical substitutionalism and sometimes engendered undue political pessimism.

Yet, the permanent crisis of modern experience engenders a practical need only satisfied by the re-articulation of the basic conceptual elements of the concept of totality. Habermas, Heller and others have submitted their own tradition to an uncompromisingly critique. At the same time, they strive to reconstruct its practical, immanent, open-ended understanding of human historical self-creation from the standpoint of future emancipation. In this they preserve the essential spirit of radical historicism and its commitment to a better social order based on conscious human solidarity and self-determination.

Notes

Introduction

1 This is so despite the fact that his later work was an important influence in shaping the contemporary thought of the Budapest School which presently carries on the historicist tradition. Shortly before his death, Lukács drew attention to a small group of young colleagues and ex-students who were then just beginning to make a name for themselves. He called this circle the Budapest School. The core of this group – Ferenc Fehér, Agnes Heller, György and Maria Markus – subsequently emigrated from Hungary after political dismissal from their academic positions. Their writings aim at a critical continuation of the historicist tradition. Substantial but still very much in progress, their works are intended to preserve the spirit of the historicist tradition in the face of contemporary theoretical and political realities.

2 In her recent work *A Theory of History*, Routledge & Kegan Paul, London 1982, Agnes Heller offers a phenomenology of the forms of historical consciousness which addresses this distinction.

3 Arendt H., *Between the Past and the Future,* Faber and Faber, London, 1954, p64.

4 Ibid., p68.

5 Löwith, K., *Meaning in History*, University of Chicago Press, Chicago, 1949, p4.

6 For the standard account of medieval millenarianism, see Norman Cohn's *The Pursuit of the Millenium*, Mercury Books, London, 1962.

7 Habermas, J., *Theory and Practice*, Heinemann, London, 1974, p244.

8 Löwith op.cit., pp145-59.

9 Cassirer, E., *The Individual and the Cosmos in Renaissance Philosophy*, Harper Torchbook, New York, 1963, p71.

10 Cassirer, E., *Kant's Life and Thought*, Yale University Press, New Haven, 1981, p287.

11 Blumenberg, H., *The Legitimacy of the Modern Age*, MIT Press, Cambridge Massachusetts, 1983, pp54-5.

12 Lovejoy, A.O., *The Great Chain of Being*, Harvard University Press, Massachusetts, 1970, pp248-56.

13 Blumenberg, op. cit., p55.

14 Habermas, op. cit., p245.

15 Ibid., pp249-50.

16 Riedel, M., 'Kant und die Geschichtswissenschaft' Einleitung zu Kant's *Schriften*

zur Geschichtesphilosophie, Phillip Reclam Jun, Stuttgart, 1974, p15.

17 Meinecke, F., *Historism*, Routledge & Kegan Paul, London, 1972.
18 Ripalda, J.M., *The Divided Nation*, Van Gorcum, Amsterdam, 1977, p7.

Section One: Chapter One: Hegel: between metaphysics and history

1 Hegel, G.F.W., *Werke*, Band 2, 'In Zwangig Bänden', Moldenhauer, E. and Michel, K.M. (eds), Suhrkamp, Frankfurt am Main, 1970, p20. Hereafter referred to as the *Difference* essay.
2 Schiller, F., *On the Aesthetic Education on Man,* Ungar, New York, 1980, p40, originally published 1795.
3 Hegel, *Dokumente zu Hegels Entwicklung*, J. Hoffmeister (ed.), Stuttgart, 1936, p49.
4 Plant, R., *Hegel*, Allen & Unwin, London, 1973, pp25-6.
5 Hegel, *Werke,* Band 1, pp204–5; (trans.) *Early Theological Writings,* University of Pennsylvania Press, Philadelphia, 1948, p154.
6 Ibid., p199; (trans.) ibid., p148.
7 Ibid., p198; (trans.) ibid., p148.
8 Hegel, ibid., pp199-200; (trans.) ibid., p149.
9 Hegel, ibid., p105; (trans.) ibid., p68.
10 Hegel, ibid., p188; (trans.) ibid., p143.
11 Hegel, ibid., pp204–5; (trans.) ibid. p154.
12 Lukács, G., *The Young Hegel*, Merlin, London, 1975, p55.
13 Hegel, Band 1, op.cit., p120; (trans.) op.cit. p82.
14 Hegel, ibid., pp274–85; (trans.) ibid., pp182-93.
15 Ibid., pp400-1; (trans.) ibid., p285.
16 Ibid., p418; (trans.) ibid., p301.
17 This is the explanation offered by Richard Kroner in his Introduction to Hegel's *Early Theological Writings*, p13. Yet, without supporting evidence, it appears to be more a restatement of the interpretative problem than a convincing solution to it.
18 See *Werke*, Band 3, p431; (trans.) *Phenomenology of Spirit*, Oxford University Press, Oxford, 1977, p355.
19 Plant, op.cit., pp65-7.
20 Ibid., pp68-9.
21 Henrich D., *Hegel im Kontext*, Suhrkamp, Frankfurt am Main, 1975, p23.
22 Hegel, op.cit., Band 1, p352; (trans.) op.cit., p237.
23 Ibid., p343; (trans.) ibid., p230.
24 Ibid., p342; (trans.) ibid., p229.
25 Ibid., p343; (trans.) ibid., p230
26 Ibid., p246; (trans.) ibid., p305.
27 Ibid., p422; (trans.) ibid., p312.
28 Plant., op.cit., p87.
29 On the general question of the influence exercised by the Christian idea of the fortunate fall on late eighteenth century German culture, see M. H. Abrams' *Natural Supernaturalism : Tradition and Revolution in Romantic Literature,* W.W. Norton, New York, 1971, Chapter 4.
30 Hegel, op. cit., Band 1, pp389-90; (trans.) op. cit., p273.
31 Ibid., pp389-90 (trans.) ibid., p273.
32 Hegel, *Werke*, Band 3, p24; (trans.) op.cit., p11.
33 Hegel, *Vorlesungen über die Philiosophie der Weltgeschichte*, Band 1, J. Hoffmeister (ed.), Akademic Verlag, Berlin 1973, pp58-9; (trans.) *Lectures on the Philosophy of World History*, Cambridge University Press, 1975, p51.

34 Subsequently referred to as the *Encyclopaedia*.
35 Hegel, *Werke*, Band 9, p23; (trans.) *Hegel's Philosophy of Nature*, Oxford University Press, Oxford, 1971, p13.
36 Ibid., p24; (trans.) ibid., p14.
37 Ibid., p27; (trans.) ibid., p17.
38 Ibid., p24 (trans.) ibid., p14.
39 Such a characterisation is especially interesting in the light of the later Marxian critiques of Hegel's idealism from the standpoint of Feuerbachian naturalism. This is not to say that this justly famous critique is misplaced but rather to indicate that it hardly does full justice to Hegel's understanding of human dependence upon nature.
40 Hegel, *Werke*, Band 10, p21; (trans.) *Hegel's Philosophy of Mind*, Oxford University Press, 1971, p11.
41 Ibid., p21 (trans.) ibid., p11.
42 Riedel, M., *Theorie und Praxis im Denkens Hegel*, Ulstein, Frankfurt am Main, 1976, p34.
43 Ibid., p34.
44 Hegel, *Vorlesungen über die Philosophie der Weltgeschichte,* Band 1, pp59-60; (trans.) op. cit., p52.
45 Ibid., pp59-60; ibid., p52.
46 Ibid., p64 (trans.) ibid., p55.
47 Hegel, *Werke*, Band 3, p145; (trans.) op. cit., p58.
48 Ibid., pp154-5; (trans.) ibid., p118.
49 Ibid., pp154-5; (trans.) ibid., p118.
50 Ibid., p67; (trans.) Ibid., p58
51 Ibid., p64; (trans.) ibid., p55.
52 Ibid., p60; (trans.) ibid., pp52-3.
53 Ibid., pp60-61; (trans.) ibid., p53.
54 Ibid., pp74-5; (trans.) ibid., pp64-5.
55 Ibid., p67; (trans.) ibid., p58.
56 Ibid., pp70-1; (trans.) ibid., pp60-1.
57 Ibid., p72 (trans.) ibid., p61.
58 On the history of the later disputes amongst Hegelians, see John E. Toew's *Hegelianism,* Cambridge University Press, Cambridge, 1980.
59 See Plant's account, op.cit., pp93-4.
60 Márkus, G., 'Hegel and the Antinomies of Modernity', *Antipodean Enlightenments: Festschrift Für Leslie Bodi*, Peter Lang, Frankfurt am Main, 1987, p291.
61 Hegel, *Werke*, Band 7, p350; (trans.) *Philosophy of Right*, Oxford University Press, Oxford, 1942, p128.
62 Ibid., pp352-3; (trans.) ibid., p129.
63 Ibid., p389; (trans.) ibid., pp149-50.
64 Plant provides an illuminating discussion of this initial attempt, op. cit., pp115-16.
65 Hegel, *Werke*, Band 3, pp394-5; (trans.) op.cit., p153.
66 Ibid, pp394-5; (trans.) Ibid., p153.
67 Ibid., p384; (trans.) ibid., p147.
68 Ibid., p385; (trans.) ibid., pp147-8.
69 For a fuller discussion of Hegel's view of bureaucracy and the modern state, see Shlomo Avineri's *Hegel's Theory of the Modern State*, Cambridge University Press, Cambridge, 1972.
70 Hegel, *Werke,* Band 3, p399; (trans.) op.cit., p156.
71 Hegel, *Philosophy of History*, Dover Press, New York, 1956, p38.
72 Plant, op. cit., p96.

Chapter 2: Marx: from history to praxis

1 See Note 58, Chapter One.
2 Marx K. and Engels, F., *Werke*, Band 1/2, Dietz Verlag, Berlin, 1980, p378; (trans.) *Collected Works*, Vol.1, Lawrence and Wishart, London, 1975, p491.
3 Henrich, D., 'Karl Marx als Schüler Hegels', *Hegel im Kontext,* Suhrkamp, Frankfurt am Main, 1975.
4 Marx, K and Engels F., op. cit., p213; (trans.) *Early Writings*, Penguin, 1975, p69.
5 Ibid., pp241-2; (trans.) ibid., p98.
6 Ibid., p386; (trans.) ibid., p252.
7 Several commentators, including thinkers within the Budapest School and the sociologist Alvin Gouldner, have drawn attention to various aspects of the strain in this identification between critical theory and the self-consciousness of the proletariat. While Marx viewed his theory as an expression of the proletariat's real needs and long-term interests, the subsequent history of the worker's movement has hardly confirmed this identification. This difficulty is evident in Marx's shifting terminology which vacillates between worker's 'needs' and their 'objective interests'. The tension received perhaps its starkest representation in the Lukácsian distinction between 'empirical' and 'imputed class consciousness'. Gouldner's last works focused on the sociological dimension of this problem. He views Marxism as a product of a new social stratum 'the secular intelligentsia' that has its own special interests and politics and therefore problematizes Marx's identification with the struggle of the working class. See Gouldner *The Two Marxisms*, Macmillan Press, London, 1980, and *Against Fragmentation,* Oxford University Press, Oxford, 1985. Although Gouldner raises a very important issue and offers an interesting sociological investigation of the relation between Marxism and the working class, some of his conclusions are very questionable and even fanciful. The proposition that Marxism expresses the interest of the intellectuals in as much as it advocates the extension of the modern state and therefore provides new opportunities for the intellectuals (*Against Fragmentation*, p36) can hardly be taken seriously as an explanation of Marx's conscious or unconscious motives. In fact, Gouldner's assertion that Marxian socialism sought the extension of state control relies on a single passage from the *Communist Manifesto* and is contradicted by most of Marx's other statements about socialism which move in the other direction towards the abolition of state power. Gouldner clearly reads Marx here from the perspective of both official institutionalised Marxism and the academicisation of Marxism in the industrialised west.
8 See Iring Fetscher's 'Das Verhältnis des Marxismus zu Hegel', in *Marxismus Studien*, Dritte Folge, J.C.B.Mohr (Paul Siebeck), Tübingen, 1960, pp 74-5.
9 For the impact of French socialism and the work of Von Stein, see Thomas Meyer's *Der Zweispalt in der Marx'schen Emanzipationstheorie,* Scriptor Verlag, Kronberg Ts, 1973.
10 Marx and Engels, *Werke,* Band 3, op. cit. p27; (trans.) *Collected Works*, Vol.5 p37.
11 Marx and Engels, *Gesamtausgabe* 1/2, Dietz Verlag, Berlin, 1982, p404; (trans.) *Early Writings*, p385.
12 Ibid., p404; (trans.) ibid., p386.
13 Ibid., p414; (trans.) ibid., p396.
14 Interpretations taking their lead from the work of Louis Althusser typically view the early Marx as a Feuerbachian humanist and, in so doing, completely underplay the very positive side of Marx's relation to Hegel. See, for example, W. Suchtings, *Marx: An Introduction,* Sussex, London, 1983.
15 Marx and Engels, op cit., p408; (trans.) op.cit., p389.
16 Marx and Engels, op. cit., p394; (trans.) *Collected Works,* Vol.3, p302.

17 Ibid., p408-9 (trans.) ibid., p390.
18 Ibid., p396; (trans.) ibid. p303.
19 Ibid., p389; (trans.) ibid., p296.
20 Marx and Engels, *Werke*, Band 5, p18; (trans.) *Collected Works* Vol. 5, p28.
21 Ibid., p69; (trans.) ibid., pp88-9.
22 Ibid., p38; (trans.) ibid., p54.
23 Ibid., p34; (trans.) ibid., p48.
24 On this revolution in the understanding of theory, see G.Márkus' *Language and Production : A Critique of Paradigms*, Reidel, Dordrecht, 1986, pp41-3.
25 See Note 7 for a brief discussion for some of the very real tensions and difficulties inherent in Marx identification of his own theoretical standpoint with the perspective of the proletariat.
26 Marx and Engels, *Werke*, Band 5, p69; (trans.) *Collected Works,* Vol.5, pp88-9.
27 See, for example, the early writings of Louis Althusser : *For Marx,* Penguin, London, 1969.
28 Marx and Engels, op. cit., Band 3, p38; (trans.) op. cit., Vol.5, p58.
29 Ibid., p42; (trans.) ibid., p58.
30 Ibid., p6; (trans.) ibid., pp7-8.
31 Ibid., p38; (trans.) ibid., p54.
32 Márkus, G., *Marxism and Anthropology*, Van Gorcum, Assen, 1978, pp39-40.
33 Quoted in Helmut Fleischer's *Marxismus und Geschichte*, Suhrkamp, Frankfurt am Main, 1975, p80.
34 Marx and Engels, Band 3, p46; (trans.) Vol. 5, p51.
35 Ibid., p60; (trans.) ibid., p73.
36 Marx and Engels, *Werke*, Band 4, p467; (trans.) *Collected Works,* Vol. 6, p489.
37 Ibid., p473; (trans.) ibid., p495.
38 Ibid., p390; (trans.) *Early Writings*, op. cit., p256.
39 Morf, O., 'Totalität und Dialektik', Marxismus und Anthropologie, Germinal Verlag, Buchum, 1980, p103.
40 Marx, *Grundrisse der Kritik der Politischen Ökonomie*, Dietz Verlag, Berlin, 1974, p189; (trans.) *Grundrisse*, Penguin, London, 1973, p278.
41 Ibid., pp364-5; (trans.) ibid., p461.
42 Ibid., pp79-80; (trans.) ibid., p162.
43 Ibid., p111; (trans.) ibid., p197.
44 Ibid., pp79-80; (trans.) ibid., p162.
45 Ibid., pp583-92; (trans.) ibid., pp690-704.
46 Marx, *Werke*, Band 25, p859; (trans.) *Capital*, Vol. 3, Progress Publishers, Moscow, 1971, p851.
47 Ibid., p828; (trans.) ibid., p820.
48 Ibid., pp266-7; (trans.) ibid., pp256-7.
49 Marx and Engels, *Werke*, Band 4, pp150-2; (trans.) *Collected Works,* Vol. 6, p184.
50 Marx, *Grundrisse*, op. cit., pp387-8; (trans.) op. cit., p488.
51 Ibid., pp715-17; (trans.) ibid., pp831-3.
52 Márkus G., 'Four Forms of Critical Theory : Some Theses on Marx's Development', *Thesis Eleven*, No.1, Melbourne, 1980, p88.
53 Ibid., p88.
54 Ibid., p91.
55 Marx, *Werke*, Band 25, pp269, 272; (trans.) *Capital*, Vol. 3, pp259-62.
56 For a full exposition of all the implications of Marx's paradigm of production, see G. Márkus 'important study' 'On the Paradigm of Production : Marxian Materialism and the Problem of the Constituion of the Social World', in *Language and Production*, op. cit., pp41-125.

Section Two: Chapter Three: The *Geisteswissenschaften:* the use of a negative concept of totality

1   Simmel, Rickert and Weber were also responsible for similar theoretical efforts to legitimate the methodological autonomy of the historical sciences.
2   Willey, T.E., *Back To Kant*, Wayne University Press, Detroit, 1978, pp28-9.
3   Schnädelbach, H., *Philosophie in Deutschland 1831-1933,* Suhrkamp, Frankfurt am Main, 1983, p49.
4   Especially the view of history as a spiritual process which expressed the idea of freedom. See Schnädelbach, ibid., p63.
5   Ibid., p52.
6   Arato, A., 'The Neo-Idealist Defence of Subjectivity', *Telos*, No. 21, Washington University Press, St Louis, Fall 1974, p108.
7   Hughes, H.S., *Consciousness and Society*, Paladin Books, Frogmore St. Albans, Herts, Chapter Two, 1974.
8   Ringer, F.K., *The Decline of the German Mandarins : The German Academic Community 1890-1933*, Harvard University Press, Cambridge, Massachusetts, 1969.
9   Schnädelbach, op. cit., p49
10 Gadamer, H.G., *Truth and Method,* Shead and Ward, London, 1978, p193.
11 Dilthey, W., *Der Aufbau der Geschichtlichen Welt in den Geisteswissenschaften*, Suhrkamp, Frankfurt am Main, 1981, p168; (trans.) *Selected Writings*, H.P. Rickman (ed.), Cambridge University Press, Cambridge, 1976, p184.
12 Redding, P., 'Action, Language and Text : Dilthey's Conception of the Understanding', *Philosophy and Social Criticism*, No.2, Vol. 9, 1982, p231.
13 It is worthwhile noting that Dilthey quite consciously abandoned Hegel's atemporal notion of absolute spirit and assimilated all cultural objectifications into the essentially historical realm of objective spirit. See Dilthey, op. cit., p184.
14 Dilthey, ibid., p176; (trans.) ibid., p189.
15 Ibid., p302; (trans.) ibid., p244.
16 Ibid., pp286-92; (trans.) ibid., pp235-8.
17 Ibid., p179; (trans.) ibid., p192.
18 Ibid., p179; (trans.) ibid., p192.
19 Dilthey, *Gesammelte Schriften*, Band 1, B.G. Teubner Verlag, Stuttgart, 1959, p92.
20 Dilthey, *Der Aufbau*, p186; (trans.) *Selected Writings*, p196.
21 Ibid., p189; (trans.) ibid., p198.
22 Ibid., p171; (trans.) ibid., p186.
23 Redding, op. cit., pp233-4.
24 Dilthey, *Gesammelte Schriften*, Band 1, p401.
25 Schnädelbach, op. cit., p76.
26 Dilthey, op. cit., p291; (trans.) op. cit., p238.
27 Ibid., p202; (trans.) ibid., p206.
28 Gadamer, op. cit., pp202-4.
29 Hodges, *Wilhelm Dilthey: An Introduction*, Kegan Paul, Trench, Trubner & Co., London, 1944, pp33-4.
30 Dilthey, *Der Aufbau*, p183; (trans.) op. cit., p194.
31 See Michael Landmann's Introduction to a German compilation of Simmel's writings where he distinguishes a positivist, a neo-Kantian and a vitalist stage. 'Einleitung des Herausgebers', in *George Simmel Das Individelle Gesetz : Philosophische Exkurse,* Suhrkamp, Frankfurt am Main, 1965.
32 Simmel, 'The Meaning of Culture', in Peter Lawrence (ed.) *Georg Simmel : Sociologist and European*, Nelson, Middlsex, 1976, p245.

33 Ibid., p245.
34 This concept of the soul was present as early as *Philosophie des Geldes*, von Duncker und Humbolt, Leipzig, 1907, p528; (trans.) *Philosophy of Money*, Routledge & Kegan Paul, London, 1978, p466.
35 Simmel, 'The Meaning of Culture' p246.
36 Arato, op. cit., p152.
37 Simmel, 'Der Begriff und die Tragödie der Kultur', *Philosophische Kultur*, Verlag von Dr W. Kinkhardt, Leipzig, 1911, p249.
38 Ibid., p248.
39 Simmel, 'The Conflict of Modern Culture', p233.
40 Simmel, 'Der Begriff', from Lawrence (ed.), p264.
41 See especially *Gemeinschaft und Gesellschaft*, Hans Wuste, Verlag, Leipzig, 1935.
42 Simmel, op. cit., p270.
43 Simmel, op. cit., pviii.
44 Simmel, 'The Future of Our Culture', in Lawrence (ed.), pp251-2.
45 Amongst the spate of recent books on Weber, Rogers Brubaker's *Limits of Rationality*, Allen and Unwin, London, 1984, has drawn particular attention to this Introduction and its thematic significance.
46 Cohen, J., 'Weber and the Dynamics of Domination' *Telos*, No. 14, Winter, 1972.
47 Weber, *Economy and Society*, Vol. 1, University of California Press, California, 1978, p506.
48 Weber, *Gesammelte Aufsatze Zur Wissenschaftslehre*, Tübingen, 1951, p596.
49 Weber, in Gerth, H. and Mill, C.W. (eds) *From Max Weber*, London, 1948, p328.
50 Arnason, J.P., 'Rationalisation and Modernity', *Incidental Paper No. 9*, Department of Sociology, University of La Trobe, 1982, p10.
51 Weber, op. cit., p154; (trans.) *The Methodology of the Social Sciences*, The Free Press, New York, 1949, p57.
52 Weber, op. cit., p132; (trans.) *Roscher and Knies*, The Free Press, New York, 1975, p192.
53 In particular see W.J. Mommsen's *Max Weber and German Politics 1890-1920*, University of Chicago Press, Chicago, 1984.
54 Weber, *From Max Weber*, p55.
55 Weber, *The Protestant Ethic and the Spirit of Capitalism*, Unwin University Books, London, 1930, p181.
56 Weber, *From Max Weber*, p229.
57 Ibid., p243.
58 On the extent of these borrowings see Thomas Burger, *Max Weber's Theory of Concept Formation*, Duke University Press, Durham, 1976.
59 Weber, *Gesammelte Aufsatze*, p180; (trans.) op. cit., p81.
60 Tenbruck, F.H., 'The problem of the Thematic Unity in the Works of Max Weber', *British Journal of Sociology*, Vol. 13, No. 3, September 1980.
61 Weber, op. cit., p184; (trans.) op. cit., pp84-5.
62 Ibid., p152; (trans.) ibid., p55.
63 Ibid., p152; (trans.) ibid., p55.
64 Ibid., p152; (trans.) ibid., p55.
65 Löwith, K., *Max Weber and Karl Marx*, Allen and Unwin, London, 1982, p38.
66 Weber, op. cit., p156; (trans.) op. cit., pp58-9.
67 Benhabib, S., 'Rationality and Social Action : Critical Reflections on Max Weber's Methodological Writings', *Philosophical Forum*, Vol.XII, No. 4, Boston University, Boston, 1981, p361.
68 Quoted in Benhabib, ibid., p361.
69 Ibid., p369.
70 Ibid., p369.

Chapter 4: The pre-Marxist Lukács: the longing for totality

1 Arato, A. and Breines, P., *The Young Lukács and the Origins of Western Marxism*, Pluto Press, London, 1979, p10.
2 This is the rather superficial view of George Lichtheim who even questions Lukács' originality. See his *Lukács*, Fontana, London, 1970, p21. Lukács similarly was also inclined to minimise the significance of his retrospectively pre-Marxist thought. See his 1962 Introduction to the re-publication of the *Theory of the Novel*.
3 Quoted in F.L. Lendvai's 'The Young Lukács' Philosophy of History', *New Hungarian Quarterly*, No. 67, Budapest, 1976, p155.
4 Márkus, G., 'Life and the Soul', *Lukács Revalued*, Agnes Heller (ed.), Blackwell, Oxford, 1983, p4.
5 Lukács, G., 'Zur Soziologie des Modernen Dramas', p294-5. Originally the second chapter of his two-volume work on the development of modern drama. This was translated and published in German in the *Archiv für Sozialwissenschaft und Sozial Politik*, XXXVIII (1914), republished in Lukács G., *Schriften zur Literatursoziologie*, Luchterland, 1961.
6 Honigsheim, P., *On Max Weber*, The Free Press, New York, 1968, p27.
7 Quoted in Arato and Breines, op. cit., p19.
8 The death of Leo Popper – Lukács' closest friend – and the suicide of Irma Seidler – his first lover – both in 1911 was soon followed by the outbreak of the First World War.
9 Arato and Breines, op. cit., p18.
10 Quoted in translation from the original Hungarian in Arato's 'Lukács' Path to Marxism (1910-1923)', *Telos*, No. 6, Washington University, St. Louis, Summer 1970, p131.
11 Arato and Breines, op. cit., p19.
12 Ibid., p19.
13 Goldmann, L., *Dialektische Untersuchungen*, Luchterland, Darmstadt und Neuwied, 1966, p289.
14 See the works by Arato and Breines referred to above; Michael Löwy's *Georg Lukács : From Romanticism to Bolshevism*, NLB, London, 1979; and the recently translated collection of older essays from the Budapest School edited by Heller, op. cit.
15 Márkus, op. cit., pp4-5.
16 See Note 5.
17 Arato and Breines, op. cit., p22.
18 Ibid., p22.
19 Ibid., p15.
20 These scenarios are discussed by Ferenc Fehér in his 'Die Geschichtesphilosophie des Drama, die Metaphysik der Tragödie und die Utopia des Untragischen Dramas. Scheidwege der Drametheorie des Jungen Lukács' in *Die Seele und das Leben : Studien zum Frühen Lukács*, A Heller et. al., Suhrkamp, Baden-Baden, 1977, p29.
21 Lukács, 'Croce Benedetto : Zur Theorie und Geschichte der Historiographie', *Archiv für Sozialwissenschaft und Sozialpolitik*, Band 39, Heft 3, Tübingen, 1915, pp884-5.
22 Lukács, 'Zur Theorie der Literaturgeschichte', *Text und Kritik*, 39/40, (ed.), Heinz L. Arnok, Munich, 1973, p45.
23 Ibid., p29.
24 Lukács, *Die Seele und die Formen*, Luchterland, Neuwied, 1971, p9; (trans.) *Soul and Form*, Merlin Press, London, 1974, p3.

25 Lukács, *Die Theorie des Romans*, Luchterland, Darmstadt und Neuwied, 1963, pp22-3; (trans.) *Theory of the Novel,* Merlin Press, London, 1971, pp29-31.
26 Ibid., p28; (trans.) ibid., p35.
27 Ibid., pp27-8; (trans.) ibid., p34.
28 Ibid., p79; (trans.) ibid., p80.
29 Ibid., p64; (trans.) ibid., p66.
30 Ibid., p65; (trans.) ibid., p67.
31 Ibid., p89; (trans.) ibid., p89.
32 Ibid., p39; (trans.) ibid., p44.
33 Lukács, 'Zur Soziologie des Modernen Drama', p265.
34 Lukács, *Werke*, Band 15, p114.
35 Ibid., p114.
36 Ibid., p113.
37 Lukács, *Die Theorie des Romans*, p29; (trans.) op. cit., p34.
38 Ibid., p27; (trans.) ibid., p34.
39 Ibid., p53; (trans.) ibid., p56.
40 Ibid., p31; (trans.) ibid., p37.
41 Ibid., p68; (trans.) ibid., p70.
42 Ibid., p71; (trans.) ibid., pp72-3.
43 Ibid., p71; (trans.) ibid., pp72-3.
44 Lukács 'Zur Soziologie des Modernen Drama', p287.
45 Ibid., p288.
46 Ibid., p285.
47 Honigsheim, op. cit., pp25-6.
48 Quoted in Arato and Breines, op. cit., p30.
49 Fehér, op. cit., p29.
50 Lukács, *Theorie des Romans*, pp 157-8; (trans.) *Theory of the Novel*, pp152-3.
51 See Ferenc Fehér's 'The Last Phase of Romantic Anti-Capitalism – Lukács' Response to the War', *New German Critique,* No. 10, University of Wisconsin, Milwaukee, Winter 1977, pp41-2.
52 Lukács, 'Letters to Paul Ernst', *New Hungarian Quarterly*, Vol. XIII, No. 47, Budapest, Autumn 1972, p93.
53 Lukács, *Die Seele und die Formen*, p219; (trans.) *Soul and Form,* p153.
54 Ibid., p214; (trans.) ibid., p153.
55 Márkus, op. cit., pp8-9.
56 Lukács, *Die Seele und die Formen*, p230; (trans.) p160.
57 Lukács, 'Zur Theorie der Literaturgeschichte; p32.
58 Lukács, *Die Seele und Formen*, p248; (trans.) *Soul and Form*, p172.
59 Ibid., p214; (trans.) ibid., p149.
60 Lukács, *Philosophie der Kunst, Werke,* Band 16, Luchterland, Darmstadt und Neuwied, 1974, p19.
61 Ibid., p19.
62 Ibid., p20.
63 Ibid., pp31-2.
64 Ibid., p15.
65 Ibid., p54.
66 Ibid., p58.
67 Ibid., p58.
68 Quoted from Béla Balázs' 'Notes from a Diary', *New Hungarian Quarterly*, p124.
69 Lukács, *Philosophie der Kunst,* p27.
70 Ibid., p72.
71 See Note 68.

72 Lukács' correspondence to Ernst quoted in Lee Congdon's *The Young Lukács,*
    University of North Carolina Press, Chapel Hill and London, 1983, p104.
73 See Lukács' essay on Theodor Storm in *Die Seele und die Formen.*
74 Lukács, 'On the Poverty of the Spirit', *The Philosophical Forum,* Vol. 13, No. 3-4,
    Department of Philosophy, University of Boston Massachusetts, Spring/Summer
    1972, p374.
75 Ibid., p376.
76 Ibid., p375.
77 Ibid., p375.
78 Ibid., p377.
79 Goldmann, op. cit., p289.
80 See Lukács, 'Die Subjekt-Objekt Beziehung in der Äesthetik', *Heidelberger
    Äesthetik, Werke,* Band 17.
81 Ibid., p173.
82 Ibid., p221.

**Section Three: Chapter Five: The Marxist Lukács: 'totality' – principle of
revolution**

1   Lukács, *Geschichte und Klassenbewusstsein, Werke,* Band 2, p202; (trans.) *History
    and Class Consciousness,* Merlin, London, 1969, p29.
2   For the fascinating story, see 'The Wager on Communism; in Arato and Breines,
    The Young Lukács and the Origins of Western Marxism.
3   Lukács, op. cit., p164; (trans.) op. cit., Preface xliii.
4   See Rudolf Schlesinger's 'Historical Setting of Lukács' History and Class
    Consciousness', in *Aspects of History and Class Consciousness,* István Mészáros,
    (ed.), Routledge & Kegan Paul, London, 1971.
5   Arato and Breines, op. cit., p114.
6   Lukács, *Werke,* Band 2, pp362-3; (trans.) op. cit., pp177-8.
7   Ibid., pp334-5; (trans.) ibid., p152.
8   Ibid., p216; (trans.) ibid., p181.
9   Ibid., p365; (trans.) ibid., p43.
10 Ibid., p375; (trans.) ibid., p188.
11 Ibid., p372; (trans.) ibid., pp185-6.
12 Ibid., p372; (trans.) ibid., p186.
13 Ibid., p223; (trans.) ibid., p50.
14 Ibid., p187; (trans.) ibid., p15.
15 Ibid., p260; (trans.) ibid., p86.
16 Ibid., pp192-3; (trans.) ibid., p19.
17 Ibid., pp265-6; (trans.) ibid., p91.
18 Ibid., p261; (trans.) ibid., p87.
19 Ibid., p261; (trans.) ibid., p87.
20 Ibid., pp261-2; (trans.) ibid., pp87-8.
21 Ibid., pp263-4; (trans.) ibid., p89.
22 Ibid., pp263-4; (trans.) ibid., p89.
23 Ibid., pp264-5; (trans.) ibid., p90.
24 See Arato and Breines, op. cit., pp116-17.
25 Lukács, op. cit., p266; (trans.) op. cit., p91.
26 Ibid., p266-7; (trans.) ibid., p92.
27 Ibid., p278; (trans.) ibid., pp102-3.
28 Ibid., pp177-8; (trans.) ibid., pp6-7.
29 Ibid., pp174-5; (trans.) ibid., pp4-5.

30   Ibid., p186; (trans.) ibid., p14.
31   Ibid., p279; (trans.) ibid., p103.
32   Ibid., p200; (trans.) ibid., p28.
33   Ibid., p200; (trans.) ibid., p28.
34   Engels, *Ludwig Feuerbach and the End of Classical German Philosophy*, Foreign Languages Press, Moscow, 1950, pp77-8.
35   Kautsky, K., *The Class Struggle*, Norton Library, New York, 1971, pp200-1.
36   For Lukács' own early Marxist elaboration of the idea of socialism, see the 1920 essay 'Old Culture, New Culture' in *Telos* No. 6, University Press, Buffalo, Winter 1970.
37   Lukács, op. cit., p255; (trans.) op. cit., p79.
38   Ibid., p363; (trans.) ibid., p178.
39   Ibid., p223; (trans.) ibid., p50.
40   Ibid., p223; (trans.) ibid., p50.
41   Ibid., p223; (trans.) ibid., p50.
42   Ibid., p223; (trans.) ibid., p51.
43   Ibid., p223; (trans.) ibid., p50.
44   Ibid., p224; (trans.) ibid., p50.
45   Ibid., p228; (trans.) ibid., p52.
46   Ibid., p231-2; (trans.) ibid., p55.
47   Ibid., p228-9; (trans.) ibid., p58.
48   Ibid., p235; (trans.) ibid., p61.
49   Ibid., p234; (trans.) ibid., p60.
50   Ibid., p233; (trans.) ibid., p59.
51   Ibid., p236-9; (trans.) ibid., pp62-4.
52   Ibid., p239; (trans.) ibid., p64.
53   Ibid., p240; (trans.) ibid., p65.
54   Ibid., p356; (trans.) ibid., p171.
55   Ibid., pp246-7; (trans.) ibid., p71.
56   Ibid., pp246-7; (trans.) ibid., p71.
57   Ibid., pp246-7; (trans.) ibid., p71.
58   Ibid., pp246-7; (trans.) ibid., p71.
59   Ibid., p248; (trans.) ibid., p72.
60   Ibid., p349; (trans.) ibid., pp165-6.
61   Ibid., p351; (trans.) ibid., p167.
62   Ibid., p350; (trans.) ibid., p166.
63   Ibid., p356; (trans.) ibid., p172.
64   See Jürgen Habermas's recent Lukács interpretation in Volume One of *Theorie des kommunikativen Handelns*, Band 1, Suhrkamp, Frankfurt am Main, 1981, pp491-2.
65   Lukács, op. cit., pp375-6; (trans.) op. cit., p189.
66   Ibid., pp375-6; (trans.) ibid., p189.
67   Ibid., p377; (trans.) ibid., p190.
68   Ibid., p377 (trans.) ibid., p190.
69   Ibid., p352; (trans.) ibid., p168.
70   See Arato and Breines' chapter 'The Wager on Communism', op. cit.
71   Lukács, op. cit., p506; (trans.) ibid., pp328-9.
72   See Arato and Breines, op. cit., pp145, 156-60.
73   Clearly aimed at the bureaucratisation and hierarchisation of the Comintern parties, ibid., pp158-9.
74   Lukács, op. cit., pp24-5; (trans.) op. cit. pxxiii.
75   Lukács never claimed, for example, that the *material character of human life activities* was a source of alienation. For an elaboration of this argument, see

George Márkus' 'Reification and Alienation in Marx and Lukacs', *Thesis Eleven*, 5/6, Monash University, Clayton Victoria, 1982, p155.

76 Márkus, ibid., p155.
77 Fehér, F. and Heller, A., 'Class, Modernity, Democracy' *Eastern Left, Western Left : Totalitarianism, Freedom and Democracy,* Polity Press, Cambridge, 1986, p217.
78 Arato and Breines, op. cit., p130.

Chapter Six: The crisis of enlightenment: Horkheimer and Adorno against the administered totality

1 Probably the most serious problem here results from treating the Institute's development in the 1930s as one phase. Helmet Dubiel's major study *Wissenschafsorganisation und Politische Erfahrung: Studien zur frühen Kritischen Theorie*, Suhrkamp, 1978, convincingly discerns two clear phases.
2 Adorno, T.W., *Negative Dialectics*, (trans. E.B. Ashton), Routledge & Kegan Paul, London, 1973, p3.
3 For Horkheimer's initial suspicions regarding Soviet developments see the collection of aphorisms published under the pseudonym, Heinrich Regius, as *Dämmerung*. Translated with some additional aphorisms from the post-war period as *Dawn and Decline: Notes 1926-31 and 1950-69*, Seabury Press, New York, 1978. For his analysis of the German proletariat, see the aphorism 'The Impotence of the German Working Class', pp61-5.
4 Horkheimer, ibid., pp61-5.
5 Ibid., pp61-5.
6 Ibid., pp61-5.
7 Ibid., pp61-5.
8 Horkheimer, 'Hegel und das Problem der Metaphysik', *Festschrift Für Carl Grünberg*, C.L. Hirschfeld, Leipzig, 1932.
9 Ibid., p191.
10 Horkheimer, M., *Kritische Theorie*, Bänden 1 and 2, S. Fischer, Frankfurt am Main, 1977, p49; (trans.) *Critical Theory*, Seabury Press, New York, 1972, p29.
11 Ibid., p53; (trans.) ibid., p32.
12 Ibid., pp38-9; (trans.) ibid., pp17-18.
13 Ibid., p42; (trans.) ibid., p21.
14 Ibid., p56; (trans.) ibid., p35.
15 Mannheim, K., *Ideology and Utopia*, Kegan Paul, Trench, Trubner & Co., Ltd., London, 1940; translation of the 1929 German edition.
16 Ibid., p236.
17 Ibid., p48; (trans.) ibid., p28.
18 Horkheimer, *Dawn and Decline,* p103.
19 Ibid., p103.
20 Horkheimer, *Kritische Theorie*, p571; (trans.) *Critical Theory*, p239.
21 Ibid., p574; (trans.) ibid., p242.
22 Ibid., p566; (trans.) ibid., p234.
23 Horkheimer, op. cit., p93.
24 Quoted in Alfred Schmidt's *Zur Idee der Kritische Theorie*, Carl Hanser, Munich, 1974, p129.
25 Horkheimer, *Kritische Theorie*, p47; (trans.) op. cit., p26.
26 Ibid., pp547-8; (trans.) ibid., pp214-15.
27 Ibid., pp547-8; (trans.) ibid., pp214-15.
28 Ibid., p548; (trans.) ibid., p215.
29 Ibid., p548; (trans.) ibid., p216.

30 The conclusions of these empirical projects were only published in 1977 due to differences between Eric Fromm and the Institute's directorship. See Dubiel, op. cit., p11.
31 Ibid., pp582-3; (trans.) ibid., p251.
32 Ibid., p574; (trans.) ibid., p242.
33 Ibid., p571; (trans.) ibid., p239.
34 Ibid., p546; (trans.) ibid., p213.
35 Ibid., p43; (trans.) ibid., p22.
36 It is worth pointing out here that Horkheimer had difficulty in drawing a distinction between eradicable and ineradicable suffering as a basis for negative values. Furthermore, as his critical standpoint was radicalised, his critical values became more abstract to avoid contamination by the increasingly reified, 'false' reality.
37 Adorno, *Gesammelte Schriften*, Band 1, Suhrkamp, Frankfurt am Main, 1973, p325.
38 Ibid., p325.
39 Ibid., p359.
40 Ibid., p359.
41 Rose, G., *The Melancholy Science*, Macmillan, London, 1978, pp39-40.
42 Ibid., pp39-40.
43 Adorno, op. cit., p364.
44 Buck-Morss, S., *The Origins of Negative Dialectics*, Harvester, Sussex, 1977, p49.
45 Ibid., p49.
46 Adorno, op. cit., pp354-5.
47 Wolin, R., *Walter Benjamin – An Aesthetic of Redemption*, Columbia University Press, New York, 1982, pp37-8.
48 Ibid., p38-9.
49 On this theory see Jürgen Habermas's, 'Consciousness Raising or Redemptive Criticism', *New German Critique*, No. 17, University of Wisconsin, Milwaukee, Spring 1979, p48.
50 Wolin, op. cit., pp94-5.
51 Ibid., p71.
52 Adorno, op. cit., p364.
53 Ibid., p334.
54 Ibid., p335-6.
55 Ibid., p335-6.
56 Wolin, op. cit., p93.
57 Benjamin, W., *The Origins of German Tragedy,* New Left Books, London, 1977. p36.
58 Buck-Morss, op. cit., p59.
59 Ibid., p59.
60 Adorno, T.W. and Horkheimer, M., *Dialektik der Aufkarung*, S. Fischer, Frankfurt am Main, 1971, p29; (trans.) *Dialectic of Enlightenment*, Allen Lane, London, 1973, p28.
61 Ibid., p23; (trans.) ibid., p21.
62 Ibid., p51; (trans.) ibid., p54.
63 Ibid., p51; (trans.) ibid., pp54-5.
64 Ibid., pp51-2; (trans.) ibid., p55.
65 Ibid., p23; (trans.) ibid., p21.
66 Ibid., p11; (trans.) ibid., p8.
67 Ibid., p11; (trans.) ibid., p8.
68 Ibid., p14; (trans.) ibid., p11.
69 Ibid., p14; (trans.) ibid., p12.
70 Ibid., p26; (trans.) ibid., p25.

71 Adorno, op. cit., p318.
72 Adorno and Horkheimer, op. cit., p5; (trans.) op. cit., pxv.
73 Ibid., p36; (trans.) ibid., p36.
74 Ibid., p30; (trans.) ibid., p30.
75 Ibid., pp37-8; (trans.) ibid., p38.
76 This point is emphasised by Dubiel, op. cit., pp129-30.
77 Adorno and Horkheimer, op. cit., p198; (trans.) op. cit., p222.
78 Adorno, op. cit., p320.
79 Adorno and Horkheimer, op. cit., pp45-6; (trans.) op. cit., pp47-8.
80 Quoted in Martin Jay's *Adorno*, Fontana, London, 1984, p100.
81 Ibid., p100.
82 Buck-Morss, op. cit., p61.
83 Dubiel, op. cit., pp90-1.
84 Adorno and Horkheimer, op. cit., pp40-1; (trans.) op. cit., p42.
85 A criticism articulated by several critics including Leszek Kolakowski. See his *Main Currents in Marxism,* Vol. 3 *The Breakdown,* Oxford University Press, Oxford, 1978, p395.
86 Adorno and Horkheimer, op. cit., p38; (trans.) op. cit., p38.
87 Ibid., p16; (trans.) ibid., p14.
88 Ibid., p23; (trans.) ibid., p21.
89 Habermas, op. cit., p516-18.
90 Ibid., p508-11.
91 Ibid., p512.
92 Ibid., p512.

Section Four: Chapter Seven: Michel Foucault: anti-totalising scepticism or totalising prophecy

1   The clearest evidence of this turn in Foucault's thought is the late lecture 'What is Enlightenment', *The Foucault Reader*, Paul Rabinow (ed.), Penguin, London, 1984.
2   White, H., 'Foucault Decoded', *Tropics of Discourse*, The John Hopkins University Press, Baltimore, 1978, p245.
3   Many times Foucault has linked his own historical works to the political interests stemming from his own practical experience in the psychiatric hospitals. See 'Questions on Geography' in *Michel Foucault: Power/Knowledge: Selected Interviews and Other Writings,* (ed.) Colin Gordon, Harvester Press, Sussex, 1980, p64; and Megill, A., *Prophets of Extremity*, University of California Press, California, 1985, p199-200.
4   'Power and Sex: An Interview with Michel Foucault', by Bernard-Henri Levy, *Telos* No. 32, Washington University, St. Louis, Summer 1977, p1578.
5   Habermas, J., *Der Philosophische Diskurs der Moderne: Zwölf Vorlesungen*, Suhrkamp, Frankfurt am Main, 1985, pp306-7; (trans.) *The Philosophical Discourse of Modernity*, Polity Press, Cambridge, 1987, p260-1.
6   Foucault, M., *The Order of Things,* Tavistock, London, 1970, pp318-35.
7   Habermas, op. cit., pp307-308; (trans.) op. cit., p262.
8   Jay, *Marxism and Totality*, p521.
9   Foucault, M., *The Archeology of Knowledge*, Harper and Row, New York, 1972, p8.
10 Megill, op. cit., p187.
11 Habermas, op. cit., p293; (trans.) op. cit., p249-50.
12 Foucault, M., 'On Structuralism and Post-structuralism', *Telos* No. 55, Washington University St. Louis, Spring 1983.
13 Foucault, *The Archeology of Knowledge*, p10.

14   Ibid., p9.
15   Foucault, M., 'Revolutionary Action: "Until Now": A discussion with Michel
      Foucault under the auspices of *Actuel', Language, Counter-Memory, Practice*,
      Donald F. Bouchard (ed.), Blackwell, Oxford, 1977, p232-3.
16   For Foucault's own anti-Marxist interpretation of the May events see, Body/Power',
      Michel Foucault: Power/knowledge, p57.
17   Foucault, M., 'Politics and Ethics: An Interview', *The Foucault Reader*, p375-6.
18   Ibid., p231.
19   Horkheimer relocates the totalising perspective from the party to engaged
      intellectuals while Foucault completely repudiates the intellectuals as bearers of a
      totalising perspective.
20   Clearly, the shared historical experiences of totalitarianism and Fascism accounts
      for this theoretical convergence, although Foucault was quite unaware of the
      Frankfurt School until quite late in own career. He has remarked that knowledge of
      their work would have enabled him to 'avoid many detours'. See 'On Structuralism
      and Post-structuralism', op. cit., p200.
21   Foucault, M., *Discipline and Punish*, Penguin, London, 1977, p194.
22   Foucault, 'Two Lectures', *Michel Foucault: Power/Knowledge*, p98.
23   Habermas, op. cit., p294; (trans.) op. cit., p250.
24   Foucault, 'Truth and Power', an interview with Alessandro Fontana and Pasquale
      Pasquino, *Michel Foucault: Power/Knowledge*, p117.
25   Foucault, 'Two Lectures', *Michel Foucault: Power/Knowledge*, p97.
26   Hayden White notes the irony of this when he says 'Foucault works in the grand
      tradition of Continental European philosophy, the tradition of Leibniz, Hegel,
      Comte, Bergson, and Heidegger, which is to say that he is a metaphysician, however
      much he may stress his descent from the positivist convention.... For with the
      successive appearance of six books, Foucault has established himself as a
      philosopher of history in the 'speculative' manner of Vico, Hegel, and Spengler', op.
      cit., p255.
27   Fraser, N., 'Foucault On Modern Power: Empirical Insights and Normative
      Confusions', *Praxis International*, October, 1981, p276.
28   Foucault, *Discipline and Punish*, p302-3.
29   Walzer, M., 'The Politics of Michel Foucault', *Foucault: A Critical Reader*, D.C.
      Hoy (ed.), Blackwell, Oxford, 1986, p57.
30   Honneth, A., 'Foucault and Adorno: Two Forms of the Critique of Modernity',
      Thesis Eleven No. 15, Monash University, Clayton Victoria, 1986, p56.
31   Honneth, ibid., p56.
32   Foucault stubbornly refuses to acknowledge a theory of power in his work. He
      maintains he is not interested in power 'as an autonomous question' but only in so
      far as various discourses of truth were inter-meshed with specific historical relations
      of power. See Foucault's own objections to characterisations that interpret him as a
      theoretican of power in the interview with Gerard Raulet, 'Structuralism and Post-
      structuralism', op. cit., p207.
33   Foucault, M., *History of Sexuality,* Vol. 1, Penguin Books, 1978, p92-3.
34   Ibid., pp95-6.
35   Foucault, 'Power and Sex', op. cit., p160.
36   Foucault explains the failure of Marxist vocabulary and its conceptual 'lack' in
      relation to the new local struggles in terms of its historical assimilation to the
      paradigm of science. This view indicates the overwhelming predominance of
      Althusserian Marxism in France during this period and Foucault's ignorance of the
      tradition of historicist Marxism reconstructed in the previous chapters. See the
      interview 'Truth and Power', op. cit., p110.

37 Habermas, op. cit., p316-17; (trans.) op. cit., p269-70.
38 Foucault M., 'Power and Strategies' in *Michel Foucault: Power/Knowledge*, p138.
39 Foucault, 'Questions on Geography', in *Michel Foucault: Power/Knowledge,* p64.
40 Here, the notion of strategies clearly extends Foucault's metaphor of the ceaseless battle used to describe the shifting terrain, and alignment of forces in the struggles between power and resistance. Unlike a universal, stable 'truth', the 'strategy' betrays its own fluid, transient status in the constant movement of the battle.
41 For this distinction between the universal and specific intellectual, see the interview 'Truth and Power', p129-33.
42 Foucault 'Power and Sex', p159.
43 Habermas, op. cit., pp325-32; (trans.) op. cit., pp276-82.
44 Taylor, C., 'Foucault on Freedom and Truth', *Foucault: A Critical Reader,* p98.
45 Virtually every one of Foucault's major critics and even some of his followers have treated this problem in his work. For a representative selection, see C. Taylor, op. cit., pp69, 73, 91-2; Fraser, op. cit.; Habermas, op. cit., p284; Jay, op. cit., p528; Philp Mark, 'Michel Foucault' in *The Return of The Grand Theory of the Human Sciences*, Quentin Skinner (ed.), Cambridge University Press, Cambridge, 1985, p79; Peter Dews (ed.), 'Nouvelle Philosophie and Foucault', *Economy and Society* Vol. 8, No. 2, Routledge & Kegan Paul, London, May 1979, p147.
46 Fraser, N., op. cit., p283.
47 Nancy Fraser in the article 'Foucault's Body Language', *Salmagundi* No. 61, Skidmore College, Fall 1983, argues that Foucault is not content with this negative position. She sees a side of his work that articulates a 'transgressive' moment which 'aspires to transcend humanism and replace it with something new'. While traces of this cannot be denied, I think it goes too far to elevate them to 'another side' of Foucault. Fraser's textual support for this 'other side' is rather insubstantial, relying mainly on one formulation from the end of the *History of Sexuality*. Rather than being another side of Foucault, they do seem to evidence his difficulty in eliminating all *positive, utopian residues from his own thinking*.
48 Foucault, 'On the Genealogy of Ethics: An Overview of Work in Progress', *The Foucault Reader*, p343.
49 Alan Megill's work, op. cit., represents a tightly argued interpretation of Foucault along these lines viewing him principally as a rhetorician.
50 Foucault, *Discipline and Punish*, p282.
51 Lentricchia, F., 'Reading Foucault (11)' *Raritan,* 2:4, Summer 1982, p51.
52 As Habermas has pointed out, Foucault's concept of power fuses this synthetic role with another empirical one explaining the specific historical constellation of power relationships as a social functional network. See Habermas, op. cit., p322-3; (trans.) op. cit., p274.
53 Even some of Foucault's critics acknowledge that his writings supplied an impetus for treating a whole range of social phenomena as political problems. See Nancy Fraser, op. cit., p280.
54 Fraser, N., 'Foucault On Modern Power: Empirical insights and Normative Confusions', *Praxis International*, October 1981.
55 Hoy, D.C., 'Power, Repression, Progress', *Foucault: A Critical Reader*, p137.
56 Foucault, *Discipline and Punish*, p222.
57 Habermas, p340; (trans.) p290.
58 Foucault, 'What is Enlightenment', *The Foucault Reader*, p50.
59 Ibid., p50.
60 Wolin, R., 'Foucault's Aesthetic Decisionism', *Telos* No. 67, Washington University, St. Louis, Spring 1986, p86.

Conclusion

1 It is difficult to write off this recourse to the concept of totality as a mere polemical, rhetorical device. Foucault obviously views modernity as a complex interwoven and interlocked system of institutions and practices. In this very important sense, the concept of totality has, for him, substantive theoretical meaning in application to modernity.

2 Heller, A., *A Theory of History*, Routledge & Kegan Paul, London, 1982, p3.

3 Habermas, J., 'Das Subjekt der Geschichte', *Zur Logik der Socialwissenschaften*, Frankfurt am Main, 1982.

4 Ibid., pp530-2.

5 Heller, op. cit., p218.

6 Ibid., p71.

7 Habermas, op. cit., p538.

8 Habermas, J., 'History and Evolution', *Telos* No. 39, Washington University, St. Louis, Spring 1979, pp10-11.

9 Heller, A., 'Is a Radical Philosophy Possible?', *Thesis Eleven* 1, Monash University, Clayton Victoria, 1980.

10 Márkus, G., *Language and Production,* p120.

11 Heller, A., 'Habermas and Marxism', *Habermas: Critical Debates*, Macmillan, London, 1982, p30.

12 The ultimate success of this reformulated distinction is of no concern here. For a critique see Honneth, A., *Kritik der Macht: Reflexionstufen einer kritische Gesellschafstheorie*, Suhrkamp, Frankfurt am Main, 1985.

13 Habermas, *Theorie des Kommunikativen Handelns*, Band 1, p537.

14 Jay, op. cit., pp486-7.

15 Heller, op. cit., p236.

16 Márkus, op. cit., p107-8.

17 Ibid., p107.

18 Habermas, J., 'The Entwinement of Myth and Enlightenment: Rereading Dialectic of Enlightenment', *New German Critique* No. 26, University of Wisconsin, Milwaukee, Summer/Spring 1982, p18.

19 Habermas, J., *Theorie des Kommunikativen Handeln*, Band 1, Suhrkamp, Frankfurt am Main, 1981, p533.

20 Fehér, F. and Heller, A., *Easter Left, Western Left*: Totalitarianism, Freedom and Democracy, Polity, Cambridge, 1987, p201.

21 See an interview with Agnes Heller by Patrick Wright in *New Socialist*, London, July 1985. On this point of the Budapest School's reinterpretation of the idea of Socialism as radicalised democracy see also Mihaly Vajda's *The State and Socialism*, Allison & Busby, London, 1981.

22 Habermas, J., 'Modernity vs Postmodernity', *New German Critique* No. 22, Winter 1981.

Bibliography

Abrams, M.H., *Natural Supernaturalism : Tradition and Revolution in Romantic Literature*, W.W. Norton, New York, 1971.

Adorno, T.W., *Gesammelte Schriften*, Band 1, Suhrkamp, Frankfurt am Main, 1973. *Negative Dialectics*, Routledge & Kegan Paul, London, 1973; Horkheimer, M., *Dialektik der Aufklarung*, S. Fischer, Frankfurt am Main, 1971; (trans.) *Dialectic of Enlightenment*, Allen Lane, London, 1973.

Althusser, L., *For Marx*, Penguin, London, 1969; *Reading Capital*, New Left Books, London, 1970.

Arato, A., 'The Neo-Idealist Defence of Subjectivity', *Telos* No. 21, Washington University Press, St. Louis, Fall 1974; 'Lukács' Path to Marxism 1910-1923', *Telos* No. 6, Washington University Press, St. Louis, Summer 1970; and Breines, P., *The Young Lukacs and the Origins of Western Marxism*, Pluto Press, London, 1979.

Arendt A., *Between the Past and the Future*, Faber and Faber, London, 1954.

Arnason, J.P., 'Rationalisation and Modernity', *Incidental Paper No. 9*, Department of Sociology, University of La Trobe, 1982.

Avineri, S., *Hegel's Theory of the Modern State*, Cambridge University Press, Cambridge, 1972.

Benjamin, W., *The Origins of German Tragedy*, New Left Books, London, p36.

Belázs, B., 'Notes from a Diary', *New Hungarian Quarterly*, Vol. XIII, No. 47, Budapest, Autumn 1972.

Benhabib, S., 'Rationality and Social Action : Critical Reflections on Max Weber's Methodological Writings', *The Philosophical Forum* Vol XII, No. 4, Boston University, Boston, Summer 1981.

Blumenberg, H., *The Legitimacy of the Modern Age*, MIT Press, Cambridge, Massachusetts, 1983.

Brubaker, R., *The Limits of Rationality*, Allen and Unwin, London, 1984.
Buck-Morss, S., *The Origins of Negative Dialectics*, Harvester, Sussex, 1977.

Burger, T., *Max Weber's Theory of Concept Formation*, Duke University Press, Durham, 1978.

Cassirer, E., *The Individual and the Cosmos in Renaissance Philosophy*, Harper Torchbook, New York, 1963; *Kant's Life and Thought*, Yale University Press, New Haven, 1981.

Cohen, J., 'Weber and the Dynamics of Domination' , *Telos*, No. 14, Washington University Press, St. Louis, Winter 1972.

Cohn, N., *The Pursuit of the Millenium*, Mercury Books, London, 1962.

Congdon, L., *The Young Lukács*, University of North Carolina Press, Chapel Hill and London, 1983.

Dews, P., 'Nouvelle Philosophie and Foucault', *Economy and Society* Vol. 8, No. 2, Routledge & Kegan Paul, London, May 1979.

Dilthey, W., *Gesammelte Schriften*, Band 1, B.G. Teubner Verlag, Stuggart, 1959; *Der Aufbau der Geschichtlichen Welt in Der Geisteswissenschaften*, Suhrkamp, Frankfurt am Main, 1981; (trans.) *Selected Writings*, Rickman, H.P. (ed.), Cambridge University Press, Cambridge, 1976.

Dubiel, H., *Wissenschaftsorganisation und Politische Erfahrung : Studien zur frühen Kritischen Theorie*, Suhrkamp, Frankfurt am Main, 1978.

Engels, F., *Ludwig Feuerbach and the End of German Classical Philosophy*, Foreign Languages Press, Moscow, 1950.

Fehér, F., 'Die Geschichtesphilosophie des Drama, die Metaphysik der Trägodie und die Utopia des Untragischen Dramas. Scheidewege der Dramatheorie des Jungen Lukács', in *Die Seele und das Leben: Studien zum Frühen Lukacs*, A. Heller et. al., Suhrkamp, Baden-Baden, 1977; 'The last Phase of Romantic Anti-Capitalism – Lukács' Response to the War', *New German Critique* No. 10, University of Wisconsin, Milwaukee, Winter 1977.

Fehér, F. and Heller, A., 'Class, Modernity, Democracy', *Eastern Left, Western Left: Totalitarianism, Freedom und Democracy,* Polity Press, Cambridge, 1986.

Fetscher, I., Das Verhältnis des Marxismus zu Hegel, in Marxismus Studien, Dritte Folge, J.C.B. Mohr (Paul Siebeck), Tübingen, 1960.

Fleischer, H., *Marxismus und Geschichte,* Suhrkamp, Frankfurt am Main, 1975.

Foucault M., *The Order of Things*, Tavistock, London, 1970; The *Archaeology of Knowledge*, Harper and Row, New York, 1972; *Discipline and Punish*, Penguin, London, 1977; *History of Sexuality*, Vol. 1 'An Introduction', Penguin Books, London, 1978; 'What is Enlightenment', *The Foucault Reader*, Rabinow, P., (ed.), Penguin, London, 1984; *Power/Knowledge : Selected Interviews and Other Writings*, Gordon, C., (ed.) Harvester Press, Sussex, 1980; 'Power and Sex : An interview with Michel Foucault', by Bernard-Henri Levy, *Telos* No. 32, Washington University, St. Louis, Summer 1977; 'On Structuralism and Post-structuralism', *Telos* No. 55, Washington University, St. Louis, Spring 1983; 'Revolutionary Action', *Language, Counter-Memory and Practice*, Bouchard D., (ed.), Blackwell, Oxford, 1977.

Fraser, N., 'Foucault On Modern Power : Empirical Insights and Normative Confusions', *Praxis International*, October 1981; 'Foucault's Body Language', *Salmagundi* No. 61, Skidmore College, Fall 1983.

Gadamer, H.G., *Truth and Method*, Shead and Ward, London, 1978.

Goldmann, L., *Dialektische Untersuchungen*, Luchterland, Darmstadt and Neuwied, 1966.

Gouldner, A., *The Two Marxisms*, Macmillan Press, London, 1980; *Against Fragmentation*, Oxford University Press, Oxford, 1985.

Habermas J., *Philosophische-Politische Profile*, Suhrkamp, Frankfurt am Main, 1971; *Theorie des Kommunikativen Handelns*, Band 1, Suhrkamp, Frankfurt am Main, 1981; *Zur Logik der Sozialwissenschaften*, Suhrkamp, Frankfurt am Main, 1982; *Der Philosophische Diskurs der Moderne: Zwölf Vorlesungen*, Suhrkamp, Frankfurt am Main, 1985; *Theory and Practice*, Heinemann, London, 1974; *Legitimation Crisis*, Beacon Press, Boston, 1975. 'Consciousness Raising or Redemptive Criticism', *New German Critique* No. 17, University of Wisconsin, Milwaukee, Spring 1979; 'History and Evolution', *Telos* No. 39, Washington University, St. Louis, Spring 1979; 'The Entwinement of Myth and Enlightenment', New German

Critique No. 26, University of Wisconsin, Milwaukee, Summer/Spring 1982; 'Modernity vs Postmodernity', *New German Critique* 22, University of Wisconsin, Milwaukee, Winter, 1981.

Hegel, G.F.W., *Werke* in Zwanzig Bänden, Moldendauer, E. and Michel, K.M. (eds), Suhrkamp, Frankfurt am Main, 1970; Dokumente zu Hegels Entwicklung, J. Hoffmeister (ed.), Stuttgart, 1936; *Vorlesungen Über die Philosophie der Weltgeschichte*, Band 1, J. Hoffmeister (ed.), Akademie Verlag, Berlin, 1973. *Philosophy of Right*, Oxford University Press, Oxford, 1942; *Early Theological Writings*, University and Pennsylvania Press, Philadelphia, 1948; *Philosophy of History*, Dover Press, New York, 1956; *Hegel's Philosophy of Mind,* Oxford University Press, Oxford 1971; *Hegel's Philosophy of Nature,* Oxford University Press, Oxford, 1971; *Lectures on the Philosophy of World History*, Cambridge University Press, Cambridge, 1975; *Phenomenology of Spirit*, Oxford University Press, Oxford, 1977.

Heller, A., *A Theory of History*, Routledge & Kegan Paul, London, 1982; (ed.) *Lukács Revalued*, Blackwell, Oxford, 1983; 'Is a Radical Philosophy Possible?' *Thesis Eleven* 1, Monash University, Clayton Victoria, 1980; 'Habermas and Marxism', *Habermas : Critical Debates*, Macmillan, London, 1982; Interview with Patrick Wright, *New Socialist*, July 1985.

Henrich, D., *Hegel im Kontext*, Suhrkamp, Frankfurt am Main, 1975.

Hodges, H.A., *Wilhelm Dilthey: An Introduction*, Kegan Paul, Trench, Trubner & Co., London, 1944.

Honigsheim, P., *On Max Weber*, The Free Press, New York, 1968.

Honneth, A., *Kritik der Macht : Reflexionstufen einer kritische Gesellschaftstheorie*, Suhrkamp, Frankfurt am Main, 1985; 'Foucault and Adorno : Two Forms of the Critique of Modernity', *Thesis Eleven* No. 15, Monash University, Clayton Victoria, 1986.

Horkheimer, M., *Kritische Theorie,* Banden 1 and 2, S. Fischer, Frankfurt am Main, 1977 (trans.); *Critical Theory*, Seabury Press, New York, 1972; Hegel und das Problem der Metaphysik', *Festschrift Für Carl Grünberg,* C.L. Hirschfeld, Leipzig, 1932; *Eclipse of Reason*, Seabury Press, New York, 1974; *Dawn and Decline : Notes 1926-31 and 1950-69,* Seabury Press, New York, 1978.

Hoy, D.C., 'Power, Repression, Progress', *Foucault : A Critical Reader*, Blackwell, Oxford, 1986.

Hughes, H.S., *Consciousness and Society,* Paladin Books, Frogmore, St. Albans, Herts, 1974.

Iggers, G., *The German Conception of History*, Wesleyan University Press, Middletown Connecticut, 1968.

Jay, M., *Marxism and Totality*, Polity Press, Cambridge, 1984; *Adorno,* Fontana, London, 1984.

Kautsky, K., *The Class Struggle*, Norton Library, New York, 1971.

Kolakowski, L., *Main Currents in Marxism*, Vol. 3, *The Breakdown*, Oxford University Press, Oxford, 1978.

Kroner, R., 'Introduction', in Hegel, *Early Theological Writings.*

Landmann, M., 'Herausgegebers Einleitung', *Georg Simmel: Das Individuelle Gesetz: Philosophische* Exkurse, Suhrkamp, Frankfurt am Main, 1965.

Lendvai, F.L. 'The Young Lukács' Philosophy of History', *New Hungarian Quarterly,* No. 67, Budapest, 1976.

Lentricchia, F. 'Reading Foucault (11)', *Raritan*, 2:4, Summer 1982.

Lichtheim, G., *Lukács*, Fontana, London, 1970.

Löwith, K., *Meaning in History*, University of Chicago Press, Chicago, 1949; *Max Weber and Karl Marx*, Allen and Unwin, London, 1982.

Löwy, M., *Georg Lukács: From Romanticism To Bolshevism*, New Left Books, London, 1979.

Lovejoy, A.O., *The Great Chain of Being*, Harvard University Press, Massachusetts, 1936, paperback edn: 1970.

Lukács, G., *Werke*, Luchterland, Darmstadt und Neuwied, 1968 onwards; *Die Seele und die Form*, Luchterland, Darmstadt und Neuwied, 1971; translation, *Soul and Form*, Merlin Press, London, 1974; *Die Theorie des Romans*, Luchterland, Darmstadt und Neuwied, 1963; translation *Theory of the Novel*, Merlin Press, London, 1971; *Gelebtes Denken*, Suhrkamp, Frankfurt am Main, 1980; *History and Class Consciousness*, Merlin Press, London, 1969; *The Young Hegel*, Merlin Press, London, 1975; 'Zur Soziologie des Mordernen Dramas', *Archiv Für Sozialwissenschaft und Sozialpolitik*, XXXVIII (1914), republished in Lukács, G., *Schriften Zur Literatursoziologie*, Einletung Von Peter Ludz, Luchterland, 1961; 'Zur Theorie der Literaturgeschichte', *Text und Kritik*, 39/40, Heinz L. Arnok (ed.), München, October 1973; 'Croce Benedetto: Zur Theorie und Geschichte der Historiographie', *Archiv für Sozialwissenschaft und Sozialpolitik*, Band 39, Heft 3, Tübingen, 1915; 'On the Poverty of the Spirit', *The Philosophical Forum*, Vol. 13, No. 3-4, University of Boston, Massachusetts, Spring/Summer 1972; 'Old Culture, New Culture', *Telos* No. 6, University Press, Buffalo, Winter 1970; 'Letters to Paul Ernst', *New Hungarian Quarterly*, Vol. XIII, No. 47, Budapest, Autumn 1972.

Mannheim, K., *Ideology and Utopia*, Kegan Paul, Trench, Trubner & Co., Ltd., London, 1940; translation of the 1929 German edition.

Márkus, G., *Marxism and Anthropology*, Van Gorcum, Assen, 1978; *Language and Production, A Critique of Paradigms,* D. Reidel Publishing, Dordrecht, 1986; 'Four Forms of Critical Theory: Some Theses on Marx's Development', *Thesis Eleven* No. 1, Melbourne, 1980; 'Life and the Soul', *Lukács Revalued*, A. Heller (ed.), Blackwell, Oxford, 1983; 'Reification and Alienation in Marx and Lukács', *Thesis Eleven*, 5/6, Monash University, Clayton, Victoria, 1982; 'Hegel and the Antinomies of Modernity', *Antipodean Enlightenments: Festschrift Für Leslie Bodi*, Peter Lang, Frankfurt am Main, 1987.

Marx, K., *Grundrisse der Kritik der Politischen Ökonomie*, Dietz Verlag, Berlin, 1974; *Grundrisse,* Penguin, London, 1973; *Capital*, Vol. 3, Progress Publishers, Moscow, 1971.

Marx, K. and Engels, F., *Werke*, Dietz Verlag, Berlin, 1980; *Collected Works*, Lawrence and Wishart, London, 1975 onwards; *Early Writings*, Penguin, London, 1975.

Megill, A., *Prophets of Extremity*, University of California Press, California, 1985.

Meinecke, F., *Historism*, Routledge & Kegan Paul, London, 1972.

Meyer, T., *Der Zweispalt in der Marx'schen Emanzipationstheorie*, Scriptor Verlag, Kronberg Ts, 1973.

Mommsen, W.J., *Max Weber and German Politics 1890-1920,* University of Chicago Press, Chicago, 1984.

Morf, O., 'Totalitat und Dialektik', *Marxismus und Anthropologie: Festschrift Für Leo Koffler,* Germinal Verlag, Bochum, 1980.

Plant, R., *Hegel,* Allen and Unwin, London, 1973.

Redding, P., 'Action, Language and Text: Dilthey's Conception of the Understanding', *Philosophy and Social Criticism,* No.2, Vol. 9, Boston College, 1982.

Reidel, M., *Theorie und Praxis im Denkens Hegel,* Ulstein, Frankfurt am Main, 1976; 'Kant und die Geschichtswissenschaft', Einleitung zu Kant's *Schriften zu Geschichtsphilosophie*, Phillip Reclam Jun., Stuttgart, 1974.

Ringer, F.K., *The Decline of the German Mandarins: The German Academic Community 1890-1933*, Harvard University Press, Cambridge, Massachusetts, 1969.

Ripalda, J.M., *The Divided Nation: The Roots of a Bourgeois Thinker – G.W.F. Hegel,*

Van Gorcum, Amsterdam, 1977.

Rose, G., *The Melancholy Science*, Macmillan, London, 1978.

Schiller, F., *On the Aesthetic Education of Man,* Ungar Press, New York, 1980.

Schlesinger, R., 'Historical Setting of Lukács' History and Class Consciousness', *Aspects of History and Class Consciousness*, Istvan Mészáros, (ed.), Routledge & Kegan Paul, London, 1971.

Schmidt, A., *Zur Idee der Kritische Theorie*, Carl Hanser, Munich, 1974.

Schnädelbach, H., *Philosophie in Deutschland 1831-1933*, Suhrkamp, Frankfurt am Main, 1983.

Skinner, Q. (ed.), *The Return of the Grand Theory of the Human Sciences,* Cambridge University Press, Cambridge, 1985.

Simmel, G., *Philosophie des Geldes*, Duncker und Humbolt, Leipzig, 1907; (trans.) *Philosophy of Money*, Routledge & Kegan Paul, London, 1978; 'Der Begriff und der Tragödie der Kultur', *Philosophische Kultur*, Verlag Von Dr W. Klinckhardt, Leipzig, 1911; *Georg Simmel Das Individelle Gesetz: Philosophische Exkurse*, Suhrkamp, Frankfurt am Main, 1965; 'The Meaning of Culture', 'The Conflict of Modern Culture', 'The Future of Our Culture': all in *Georg Simmel: Sociologist and European*, Peter Lawrence, (ed.), Nelson, Middlsex, 1976.

Suchting, W., *Marx: An Introduction*, Harvester, Sussex, 1983.

Taylor, C., 'Foucault On Freedom and Truth', *Foucault: A Critical Reader,* Blackwell, Oxford, 1986.

Tenbruck, F.H., 'The Problem of the Thematic Unity in the Works of Max Weber', *British Journal of Sociology*, Vol. 13, No. 3, September 1980.

Theunissen, M., 'Die Verwicklichung der Vernuft: Zur Theorie-Praxis Diskussion im Anschluss an Hegel', *Philosophische Rundschau*, Beiheft 6, J.C.B. Mohr (Paul Siebeck), Tübingen, 1970.

Toews, J.E., *Hegelianism: The Path Towards Dialectical Humanism, 1805-1841*, Cambridge University Press, Cambridge, 1980.

Tönnies, F., *Gemeinschaft und Gesellschaft,* Hans Wuste Verlag, Leipzig, 1935.

Vajda, M., *The State and Socialism*, Allison & Busby, London, 1981.

Voltaire, *The Philosophy of History*, Citadel Press, New York, 1965.

Walzer, M., 'The Politics of Michel Foucault', *Foucault: A Critical Reader*, Blackwell, Oxford, 1986.

Weber, M., *Gesammelte Aufsatze Zur Wissenschaftslehre*, J.C.B. Mohr (Paul Siebeck), Tübingen, 1951; *Economy and Society,* Vol. 1 University of California Press, California, 1978; *From Max Weber*, Gerth, H. and Mills, C.W. (eds), Routledge & Kegan Paul, London, 1948; *The Methodology of the Social Sciences,* The Free Press, New York, 1949; *The Protestant Ethic and the Spirit of Capitalism*, Unwin University Books, London, 1930; *Roscher and Knies*, The Free Press, New York, 1975.

White, H., 'Foucault Decoded', *Tropics of Discourse*, John Hopkins University Press, Baltimore, 1978.

Willey, T.E., *Back To Kant*, Wayne University Press, Detroit, 1978.

Wolin, R., *Walter Benjamin – An Aesthetic of Redemption*, Columbia University Press, New York, 1982; 'Foucault's Aesthetic Decisionism', *Telos* No. 67, Washington University, St. Louis, Spring, 1986.